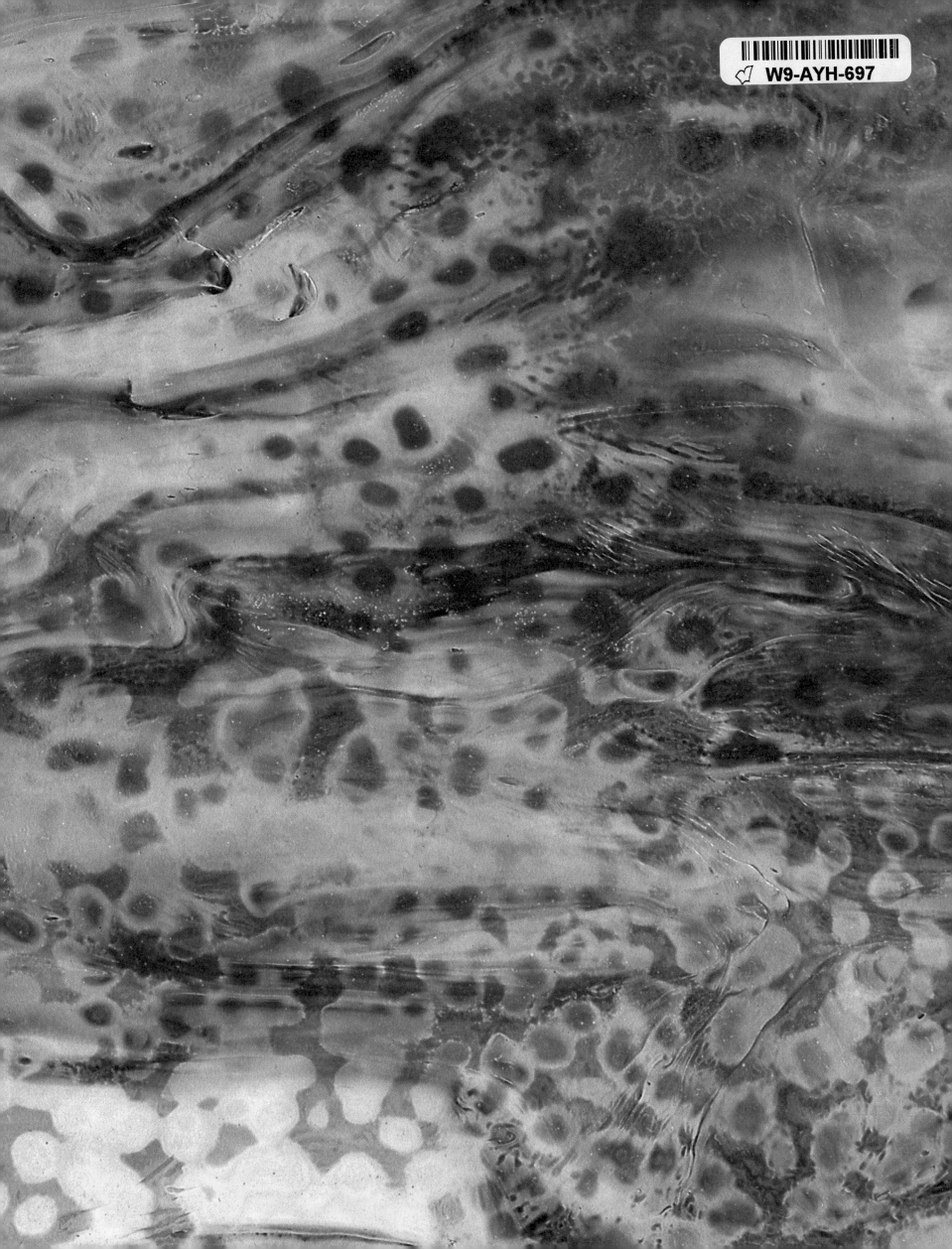

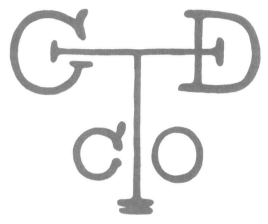

TIFFANY GLASS
AND DECORATING
COMPANY
1892–1900

FAVRILE GLASS
1894

THE LAMPS

THE FAIRFIELD PRESS, NEW YORK

OF TIFFANY

by DR. EGON NEUSTADT

Director, The Egon and Hildegard Museum of Tiffany Art.

In Memory of Hildegard

The Choicest Lamp

WE PASSED a tiny basement store,
Walked down a wooden ramp
And soon her eager eyes did spot
A strange, old-fashioned lamp.

She took me there a second time,
Entreating all the while;
The lamp was no more radiant
Than her excited smile.

At home, it soon found company
And fathered a collection
In styles of every form and size,
Of color and complexion.

When experts argue which of them
The choicest lamp may be,
I keep my peace because I know
Which one it is—for me.

FOREWORD

ONE OF Louis Comfort Tiffany's declared goals was to bring beauty into the home in order that we might live with it, absorb its substance and so enhance our existence. It was almost axiomatic with Tiffany that a functional object must also be beautiful, and he achieved this goal in such diverse media as glass, bronze, enamel and pottery.

It was in the medium of glass, and particularly in the lamps produced by Tiffany Studios, that Tiffany the artist achieved his greatest success. No other examples of his art combined to such a remarkable degree the requirements of both usefulness and decorative excellence.

At first sight, Tiffany seems to resemble Thomas A. Edison in his pragmatic approach to art. Young Tiffany was an experimenter with a definite goal, yet of necessity he stumbled often in his quest for beauty. In the realm of glass, he was exploring unknown regions, and some of his innovations produced less than wonderful results. However, when Tiffany did hit his mark, he knew it and, of equal importance, he knew the "why" of it. Each success became part of Tiffany's "repertoire," another stepping stone in search of an aspiration. His eyes always seemed focused on the future.

At the connoisseur's second look, Tiffany takes on new dimensions. His aesthetics were those of Shelley, seeking the spiritual beauty hidden in nature. His rationale was that of Ruskin, finding beauty in expressive, living things. He was the epitome of the creative artist —clarifying, intensifying and animating our most commonplace experiences. As the artist Tiffany matured, his work acquired a sense of freedom, of peace, and of unity. In his early work, he attempted to separate and abstract the concept of beauty from nature. Later, he emphasized the organic movement in its natural environment and added to it man's emotionality. This indivisibility of organic beauty and human passion is the highlight of Tiffany's genius. He is asking us "Do you see what I saw? Do you feel what I felt?"

The spiritual feeling so often engendered by his greatest works is due to this totality; it compels us to see with our hearts.

Before Tiffany, natural settings were thought to have only the reflective quality of light and the partial light of shadows. In his attempt to duplicate the glories of nature in glass, Tiffany was handicapped in that his medium was primarily translucent and often had poor reflective qualities. Then, somewhere, somehow, Tiffany became aware of the fact that nature herself was full of translucence; a brown branch behind a new leaf was greenish-brown, and the leaf itself was brownish-green. This knowledge was a new tool and he used it well. He had his art form. Now his lamp shades had the three dimensions of sculpture, the brilliant colors of the canvas, and the living glow of translucent light. With these, and his own intuitive sense of beauty, he gave his creations a uniqueness known as "The Touch of Tiffany."

Once the techniques of a craft are mastered, the inner eye of the artist becomes all-important. As Tiffany himself said in reference to the creation of a fine window, "The artist in glass cannot turn his sketch over to a foreman and expect a result worthy of his reputation. He has to superintend every stage of the work just as carefully and with the same zeal as during the evolution of an oil painting, for as in painting, the introduction of color in one part of the canvas, or of a tint or tone, has its blissful or baneful effect upon all that has gone before, so with a stained glass window: no other eyes than those of the original artist can tell whether the fresh note added to the rest is the right or the wrong one. Infinite, endless labor makes a masterpiece."

It has long been apparent that a definitive collection, encompassing the scope and virtuosity of the artist, must be assembled if ever there is to be a true appreciation of the lamps of Tiffany. Time is running out.

While most lamps are in the hands of collectors, each collector selects according to his own often highly subjective taste; no one until Dr. Neustadt has had the inclination and determination to gather together an example of each kind of lamp, regardless of his own preference, for the purpose of representation and preservation.

Another perplexing omission is that a book such as this has not been produced before. Art paintings, for example, are also one of a kind, and yet there are many excellent compilations in print. Two reasons for this lapse suggest themselves. The first is that collectors fear the increased valuation that follows in the wake of publicity. The second is that one must use the best materials and techniques available in the photographic and printing fields in order to bring the lamps to life.

Dr. Neustadt has overcome these two objections by completing his own representative collection and by sparing no effort in obtaining quality reproductions. In addition, he has dedicated endless hours and unimaginable energy to the authorship of this book. I feel that Mr. Tiffany, were he alive, would be pleased by the results. I know the "Touch of Tiffany" has guided the author.

The purpose of this book is to bring to the general public and art connoisseur alike a better understanding and appreciation of the lamps of Tiffany.

Bruce E. Randall

CONTENTS

1. The Glass

2. Lamp Bases and Fixtures

3. Favrile Shades

4. Geometric Shades

5. Transition to Flowers

6. Flowered Cones

7. Flowered Globes

8. Irregular Lower Borders

9. Irregular Upper and Lower Borders

CATEGORIES OF SHADES
Numerals refer to number of illustrations

CATEGORIES OF BASES AND FIXTURES
Numerals refer to number of illustrations

INTRODUCTION

THE LAMPS described in this book have been assembled over a period of more than thirty years. Most of them are now part of a permanent collection, which, together with the Tiffany Studios Album and a substantial reserve of Tiffany glass, will become the Egon and Hildegard Neustadt Museum for Tiffany Art, chartered by the State of New York. This arrangement has been made to maintain the integrity of the collection and to promote the acquisition of new pieces.

It is the purpose of this book to present the most important lamp designs created by Tiffany, describe them in detail, explain their basic characteristics, and in so doing classify them. While the book cannot possibly contain every type of Tiffany lamp because of their enormous diversity, all of the significant styles have been included.

Classification

For the clearest possible presentation of the subject matter, the lamps (or, more specifically, the lamp shades) have been classified into several categories in accordance with their basic features. This classification will follow a logical progression from the simplest to the most complex, from the smallest to the largest, from the plainest to the most ornate.

After a brief biography of Louis Comfort Tiffany, a chapter on the glass used in constructing the lamp shades, and a description of the lamp bases, the main section of the book begins; this analyzes every aspect of the lamps. The one-piece Favrile shades are shown first. Progressing to multiple-leaded glass shades, we start with geometric patterns; the succeeding chapter describes the transition from these geometrics to the more complex and fluid flower designs.

Finally, we arrive at the flower shades themselves in which the floral pattern covers the entire surface; these are divided, according to shape, into cones and globes. The subsequent chapter deals with an advanced design of free-flowing natural form which, unconfined by a predetermined straight-line lower edge, creates the impressive "irregular lower border." In the final chapter we find that the upper border has also become irregular; the artificial aperture has been supplanted by lifelike stems and tree branches, thus achieving the ultimate in Tiffany Studios lamp designs.

Insofar as it is feasible, the same method of classification is used within each chapter: simple to complex, small to large, elementary to elaborate. Descriptions have been based upon the actual shades rather than the (unretouched) color plates. Because of this, some slight discrepancies may be apparent as a result of the photographic process.

An effort has been made to show the shades in true proportion to their sizes. Most appear approximately one-fifth their actual dimensions. In some instances, minor deviations are the result of photographic exigencies or the desire to show specific detail. In all cases, accurate measurements of the shades have been supplied. The existence of reinforcement wires, employed for structural strength, is also noted.

Authentication

Most lamps produced by the Tiffany Studios were signed *Tiffany Studios New York*, with or without a number identifying the style of the lamp, such as 1558. Another figure code is sometimes found: this—known as a dash number—is reputedly the private cipher used by the Studios to mark those shades Tiffany thought to be exceptional. When present, the dash number follows the identification number: e.g., 1558–2. From this we may deduce that a superior shade of the same series had previously been produced, marked 1558–1.

Though these signatures are often referred to as "impressed," no metal die was ever used on the shade itself. The information was stamped upon a narrow bronze tag or plaque; this in turn was soldered to the shade, ordinarily on the inside of the lower rim [1, 2], but sometimes on the lead lines between adjoining glass sections or on bronze branches. Direct impressions were made only on the base, generally on the bottom plate of the platform, consisting of signature, base number and occasionally an insigne composed of the letters L. C. T. Co. [3]. On Favrile shades the identifying letters and numbers were etched upon the glass surface.

The Tiffany Studios' *signature* cannot always be completely relied on, however, because certain shades, such as the small cone-shaped Dragonflies, were never signed. The

1

2

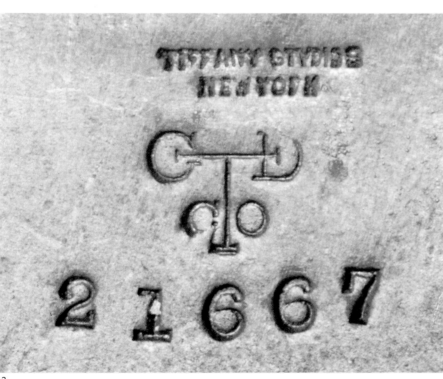

3

signature imprint has frequently been omitted from other shades and bases as well.

The *glass* itself is an important clue to the authenticity of a Tiffany Studios shade; its distinctive characteristics will be fully described.

Reinforcement wires attached to the inside of the shades are an almost exclusive feature of Tiffany Studios; several typical examples are illustrated.

The quality of *craftsmanship*, most evident in leading over copper foil, is also a dependable criterion. Used in all shades constructed of a large number of small glass segments, this leading is thin and uniformly rounded inside as well as out.

An established *design* is, of course, another indication that a shade is genuine. It appears that the following procedure was followed at the Studios:

Each lamp pattern was translated into a three-dimensional wooden form; this mock-up established the shade's exact width, height and size of aperture; with meticulous accuracy it also specified the number of leaded pieces to be used, and the precise size, shape and location of each. As a result, each shade made from a specific pattern is virtually identical in form with every other shade constructed from that same pattern, although the color schemes may differ greatly.

In the case of a Favrile shade, authenticity may be determined by the quality of the glass and by the etched initials; sometimes an identifying number and the word *Favrile* may also be found.

At the Tiffany Studios, lamps were constructed by highly trained craftsmen who cut each glass piece in accord with the pattern inscribed on the particular wooden form. In many instances, especially in the case of the more complex lamps, it is probable that special colorists selected the most suitable colors and textures from the enormous number of sheets of glass always kept in stock.

The scarcity—and thus the value—of such colorists is attributable to the fact that almost any dexterous workman might be taught technique, but only a person born with superior color perception could become expert in this area. The individuality of each artisan entrusted with these color choices explains why shades of exactly the same design were often so different. It is a valid assumption, therefore, that shades were made with the help of excellent colorists, mediocre colorists—or sometimes completely without the aid of a colorist.

In addition to craftsmen and colorists, the Studios employed several exceptional artists, who evolved the actual lamp designs. If the procedures used in the creation of Tiffany windows were also followed for lamp shades, we may assume that the more elaborate shade designs were carefully drawn, in full color, to serve as guides for those who would execute them.

Since Tiffany lamps are now almost a hundred years old, it is not surprising that a few of those shown in this book have required the replacement of broken glass pieces, new wiring, sockets, switches, and so on. Changes in the illumination of lamps and the replacement or addition of glass will be referred to in this volume as adaptations. Fortunately, access to the Tiffany Glass Reserve permitted most replacements to be made from the original Tiffany sheets.

5

Tiffany Studios Album

This photographic album which includes several hundred shade and base designs has been a great aid in the evaluation of the lamps in this book [4, 5]. Quite different from other existing catalogues, which merely contain sketches made for advertising purposes, this comprehensive Album includes large-scale photographs on 11″ × 13″ sheets, identification numbers for both shades and bases and production entries and prices. The Album was loose-leaf between hard covers so that additional pages could be inserted if required. Notations appearing on the back of some sheets indicate that the bulk of the Album was compiled between the turn of the century (when Tiffany Studios originated) and the start of World War I (when it began to close down).

Many reproductions of the original black-and-white Album photographs are included in this volume, in addition to our own new color photographs; however, since their sizes are not given, no definite proportion to the lamps could be established with the former, as was done with the latter. As to identification, there can be no doubt that any lamp that is identical with a photograph in the Album is an original Tiffany lamp.

Tiffany Glass Reserve

Part of the Neustadt Collection consists of Tiffany glass stockpiled at the Corona Furnaces plant, Tiffany's glass factory, at the time of its closing. The story of this glass reads like an American Odyssey, and is probably just as apocryphal.

When the Furnaces shut down, some 500 large crates, loaded with the precious glass, first went to a dealer in Manhattan; though the only cost to him would have been transportation charges, he refused acceptance. For lack of a buyer, the glass was bundled off to a garage in Putnam County, owned by a former Tiffany associate. Upon the man's death, his attorney accepted the glass as his fee for settling the estate.

After several decades and additional peregrinations, the glass was unceremoniously hauled back to Long Island, where for several years it was exposed to the elements in an unguarded backyard. Eventually the glass found its final haven in Manhattan as part of the Neustadt Collection; a substantial portion of it will be incorporated into the Tiffany Museum.

Fortunately, the wooden crates had been packed with the care and skill typical of the Tiffany Studios. Cardboard or heavy paper had been inserted between adjoining sheets, which range in size from 12″ × 16″ to 18″ × 30″ and of which there are an estimated total of 36,000. The larger crates, exceeding 6 feet in length, were provided with wooden dividers to assure even more protection. Despite the passage of years, the casual handling, and the mileage covered, this careful packing prevented breakage to an unbelievable degree.

The Reserve has permitted a closer study of Tiffany glass and its qualities than was previously possible. A complete analysis would require a separate volume. The multitude of types, textures, weights and colors, and the large quantity of experimental sheets, testify to the untiring expenditure of time, effort, thought, ingenuity, love—and

money—Tiffany expended in this area. It has been established, though, that it contains every conceivable type of glass, including a complete line of Tiffany jewels. Insofar as they relate to lamps, these will be described in Chapter I.

THE ARTIST

Louis Comfort Tiffany was born in 1848 into the family which owned the famous jewelry firm, Tiffany & Company. Although he made many trips abroad, he spent most of his adult life in New York City, later moving to Laurel Hollow near Oyster Bay, Long Island. His artistic inclinations became apparent when he was still a child who roamed alone through forests and along beaches, evidencing a strong interest in landscapes, trees, flowers and rocks. He disappointed his father when he decided against college and eventual entry into the family's jewelry firm, and chose instead to study art.

When he was twenty, Tiffany started the first period of his artistic career, one that was devoted to painting and lasted for about a decade. Although he continued to paint in his later years, painting was then only an avocation, and Tiffany expressed himself more fully in other art forms. He studied in Paris and visited other parts of Europe, including Spain and Morocco, where he became acquainted with Moorish and Islamic design. After his return home, he continued to paint in both oils and water colors.

In exhibiting his work, Tiffany achieved a certain amount of acclaim. Perhaps he might have gone farther in this field, but his restless nature led him to pursue a diversity of interests. Possessed of ambition and an inexhaustible store of energy, he never hesitated to abandon an old enterprise when a new venture beckoned.

His years as a painter served as stepping-stones to his next endeavors, in the area of interior decorating and architecture. The firm of Louis C. Tiffany & Associated Artists, started in 1881, was the first of several agencies and partnerships Tiffany formed and in whose behalf he engaged a number of outstanding artists. Here we notice for the first time another of the attributes that led to his success: his ability as an organizer and executive. Though he was not an eloquent public speaker or a fluent writer, he had the gift of getting along with people and inspiring them to their finest efforts.

In the years that followed, he designed or decorated theatres, churches and elaborate houses and apartments, among them the Madison Square Theatre, the Church of the Divine Paternity, his own luxurious apartment on Madison Avenue, the houses of Mark Twain, the Vanderbilts, Hamilton Fish, the Havemeyers and the White House under President Arthur.

His style of decoration did not conform to prevailing modes of taste. In the beginning he made extensive use of Moorish and Oriental patterns. Later, especially after he had visited Paris and Vienna and witnessed the emergence of the movement, he became an enthusiastic exponent of Art Nouveau. It satisfied his desire for the unusual—the unique—and supplied him a foundation upon which he could elaborate at will. It afforded him, as well, the long-sought opportunity to break even farther away from the pervading style of the era, the highly artificial Victorian Rococo. Furthermore, Art Nouveau, with its free-flowing designs based on natural objects and its esoteric symbolism, exemplified those characteristics that had always played a large part in Tiffany's own creations. With the passage of years, these elements assumed ever greater significance as he developed his individual approach to Art Nouveau. Colorful peacock feathers, mysterious mazelike webs, and variations of Moorish patterns became favorite decorative motifs.

He successfully employed multicolored embroideries and rugs in his interiors, and highly sophisticated draperies; in color and tonal qualities, these were legacies of his first career as an artist. The effects he had once obtained with oils he now achieved with woolen yarns and silken strands and velvet swatches. His patterned wallpapers were a miracle of gleam and glitter.

The interplay of light and dark, and the artistic possibilities inherent in reflected rays, had always fascinated Tiffany. For unusual refractive effects, he made use of mirrors, glass mosaics, tiles, shiny discs and metallic wallpapers. For direct illumination, he employed a variety of chandeliers, sconces, skylights and colored windows. As time went on, he grew increasingly impatient with the available glass. The drive to acquire finer glass consumed more and more of Tiffany's time and gradually led to his complete preoccupation with the production of colored glass. As his efforts were crowned with success, he became instrumental in the re-acceptance of colored-glass windows as a separate art form.

The Search for Glass

At the beginning of his search for better glass, he first attempted to produce an iridescent type such às he had seen in Europe. Ancient Roman vases, buried in the soil for centuries, had acquired a strange but pleasing luster. After innumerable experiments, Tiffany finally achieved the correct chemical interaction, and, in 1881, acquired the patent on an iridescent glass.

Subsequently he organized the Tiffany Glass Co. which in 1892 was absorbed by the Tiffany Glass and Decorating Co.; the latter continued until 1900 when the Tiffany Studios emerged. Until he acquired his own production plant, he used the facilities of other glass makers. The Tiffany-owned Corona Furnaces on Long Island were not established until 1892. From that time on, they were the focal point of all his endeavors.

Although Tiffany's search for multicolored glass (without the addition of paint) went back almost as far as that for iridescent, the secret eluded him for many more years. His efforts were eventually rewarded and in 1894 the patent for his Favrile Glass was granted. Lamp shades made of this glass were first placed on the market in 1895.

He had finally succeeded in producing polychromatic glass, whose lifelike tones enabled him to transform paintings into glass pictures. The mighty contest that had long raged in Tiffany's soul had by now resolved itself. At last he had proved to himself and would do so to the world that no painting could convey the brilliance of color and the radiance of light which endowed his stained-glass windows with the semblance of life itself.

Tiffany's windows gained him assignments for a multitude of churches, museums, theatres and distinguished homes, together with an ever more illustrious reputation. Among his best-known works were the Russell Sage Memorial windows, reputed to be the largest unit of its kind (25' × 21'); the iridescent windows in the Tiffany Chapel at the 1893 Chicago Exposition, which were seen by more than a million viewers; and the celebrated picture window "The Four Seasons," which graced Tiffany's own Laurelton Hall estate.

In addition to windows, Tiffany produced some extraordinary mosaics, among the most notable of which were the "Dream Garden," a large-scale mosaic (50' × 15') made for the Curtis Publishing Company in Philadelphia, and the famous glass Curtain designed for the Palacio de Bellas Artes in Mexico City, which magnificently depicts nearby mountain scenery.

While the spectacular windows and mosaics occupied the limelight, in the 1890s the colored-glass lampshades began to emerge from their relative obscurity. According to the legend, too many glass fragments were left from the windows to discard. Business economics demanded their utilization in some way, and the obvious solution seemed to be their inclusion in leaded lampshades and other small ornamental objects. There is good reason to doubt this explanation.

Though it is true that each individual leaf, flower petal or background piece requires only a small segment of glass,

LOUIS C. TIFFANY

each lampshade consists of hundreds of such segments, all color-keyed and properly coordinated in terms of type, tone, density and the like. This means that all must be cut from the same sheet of glass. The desired over-all effect of the shade would otherwise be lost, and gathering of congruous pieces from masses of unrelated fragments would be an almost impossibly time-consuming task. Even in the repair of broken shades, where only a few pieces have to be replaced, major difficulties are encountered, since the sheet of glass from which the shade was originally made is obviously unavailable.

To make a first-class repair, an entire sheet of glass, similar in size and color to the original, may be needed to replace five or six missing fragments. Since the tonality and the striation or mottling, as well as the transparency, changes from inch to inch, each such fragment must be cut from a different portion, destroying practically the entire sheet in the process.

Tiffany's repeatedly expressed desire to bring beauty into the average home was probably responsible for the new emphasis on lamps, vases and other small articles. In this area, his one great and lasting love, colored glass, found fresh scope and inspiration. Though closely related to his windows, the challenge was somewhat different. While the windows served to transmit the light of day, the lamps represented a new source of illumination independent of daylight. The advent of electricity at the turn of the century further enhanced their importance and universal usefulness.

Besides the leaded glass lampshades, made of many small pieces, other shades, consisting of a single piece of glass, were blown into shape by the standard methods of glass-blowing.

In addition to these, the list of decorative objects offered by the Studios included metal craft, which encompassed bronze lamp bases, stands for vases, trays, candlesticks, jewel boxes, clocks, desk sets and similar objects.

These proved popular as gifts, and their wide public acceptance spread Tiffany's name and fame. With the advancing electrification of houses and apartments, the lamp department became increasingly important, and more ceiling fixtures and hanging lampshades were added to the production. Meanwhile, the excellent reputation of the firm was attracting some of the country's finest artists and craftsmen.

Tiffany continued to manage his companies with an equanimity and efficiency not ordinarily found in a creative artist. Though strict and demanding, he was eminently fair. He had the unusual gift of inspiring his employees with his own ardor, and most stayed with him for long periods.

Laurelton Hall

Until the very end, the dynamism of this prolific man never diminished, although in Tiffany's later years it was diverted from the planning of new products to an insistence upon broader recognition of past accomplishments. This desire, which at times assumed compulsive proportions, asserted itself in a flood of newspaper and magazine articles and unceasing exhibitions in all parts of the world; in these endeavors he demanded the active assistance of his friends. He also arranged for the publication of a book entitled *Art Work of Louis C. Tiffany*, which expounded the entire range of his achievements, with one strange exception; no mention was made of his lamps. In this same spirit of self-aggrandize-

ment, Tiffany purchased an enormous estate near Oyster Bay, Long Island, which he proceeded to transform into one of the most exquisite and expensive showplaces in the world. A two-million-dollar figure has been mentioned in connection with this undertaking.

Into this estate Tiffany poured a lifetime of experience in architecture, interior decorating and landscaping. He filled it with his choicest art treasures and regarded it as the crowning glory of his career. Called Laurelton Hall, it encompassed some 500 acres and consisted of a magnificent mansion, chapel, studio and art gallery; complete with hanging gardens, waterfalls, greenhouses, stables, palm trees, flower beds, fountains, covered bridge and gatehouse, it even included a lighthouse overlooking Cold Spring Harbor. Laurelton Hall was his command post. In addition to being Tiffany's official residence and focal point for all publicity, it served as the staging area for the most elaborate parties of the period. It burned down in 1935.

This obvious display of fame and fortune can only be construed as the desperate effort of an artist to remain in the spotlight as his own era slowly faded away. Art Nouveau had receded from the scene. With its replacement by Art Moderne and Expressionism, Tiffany's reputation faded, and for several decades many of his priceless creations were relegated to the attic or simply discarded. As with other significant art forms, however, his work was too important to be long buried. Disinterred and re-evaluated, it has begun to assume its rightful permanent place in the history of the nation's art.

Tiffany died in 1933, at the age of eighty-five. Honored by the world, he was also warmly loved by all who knew him well. Sincerity and understanding marked his close familial relationships. Despite the fact that his father had originally objected to his choice of career, the two men remained on cordial terms. Though a shadow fell on Tiffany's domestic happiness when his first and dearly beloved wife died, he married again and survived his second wife.

Not content with simply being the scion of an illustrious family, he made his own fame and fortune. Though small in stature, hesitant of speech, and extremely restless by nature, he overcame his handicaps with ambition, perseverance and genius, leaving to America a precious heritage.

LAURELTON HALL

1.   THE GLASS

ANTIQUITY holds the beginnings of the art of glassmaking. The first glass was probably created more or less by accident and used solely for ornamental purposes. Subsequently it was made into utilitarian objects. Much later it was used in wall openings, affording protection against the elements and also permitting the passage of light. Later still, glass was employed to protect the flickering flame of oil lamps and, eventually, to contain the vacuum of modern electric light bulbs.

Throughout this evolution, the decorative aspect of glass was always appreciated. Fancy dishes, vases and plates assumed a place of honor in many households. The first small, almost opaque, windows developed into the breathtakingly beautiful works of art that enhance both Renaissance structures and the sweeping glass surfaces of skyscrapers. The strictly utilitarian glass bowls on old oil lamps and gas lights became the attractive lampshades we know today.

COLORED GLASS

The art of coloring glass had, of course, been known for centuries; the most splendid examples of this art form are to be found in the stained-glass windows of old-world churches. However, almost every piece of glass was a single color. Multicolor effects were produced by the artful juxtaposition of the monochromatic pieces and, in many instances, by the addition of colored paints and stains.

On his European tours Tiffany was much impressed by these masterpieces, but found their effectiveness impaired by three factors. For one thing, the monochromatic character of the glass was untrue to life, since nothing in nature is uniform in color. Secondly, the application of paint interfered with the transmission of light, one of the principal functions of any window. Finally, the glass lacked the iridescence and luster he desired. His determination to create glass that would transcend these limitations goaded Tiffany throughout his entire artistic life.

Polychromatic Glass

During his years as a decorator Tiffany had attempted to produce more interesting types of glass than any he could obtain in the market. He experimented with new formulae at several glass works in Brooklyn and eventually succeeded in manufacturing glass with a unique iridescent quality. He next aspired to improve upon the monochromatic glass available for stained-glass windows. A multitude of colored glass pieces, skillfully arranged, might produce some striking effects, but the fact that each individual segment consisted of a solid color prevented the subtle blending of chromatic tones as they occur in nature. While the unreal appearance could be ameliorated to some degree by the application of paint, the procedure deprived the glass of its transparency.

In time, Tiffany would, in his furnaces in Corona, Long Island, create a glass in which color flowed and diffused, its hues as varied and changeable as those in the natural objects. The force that impelled him was the desire to create the mood of a painting by means of colored glass instead of colored pigment. With his newly created glass he could duplicate the subtle nuances of trees, flowers, rocks, sky, feathers, fabrics—even skin tones—and achieve the acclaim that had been denied him as an artist.

For a depressingly long period, even his own furnace men told Tiffany that his aim was unattainable. It was impossible, they said, to incorporate color into glass as he envisioned it. For years they tried to combine various metallic oxides to produce different tints and hues, but the mixture would always disintegrate. However, Tiffany had a stubborn streak which, added to his extraordinary energy, led to eventual success.

He devised new firing ovens and new methods of annealing, which finally enabled him to distribute chromatic materials throughout the fused mass; the result was color-imbued glass. As the procedures were refined, glass could be produced in an almost unlimited variety of tonal and density gradations. The Favrile patent covered these innovations.

With constant work, so many color combinations were perfected that, at the peak of production, glass sheets in several thousand different color combinations were at the disposal of his craftsmen.

Only a small number of the sheets were monochromatic, and even these show tonal variations. As used throughout this book, the term *tone* will designate density or saturation of a color. The *admixture* of another color will also be indicated. In dealing with glass, white must be considered a color. In surface paints, white, added to another color, merely lightens its tone; added to colored molten glass, it becomes visible in the finished sheet in its own right. In colored glass, we must then distinguish between light blue, which contains no white; white-blue, which is basically blue with added white; and blue-white, which is essentially white with added blue.

In addition, the relative *translucence* of the glass, which

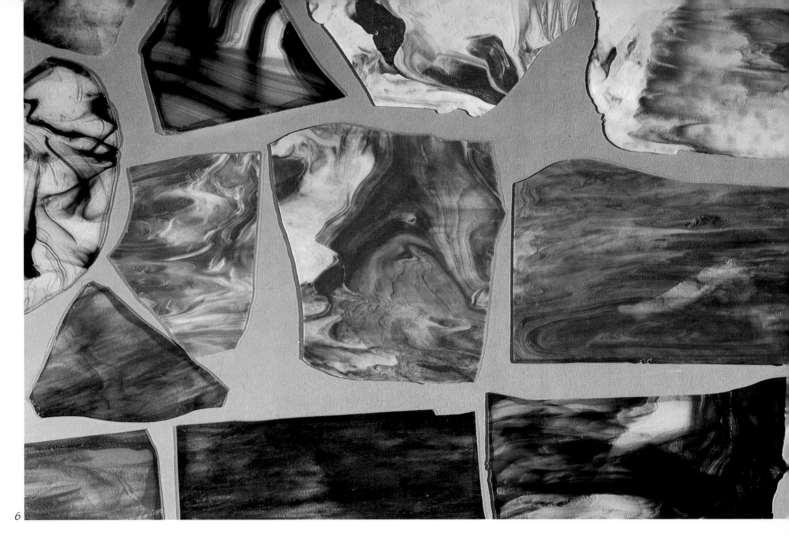

Striations viewed in reflected light.

varies from almost transparent to semi-opaque, must be considered. When the term *opaque* is used, it will be understood that the transparency is much reduced but not completely eliminated. Neither completely opaque nor completely transparent glass was ever used in Tiffany shades. A monochromatic sheet, then, might be a sheet of glass in any density of color or degree of translucence, without the addition of another color.

Actually, as we have pointed out, no color in nature is strictly monochromatic. A lake may appear blue, but closer observation will prove that the blue is not uniform over the entire expanse. These color modifications can be caused by such conditions as unequal water depth, bottom vegetation, the sun's brilliance, the surrounding landscape, surface ripples or atmospheric moisture. On inspection, then, the basic blue of the lake is altered by the addition of other colors. It is exactly this diversity that Tiffany has managed to incorporate in a single sheet of glass.

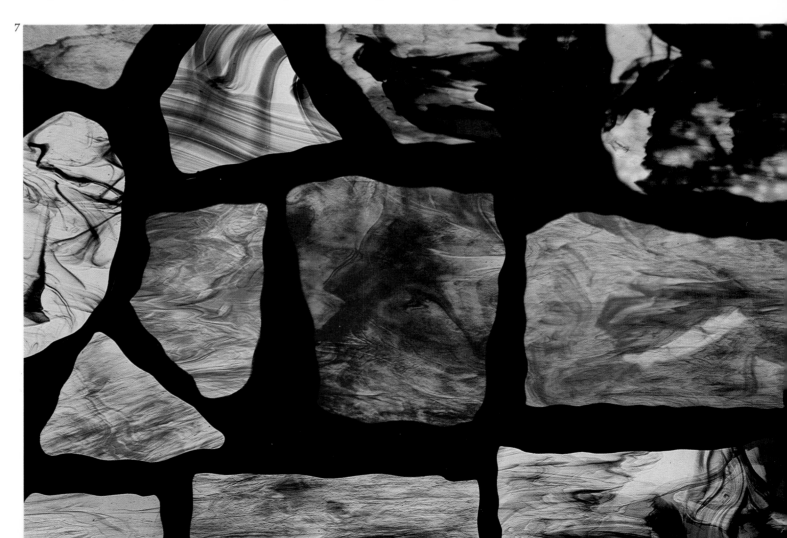

Striations viewed in transmitted light.

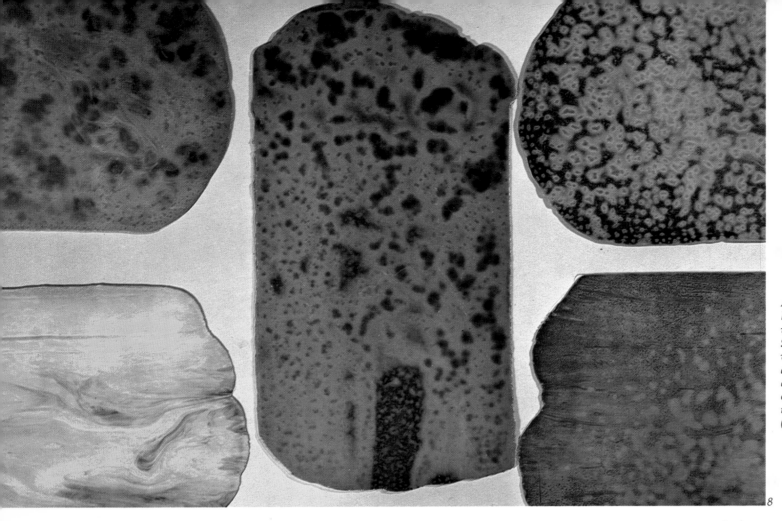

Area mottling and
localized mottling;
view in reflected light.
Secondary mottles
within primary mottles
at upper right. At
center, an entire sheet
of glass in the usual
rectangular shape
(note irregular ends).

Internal Color Patterns

The mixture of colors in a sheet resulted in the appearance of many different color patterns within that sheet. The most important of these are the striations and the mottles.

Striations

In a striated sheet, we are dealing primarily with lines and bands, which may arrange themselves longitudinally, flow in different directions or form swirls [6, 7]. Striking, often spectacular, this category can simulate such natural striations as those found in flower petals, leaves, stems, tree bark and branches, fruits, cloud formations, the wings of peacocks and dragonflies.

Mottles

Realism is also achieved by the employment of mottled glass [8, 9]. Mottling, which consists of splotches, speckles and dots of different sizes, is produced either by the addition of a second color or by a change in tonality or translucence

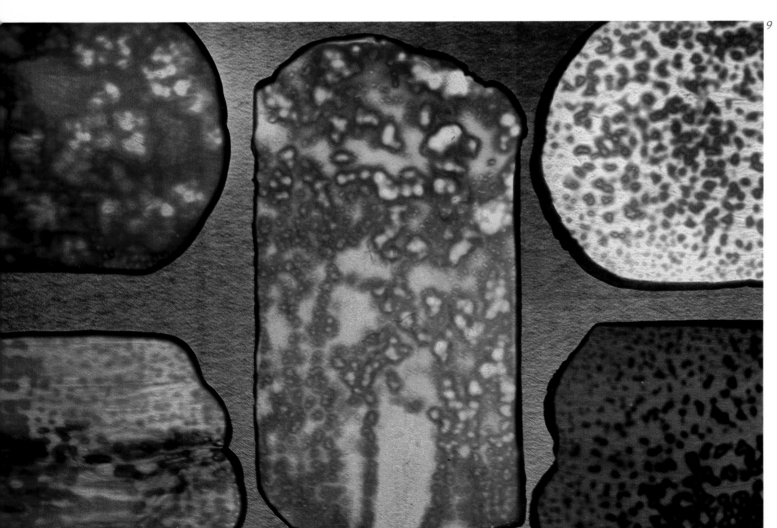

Mottling in trans-
mitted light.

Striations combined with mottles; view in reflected light. At center, an entire oval sheet.

10

from that of the basic glass (without the addition of another color). The latter is known as self-mottling.

With respect to coverage, we differentiate between area-mottling and spot-mottling. In area-mottling, the subsidiary color or the change in translucence is widespread. In spot-mottling, the mottles are smaller, sometimes as tiny as pin-points. Occasionally, large mottles are themselves spotted with tiny secondary mottles of a different color or degree of translucence.

Available as they are in such a vast assortment of sizes and shapes, mottles imitate certain living substances better than the more or less defined striations. Glass often contains both striations and mottles [10], see also end papers.

LIGHT PHENOMENA

Certain aspects of illumination require some consideration since they influence the perception of color and are essential for the evaluation of glass and of lamp shades.

Transmitted Light

Transparency is one of the most important attributes of plain glass. In a window frame, it forms part of the protective wall and, at the same time, allows the transmission of outside light into the interior of the house. The greater the transparency, the better it serves this purpose. However, in certain circumstances, it may be desirable to modify this un-filtered light by coloring, coating or otherwise treating the glass.

Since an electric bulb casts a very concentrated light, a transparent lampshade would permit glare and cause eye-strain. On the other hand, a shade made from completely opaque glass would confine the light to a highly restricted area, which is equally undesirable, since strong contrasts are also to be avoided, especially for reading and writing.

Glass used for lampshades should therefore be of mod-erate transparency, a demand most satisfactorily met by Tiffany glass, which runs the entire acceptable range of translucence. Since the density of glass is not entirely de-pendent upon its color, a whitish or grayish piece may be murky while a dark green or dark blue piece can be amaz-ingly transparent.

Occasionally we find that a shade made at the Studios, possibly for an oil lamp, is too transparent and can be uti-lized only by employing low-wattage bulbs. On the other hand, certain portions of a shade may be too dark and re-quire unusually strong bulbs behind the dull areas. This can be accounted for by the fact that the shades were handmade, and therefore subject to human error. Compensatory devices other than the selection of bulbs will be found in the chapter dealing with bases and methods of illumination. The vast majority of Tiffany shades, however, provide both an ade-quate reading light and sufficient translucence to create a pleasant level of illumination for the surrounding room.

Reflected Light

In addition to translucence, which is most evident in an otherwise dark room, glass also has a reflective quality. The

*Textured glass viewed
in transmitted light*

main reflection is produced by light striking the glass from an outside source, such as natural daylight from a nearby window, or artificial light falling upon it from another lamp or from a ceiling fixture.

While the true beauty of Tiffany lamps is brought out by transmitted light, a great many of them are also attractive and colorful in reflected light. Other of his shades, although magnificent when viewed in transmitted light, appear dull and cloudy without it.

Dichroic Effects

In this respect it is interesting to note that the color of a piece of glass in reflected light may not be the same as in transmitted light. Glass which displays this kind of color variance is called dichroic glass and was produced in the Tiffany Furnaces for this specific quality. The color change when such a lamp is lit is often startling [6-7, 8-9, 11-12]. With the touch of a finger, purple turns to red, green to yellow, blue to brown. Besides the dichroic sheets of glass seen here,

*Textured Glass viewed
in reflected light.*

Top row, left to right:
High Rippled.
Stippled, coarse.
Fibrillated.

Center row, left to right:
Fractured.
Undulating.
Drapery.

Bottom row, left to right:
Knobby.
Stippled, fine.
Low Rippled.

this feature will be illustrated by color plates of several lamps, showing them both lit and unlit.

Iridescence

Another rare attribute of Tiffany glass is its iridescence when seen in reflected light. To obtain the best effect, either the source of light or the viewer must stand at a slight angle to the glass. In transmitted light, the glass may appear to be plain and uninteresting, but when properly illuminated from the outside, exquisite rainbow tints appear as if by magic.

Iridescent glass is used in Favrile, leaded and mosaic shades. It is also extensively employed in stained-glass windows and in vases, where the same light-source requirements apply.

TEXTURED GLASS

Polychromatism and internal color patterns, dichroism and iridescense are not the only outstanding characteristics of Tiffany glass. Exceptional structural and textural qualities distinguish it as well. Most sheets of Tiffany glass are not smooth but are unevenly surfaced either on one or both sides; multitudes of folds, ripples or nodular irregularities give the glass a third dimension and also create the extraordinary light refractions which give Tiffany shades a great deal of their distinction. Other glassmakers have occasionally succeeded in producing polychromatic sheets of glass, but, without the unique textures, they invariably lack some of the qualities that give Tiffany lampshades their outstanding beauty. Textured glass may be divided into three main categories, each of which has several subdivisions: ridged textures, nodular textures and ridged-nodular textures.

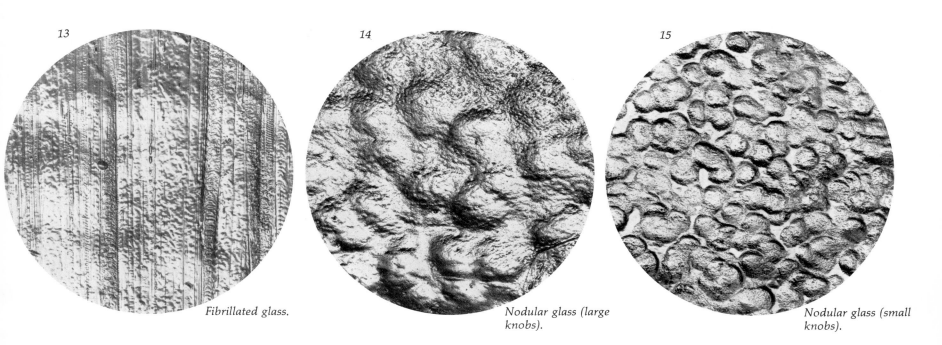

13   14   15

Fibrillated glass.   *Nodular glass (large knobs).*   *Nodular glass (small knobs).*

Ridged Textures

The greatest irregularity in texture is found in the heavy folds of *drapery glass* (so designated by Tiffany), in which the deep ridges and grooves involve both surfaces and are sometimes as much as 2" thick [11, 12]. For the most part, this glass was delegated to windows where it served to portray cloaks and gowns. Though infrequently used in shades, when drapery glass *is* employed, the effect is extraordinary. Smaller protuberances are found in the rare *sculptured glass* [23, 272].

Rippled glass, extensively used in lamp shades, has less pronounced and, as a rule, more uniform ridges. In general, only one surface is involved, but there are some exceptions. The ridges may be either high or low [11, 12].

One variety of this category is *Favrile Fabrique*. Here the ripples are arranged in a uniform fashion, creating a pleated effect similar to the "linenfold" found in English furniture, figures [23, 73, 74]. Like the following less pronounced texture, the grain in the pleated glass most frequently appears on only one surface.

The smoothest example of the ridged textures category is found in *fibrillated glass*, the surface of which is a mass of closely packed, threadlike filaments more or less parallel to each other. These tiny ridges are only slightly elevated and are separated by hair-thin grooves [11, 13]. Since the finer textures cannot be seen clearly in the color plates, which are reduced in size, they are shown in their natural size in special black-and-white illustrations.

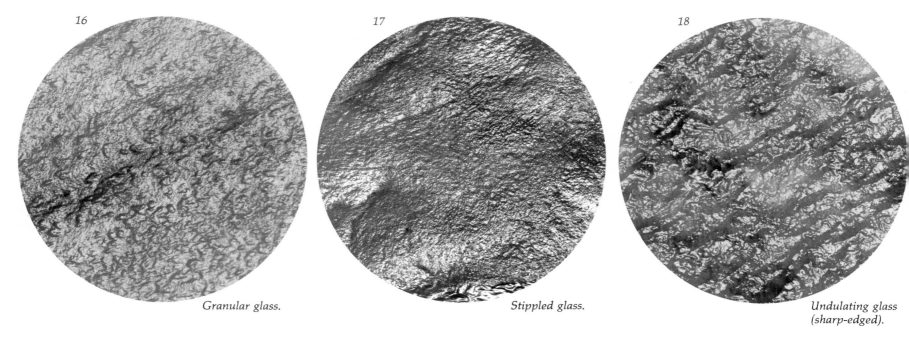

16   *17*   *18*

Granular glass.   *Stippled glass.*   *Undulating glass
(sharp-edged).*

Nodular Textures

Nodular glass is characterized by roundish or oval protuberances ⅛″ to ¼″ in diameter. The largest appear in *knobby glass*, in which the nodes are fairly well defined; they may be large, widely spaced [*14, 23*] or smaller and closely clustered [*15*]. When the surface irregularities are still smaller, the texture produced may be described as *granular or pebbled* [*16, 23*]. Decreasing in size, we subsequently arrive at *stippled* [*17*], *pinhead* and, finally, *pinpoint* textures. The surface of the latter is comparable to that of coarse sandpaper.

    Another variation of texture may be mentioned here which affects not the outside but the inside of the glass; it may be referred to as *bubble glass* and contains myriads of the tiniest air bubbles within its body. The effect is a soft diffusion of light and color.

Ridged-Nodular Textures

In this group, *undulating glass* is the most strongly textured and also the most frequently employed. Asymmetrically distributed all over the glass surface, long ridges intermingle with raised knobs, swells and sundry other formations of similar shapes. These ridges and other protrusions may either be sharp and angular [*18*] or smooth and rounded [*19, 23*].

    Configured glass also consists of ridges and nodules, but is more uniform in texture. Sometimes it is almost geometrically formal and regular [*20, 23*]; other times the figures consist of ridges and knobs in unaccountable combinations, in irregular criss-cross array or simulating patchwork [*21*].

    The various surface textures given to Tiffany glass endow it with the ability to refract and reflect light in many directions and with different intensities, thereby creating the most astonishing effects. Each of the textures described modifies the transmission of light in its own unique fashion. Rippled and undulating glasses create a fiery glitter, intensity depending on the size of the ridges; knobby and granular textures lend brilliance; configured and fibrillated textures result in a soft glow; stippled surfaces create a diffused glimmer. Since all these effects are influenced by the color of the glass as well as its saturation, transparency, striations and mottles, the Studio craftsmen could by careful selection achieve any degree of effulgence from a mellow glow to a blaze of glory.

*Undulating glass
(smooth-edged).*   *Configured glass
(regular).*   *Configured glass
(irregular).*

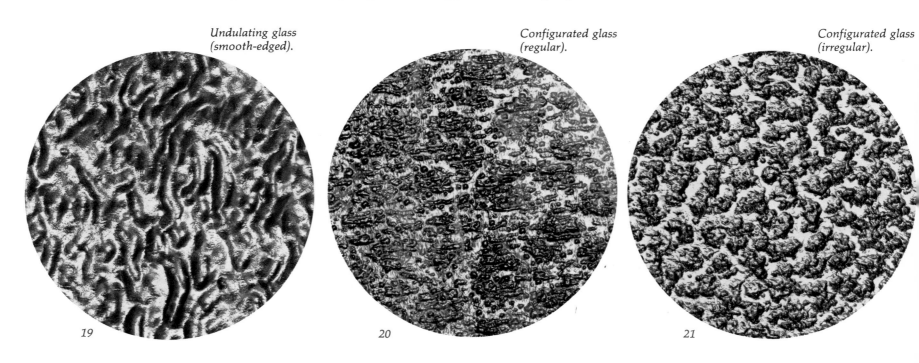

19   *20*   *21*

Fractured Glass

The foregoing types of glass were fabricated in practically all colors, with texture and tint largely unrelated to each other. *Fractured glass*, on the other hand, is a Tiffany innovation which integrates the two elements.

While a sheet of glass was in the process of hardening, but still semi-soft, small flat splinters or flakes of differently

which this fractured glass was extensively employed. The rare dimension it added to a lampshade has always been much cherished by collectors.

By making full use of the innumerable color combinations, striations, mottles and surface textures available to him, Tiffany was finally able to achieve lampshades that are truly paintings in glass, portraying a diversity of sceneries.

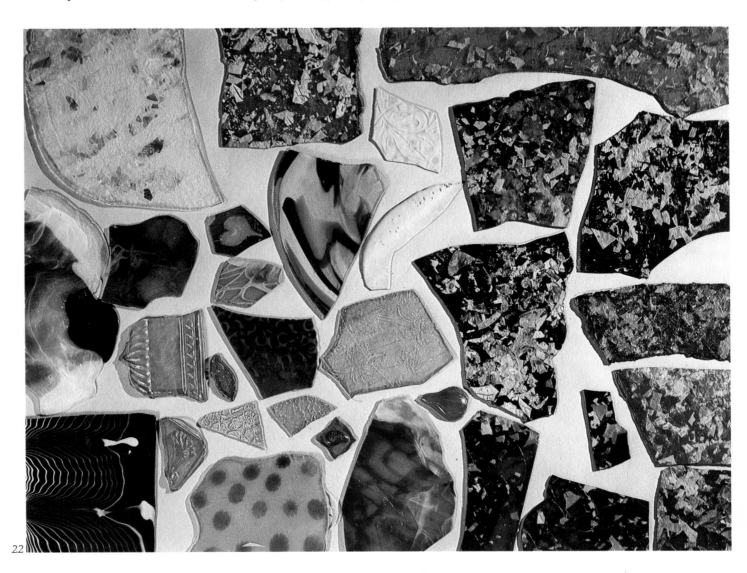

Fractured glass and patterned glass.

colored glass were pressed upon its surface. Some of the splinters were wholly incorporated; the raw edges of others would protrude, giving the glass an uneven ragged texture [22]. Splinters of many colors were used on the same background, sometimes superimposed on each other to create subtly variegated shadings. This kind of coloration lent itself superbly to such backgrounds as sunset skies, mountains, meadows, water scenes, flower gardens, for all of

From the standpoint of *usage*, Tiffany glass can be divided into ornamental glass for geometric designs; flower glass for petals; foliage glass for leaves; "twig glass" for tree bark, branches and stalks; "lace glass" for reticulated structures; "sunset glass" for distant landscapes and background; and "horizon glass" to picture sky or water. The terms in quotation marks are those used in the patent for Favrile glass.

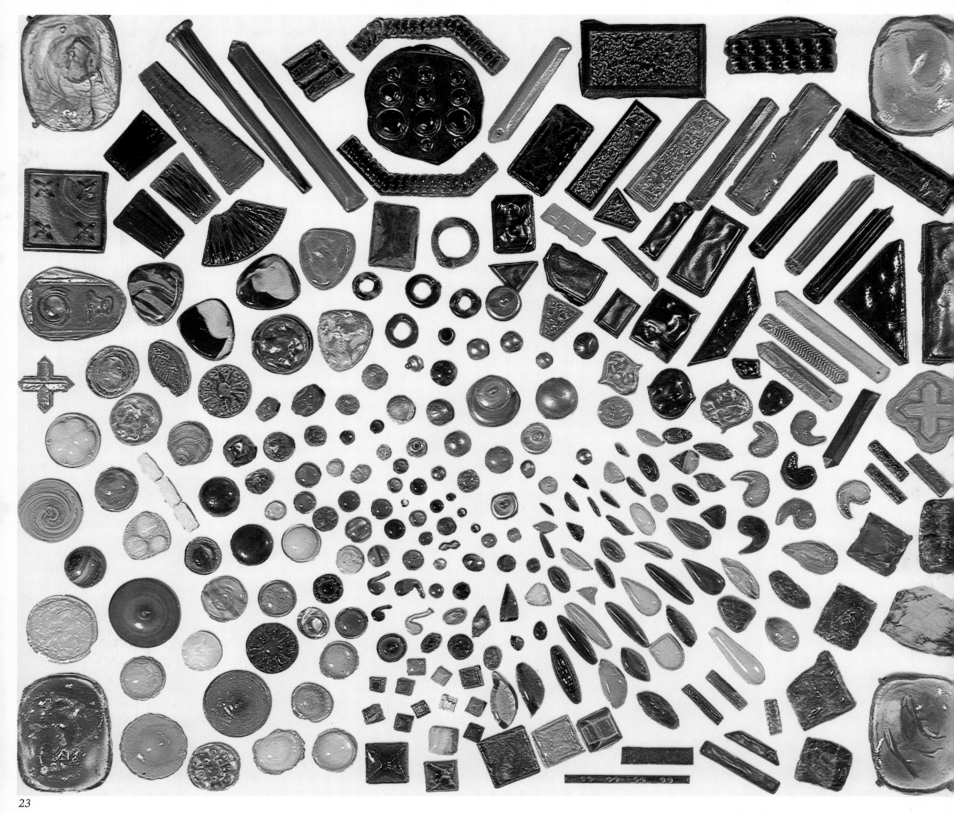

23

Glass Jewels

In addition to sheets, the Tiffany Studios also produced glass jewels in various sizes, shapes, textures and colors, some transparent, others opaque [23].

The Turtlebacks, rough-surfaced, thick pieces of glass about 4" × 6" in a wide range of colors, are seen in lamp bases, in the shades of desk lamps and in ceiling fixtures. Small oblong jewels, of various sizes and almost every known hue, adorn many shades. Iridescent balls and rhomboid jewels are also employed in many shades and bases. Multi-colored prisms hang from the bottom edges of Favrile and Geometric shades. Oddly shaped chunks of glass are occasionally used as flower centers of large blossoms. Round and half-round glass pearls form the lower borders of still other shades. With their iridescent colors, unusual surface textures and exotic shapes, the jewels play an important part in the ornamentation of many lamps. For special color effects the jewels were sometimes backed by an additional layer of glass.

Once Tiffany glass has been incorporated into a leaded shade, its *cleaning* requires a great deal of care; overly strong cleaning fluids will mar the finish of the leading. A firm nylon or fiber brush, used with warm soapy water, will rout dirt from tiny crevices; a cotton swab dipped in turpentine is useful to soften hardened incrustations. Lemon oil will remove a dull film from glass and restore its original luster. Because of its oily base, it should be used sparingly or the shade will attract dust. After applying any cleaning substance, the shade should always be wiped dry with a soft, lint-free cloth.

2. LAMP BASES AND FIXTURES

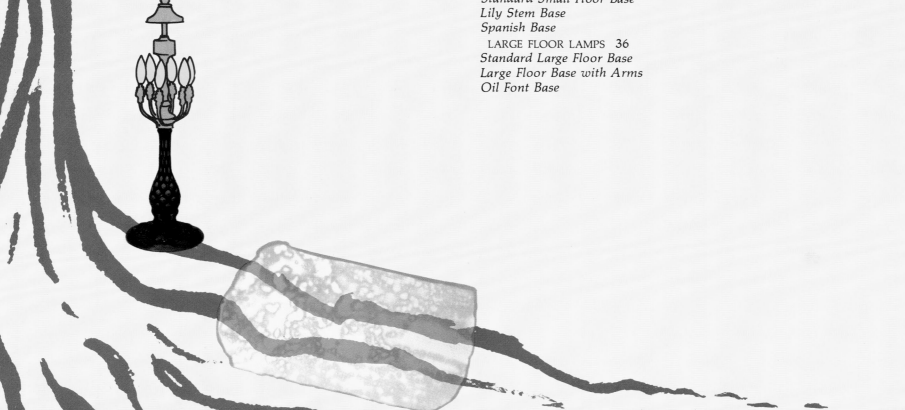

PROPER DISPLAY and function of their fine lampshades was of considerable concern to the Tiffany Studios. Almost from the beginning, therefore, they decided to provide their own bases. Only the earliest catalogues show Tiffany shades on bases made outside the Studios; some are known to have come from the Grueby Faience Company and the Rookwood Workshops.

Besides bases for table lamps, the Studios made floor-lamp bases and hanging fixtures. Most shades and bases were interchangeable. A few of the table bases were designed for specific shades so as to make them completely integrated units; in these instances, each piece enhanced the value of the other. As a general rule, however, it must be admitted that the bases are not equal to the shades in artistry.

Bases for Table Lamps

THE MOST important bases for table lamps will be shown in conjunction with the shades. The styles include Art Nouveau, Moorish, Spanish, French and Classic. The sizes range from low standards, holding individual globes and designed for use on night or vestibule tables, to desk lamps of imposing dimensions. Almost all consist of a platform, a main stem, a light cluster, a support for the shade and a finial.

The majority of table or desk lamps are between 20" and 30" high. At the start, they were actual oil lamps, complete with reservoirs which served as bases. Later models consisted of adaptations or imitations of these oil lamps. Some bases were starkly simple, others were elaborately decorated with geometric patterns or with designs of leaves, flowers and other motifs.

Shade Supports   *24, 25, 26*

The majority of table shades—those not integrated with special bases—may be used with all other nonintegrated bases by employing the proper *aperture ring*. Most shades have a circular opening (aperture) at the top, the edge of which is reinforced by a heavy metal rim. The edge of the rim fits over the aperture ring, which is attached to the top of the base [24, 25a]. The size of the apertures varies with the size of the shade, and the rings correspond to the apertures, with just enough difference in diameter to allow for correct fit. The rings are secured to threaded nipples on the bases and are also interchangeable. For example, a 4" ring on a base could be replaced with a 5" ring, and be equipped to take a larger 5" aperture shade.

For the sake of simplicity, ring and aperture sizes will be described in even inches: 2", 3", 4", 5", 6". Their exact measurements are 1⅞", 3½", 4⅛", 4⅞" and 6⅝". The apertures are slightly larger.

Some of the smaller and medium-sized bases, such as those featuring the old-fashioned oil wells, support their shades on from three to five *arms* rather than on a ring. These nonadjustable arms are principally sized to hold 10", 12", 14" and 16" shades, with a few designed to take 18" and 20"

shades [25b]. The arms are a carry-over from the old oil lamps, whose chimney prevented the use of an aperture ring.

In rare instances, support for the shade comes from a *circumferential ring* connected with the base by several extensions. The Lily Stem Base is a representative example of this type [26b].

The Tree Bases are occasionally equipped with aperture rings but most frequently they have a different type of support mechanism, consisting of a *rod and sleeve*. Ordinarily, the rod is at the top of the stem [26a] and slips into the hollow sleeve which is attached to the underside of the shade. Occasionally, this arrangement is reversed, with the sleeve being on the base, the rod on the shade.

24

25

26

Left: 25a, b, c
Right: 26a, b

Metal Finishes

The metal bases were cast in bronze and finished in shadings which range from light to extremely dark and also encompass copper tones; all these may be affected by age and atmospheric conditions. The patina finish, which adds green to the bronze, may encrust the base to any desired degree.

While Tiffany seldom resorted to plain gilding, he made much use of the gold doré finish for which he was famous. Far more complicated than ordinary plating, it is characterized by a distinctive surface texture, formed of innumerable almost microscopic wrinkles whose raised surfaces are somewhat lighter than the depressed portions. We will differentiate between a light and a dark doré. While all Tiffany finishes are difficult to restore, this one is almost impossible to recreate once it has deteriorated or been marred by overzealous cleaning.

Finally, we have the old silver finish; dull in tone, it is reminiscent of pewter and rarely seen.

In general, base finishes harmonize with that of the finial and shade leading, except that a plain gold finish rather than gold doré was used on the shades. In the descriptions the finish will be mentioned only if other than plain bronze.

Quite a few of the bronze bases have inserts of Tiffany jewels. In others, the glass is blown through a network of bronze. Some bases are set with mosaic, and a good number are of Favrile glass. Examples of each will be shown.

Light Clusters

The actual lighting for the table lamps derives, in most instances, from a cluster of bulbs attached to the top of the base stem. It consists of from two to six sockets which are arranged so that the light bulbs circle the base standard. Two important results ensue: larger bulbs can be used; the bulbs are situated farther from the shade [24, 25b], thus insuring the glass against heat burn, which causes multiple fine cracks.

It is advisable to keep a 100-watt bulb about 2″ away from the glass; smaller and larger bulbs may be placed proportionally. As a general rule, bulbs of fairly low wattage are as effective in Tiffany lamps as those of higher wattage, which are all too frequently employed.

In a few of the larger stands, such as some of the Tree Bases, sockets (and consequently bulbs) are at right angles to the base stem [26a]; this brings the bulb close to the shade and makes for spotty lighting. Some special integrated bases carry four or six candelabra (small-gauge) sockets on delicate, curved stems [25a, 25c]. Only the smallest lamps have single sockets at their centers.

Many of the larger bases are equipped with switches, some of which are so wired that, at the first turn, only half the bulbs light; the second turn operates the others; the third turn shuts them off. In other instances, the first turn lights half of the bulbs; the second twist turns them off and switches on the second group; the third turn illuminates all the bulbs and the fourth shuts them all off.

Finials   27

Finials, which correspond to the aperture rings in size, cover both rings and apertures [27]. Those designed for the smaller table lamps (2″ to 4″) are almost flat, with just a slight convexity and a small knob in the center. Like all finials, they are perforated to let the heat escape, yet the perforations are so arranged that no glaring light rays are emitted. The finials for the 5″ apertures are heavier in all respects and stand higher. The finish almost always harmonizes with that of the base. Except for integrated lamp units, which have their own special finials, these aperture covers are interchangeable. Finials are not signed.

27

Bases for Floor Lamps

BRIDGE LAMPS

The smallest floor bases are used for the bridge lamps which are designed to take Favrile shades and have single light sockets. Sometimes they carry ash trays or other accessories.

Bridge Lamp with Balance 28

The lamp shown in figure [28] is 50" tall; its plain stem narrows slightly toward the top, where it ends in a short, rather bulbous section with several metal turnings. Counterbalanced by a bronze ball in a leaf-shaped cradle, the shade may be raised or lowered. The stem is supported by five curved legs which stand on flat leaflike pads. (Similar bases were constructed with only three legs.) The base is finished in light patina and is numbered 468.

Bridge Lamp with Small Harp Design 29

This slightly larger lamp is 55" in height, and has a more elaborate stem, consisting of a number of slightly bulbous sections, connected by elongated knobs [29]. It looks much like a plant stalk, with the knobs representing joints or nodes marking the beginnings of new growth. At the top, the stem branches off into two arcs, forming a harp design, within which a 10" Favrile shade is suspended. An adjustable socket allows for the tilting of the shade. At the lower end, the stem widens into an 8" irregularly rounded platform, whose upper surface is decorated with shallow fluting, resembling roots. This lamp has a dark gold finish; its number is 670.

Bridge Lamp with Large Harp Design 30

The 60"-high fixture [30] has a stem which is heavier than that of the previously shown lamp and is plain except for a small swelling near its top. A round ashtray is affixed halfway up the stand. A harp design encloses a 12" Favrile shade, which is adjustable in two directions. The unusually heavy platform is 10" in diameter and raised some 2" above the floor; it has four straight legs on leaf-shaped pads. It is numbered 582. The finish is dark bronze.

Aladdin's Lamp 31

This design was obviously inspired by the ancient Arabian Nights legend. Its fluted stem is adjustable in height from 50" to 60" [31]. The arm, which carries a Favrile shade and is capable of a full 360° turn, is a re-creation of the original conception of Aladdin's Lamp. The central oil font is inscribed in swirling arabesques; the finely sculptured figure of a little angel holding a bird serves as cover. A winglike handle soars from one side of the font; on the other side, the elongated spout becomes part of the carrying arm; this ends in an adjustable rod from which the light socket and Favrile shade are suspended. The stem is connected by three curved legs to a triangular platform, decorated with wing motifs. The finish of the lamp is dark green patina. Rubbing will enhance its sheen but is unlikely to awaken the genie; simply in possessing the lamp, however, the owner has been richly rewarded.

28

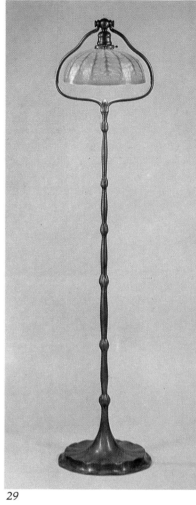

29

30

31

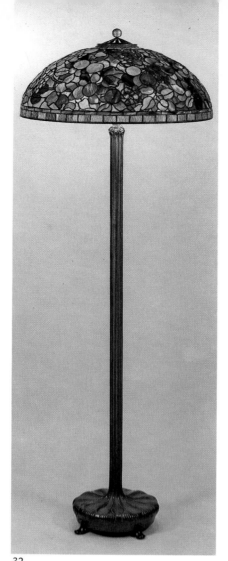
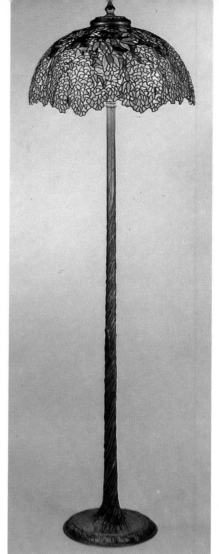
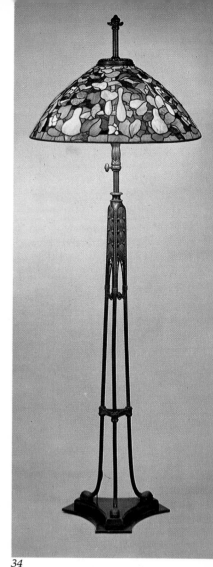

32   33   34

SMALL FLOOR LAMPS

Standard Small Floor Base   32

These bases measure 62" to the top of the shade, exclusive of finial, and rank next to the bridge bases in size and importance. They are made with plain round stems or with "foliated design" (fluted) stems, both of which are 1½" thick. Their 11" round platforms are raised from the floor on four small padlike legs. When the stem is plain, the platform surface is also smooth and unadorned. In a fluted stem base, twelve strands of wire run down the stand, cross the platform radially, and form a leaf pattern thereon. Such a base, finished in a soft patina and numbered 370, is illustrated in figure [32].

The Small Floor Bases are made to carry medium-sized shades and are equipped with 5" rings; they carry an intermediate finial 3½" high. Their lighting equipment consists of from four to six socket clusters, each socket of which is individually controlled.

Lily Stem Base   33

Also referred to as the Twisted Vine Base, this base represents one of the most beautiful of the small floor stands [33]. It is 66" high, finished in gold doré and numbered 645. The platform, 12" in diameter, sits flat on the floor, with the electric wire introduced slightly above floor level to avoid fraying. The outer rim of the platform is ringed with an elaborate root design, giving rise to twenty-four vinelike ridges; these twist and turn up the stem, flattening and thinning out as they approach the top.

This base represents a successful Art Nouveau design. Here the functional lamp base assumes the aspect of a plant, rooted in the floor, and carries a lampshade with a design of leaves and flowers in lieu of living growth. A similar design is made in Table Bases.

Spanish Base   34

Figure [34] depicts a base in Spanish style; it has an extension permitting adjustments of the shade from 62" to 69" although the delicate design of the stand does not favor usage of its maximum height. The triangular platform of this base is similar to that of the Aladdin Bridge Lamp, but larger (12") and heavier. Three leaf-patterned feet rest on this platform and give rise to three graceful stems which ascend at a slight inward angle; these are bound together at the top by a twisted-wire design in the shape of circles; four circles, vertically arranged, appear between each stem. A few inches below, we find a far less elaborate circular motif and, still farther down, another joining of the stems with essentially flat bands.

The vertical adjustability of this base is unusual in that the over-all height of the stem remains constant, while the height of the shade can be adjusted to any point between the uppermost triangular interconnection and the finial at the top. As shown in the illustration, the shade is still 3" above its lowest possible adjustment. (Note position of extension knob below center of shade.) In the Tiffany Album, the base carries the number 378.

LARGE FLOOR LAMPS

Standard Large Floor Base   35

The base [35] is taller and heavier, but otherwise similar in design to the Standard Small Floor Base. Its round platform, supported by four legs, is almost 5" high and measures 16½" in diameter. The stem, more than 2" thick and either plain round or fluted, is 72" high, exclusive of the large and elaborate finial, itself 10" in height and topped by a sprightly swirl. It is fitted with a 6" ring, the biggest made. The base shown has a fluted design and is finished in a light gold doré; it is numbered 376.

Large Floor Base with Arms   36

Though prevalent in table bases, a floor base with arms is so rare that it may have been a special-order item [36]. Its platform and stem are the same as those used in the Standard Large Floor Base, and may therefore serve as an example of the round smooth type of stand which has not previously been shown. The finish is dark bronze. The difference lies in the three arms which extend in graceful S curves from a knob on the stem to the rim of the shade, which they grasp between leaflike prongs.

Oil Font Base   37

Here a radially fluted platform supports a smaller platform which, in turn, carries the lower hollow portion of the extension stem [37]. This half of the stem is also fluted and, as in other base designs, the raised ridges continue into the platform, ending in a circular decoration. The upper portion of the stem is smooth until it reaches the extension; above that, it is embellished with the familiar longitudinal ridge design with circular motifs.

A good-sized oil receptacle, decorated with a wavy pattern, tops the stem. Four arms curve from the upper rim of the drum and hold the circumferential ring upon which a 24" shade can rest. As shown in the illustration, four extended prongs, attached to the ring as an adaptation, permit the use of a 26" shade. Without the extension, the base is 78" from floor to finial. The quaintly old-fashioned appearance of this oil-font base calls for a conservative shade, while its height and massiveness demand an extra-large (26") shade such as that pictured. The Tiffany Album gives the base the number 230.

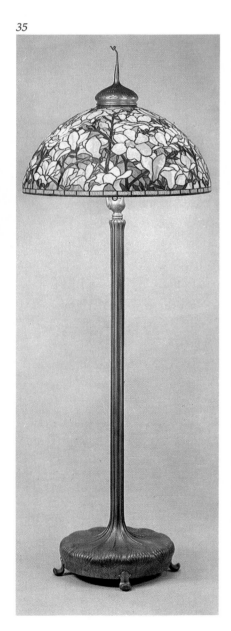

35

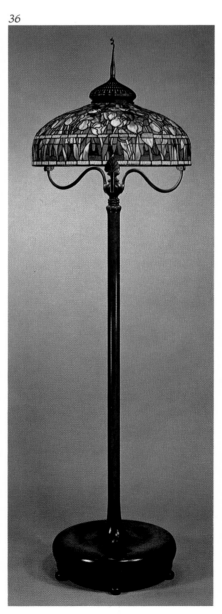

36

37

38

39

Ceiling Fixtures

FIXTURES for hanging shades are neither as varied nor as attractive as some of the table bases. They are mainly utilitarian, following in principle two methods. The simpler one attaches the shade to the ceiling by means of a heavy chain, fastened to the shade's finial. The hanging finial is constructed somewhat differently from those found on table or floor lamps. For one thing, it is firmly connected with both the aperture ring and the electric cluster. For another, its top ring, which hangs onto the last link of the chain, is bored to allow entry of the electric wire; this wire passes through both ring and finial and finally emerges on the inside of the shade. In figure [228] the wire can be seen running alongside the chain until it disappears within the hanging finial.

Another method of hanging a shade makes use of a pipe which conceals the electric wire and at the same time supports the bulb cluster. Three chains depend from the pipe and carry the weight of the shade, see figure [175]. These chains are lighter than the single chain referred to above and are made of round links. Most hanging-type shades (only the largest sizes were used in ceiling fixtures) are equipped with a heavy metal rim around the aperture, which contains three hooks; a chain is fastened to each hook.

In the largest hanging shades—those with 10″ apertures —the hooks are fastened to heavy aperture reinforcements [38]. Note that the chains are not carried all the way up to the canopy but only to an intermediary ball, also equipped with three hooks, through which the pipe passes. This arrangement was employed where ceilings were extra high, since it divided the great distance between ceiling and lampshade into two sections, one consisting of the pipe alone, the other of the pipe plus chains.

The fixtures for other unusual hanging shades will be discussed later in conjunction with the shades themselves.

The large area available for design, coupled with the excellence of the work itself, combine to make the large hanging cones some of the most memorable of all Tiffany shades. However, in order to afford a full view, such shades must be hung rather low, not more than 5′ from the floor. Because of this height restriction, which makes it impossible to walk beneath them, they must be placed above a sizeable table or desk. In modern homes, only the dining room table is likely to be large enough to cope with a 28″ shade. For best effect, the lower border of the shade should be from 16″ to 18″ above the surface of the table.

Since these considerations inhibit the use of the large hanging shades in the conventional manner, other means of display are advisable. Upside down, with their large rims facing the ceiling and their apertures about 6′6″ above the floor, they actually show to best advantage [39]. A greater height, within reasonable limits, may be desirable in order to increase the expanse of surface exposed to view. While extremely decorative in this position, even the largest shade will not interfere with normal room activities.

Since the flower designs in most shades are free-flowing, with stems, foliage and blossoms twisting and turning in every direction, often the over-all effect equals that produced when shades are hung as originally intended. Only the most formal plant patterns are unsuitable for use in this fashion.

Lighting Suggestions

Suggestions as to the improved lighting of the larger shades are in order here. The electric clusters mounted by the Tiffany Studios were of the highest quality, and most of them still function well; even some of the original wiring is still in serviceable condition. However, many electrical innovations are now available and should be investigated.

One of the most useful of these is the two-row cluster [40], which supplies two rows of sockets, thereby insuring adequate illumination of both the upper and lower portions of a large shade. The adjustable socket with movable joint, permitting the light source to be pointed in any desired direction, is another helpful development. A combination of the two-row cluster with the adjustable socket opens the door to a much better distribution of light in the large shades. It is virtually impossible to do justice to any shade exceeding 8″ in depth with only one row of lights; weak bulbs fail to illuminate the whole shade and strong bulbs produce glaring spots.

With two rows of adjustable sockets, adequately diffused light can be supplied to the entire leaded glass area, providing the proper illumination for every component of its design. Branches, stems, foliage, flowers and background, not only in the center of the shade but in every inch of it, from aperture to lower border, are equally aglow. Depending on the density of the glass, which may vary considerably from area to area, the intensity of each of the ten to sixteen electric bulbs may be modified to attain the exact degree of brightness desired in each separate section.

Other refinements in electrification have made it possible to illuminate some bases which have Tiffany glass inserts of various types. This adds still another dimension to the beauty of the lamp. Whenever this is done on lamps illustrated in this volume, it will be noted as an adaptation.

40

Care should be taken in *cleaning* Tiffany bases in order to avoid damaging the finish. Hard brushes, steel wool and strong chemical cleaners must never be used. A sponge, soft brush or cloth, along with a mild soap solution, will safely remove all dirt. For regular dusting, a soft cloth or special dusting brush is suggested. To bring up the gloss, a few drops of liquid wax may be applied to the surface and buffed well.

3. FAVRILE SHADES

ORIGINALLY, all of the new polychromatic glass developed by Tiffany was called Favrile Glass, a term derived from an old English word denoting "handcrafted." The covering patent specifically includes Favrile Sunset Glass, Favrile Horizon Glass, Favrile Twig Glass, Favrile Fabric Glass, and Favrile Lace Glass. According to the patent, these designations refer to glass used in leaded glass shades, stained-glass windows and blown shades. However, the term *Favrile* has come to mean glass shaped by blowing the molten product rather than by pouring it from the kiln. This narrowing-down of the definition is probably due to the fact that the blown pieces such as vases, bowls and lamp shades were signed "Favrile," while the leaded shapes customarily carried the Tiffany Studios signature instead.

In the making of blown shades, decorations could be added before and during the blowing process by the external application of varicolored materials to the hot surface. With poured glass this was a far less common procedure, primarily used in the production of fractured glass; in this instance, the colored flakes were added to the molten mix after it had cooled to a semiliquid state.

Since the responsibility of decorating the Favrile shades rested with the glass blower, his talents had to include those of a highly trained technician, a designer and a color expert. Thus the well-executed blown Favrile shade was a rare amalgam of art and craftmanship, which probably found its highest expression in Tiffany vases. Yet, in comparison with the flower-patterned leaded glass shades, which so masterfully imitate or abstract nature, the one-piece blown glass shades appear simple both in construction and design. For this reason, the Favriles will be the first shades discussed, followed by the least complicated leaded shades. In sequence, each succeeding chapter will deal with increasingly complex designs.

Favrile Globes

THEY TEND to be spherical in shape or represent modified spheres; in either case we will sacrifice exactitude for simplicity and refer to this group of shades as "globes." Of various sizes, the most common range from 7" to 12", though some were larger; a 14" globe is shown in figure [67]. These shades were used in table and bridge lamps, as well as in ceiling fixtures and accommodated electric bulbs suitable to their size.

SPHERICAL SHADES

Speckled Globe 41

The simplest type of Favrile shade, such as the Globe shown in figure [41], is spherical except for the interruption of the aperture. At that point, the glass turns back to form a flange into which small screws, emerging from the socket enclosure, may be wedged to support the shade from above. In the illustration, this suspension feature is not employed, and the shade rests instead on three supporting arms. The globe is 7" in diameter at its lower border, 2" across its aperture and 3¾" in height.

The Speckled Globe is dark orange at the top and light orange in its lower straighter-sided portion. Two series of bands, made up of tiny green and brown specks, create a directional design; starting at the aperture and ending at the bottom border, these bands intersect to form a new pattern.

The base symbolizes a tree, each of whose triple trunks divides into two roots, adding up to a six-legged support. The shade is supported by three arms, simulating the branches of a tree. An extension is provided to raise the shade which, in the Tiffany Album, bears the number 393. This is a rare and much-acclaimed base, which the Studios also made in several other styles and sizes, some of which will be shown.

In figure [42], taken from the Tiffany Album, we see a stand consisting of a plain straight trunk, whose two main roots divide into four rootlets; it is numbered 396. Figure [43] shows a stem with three main roots; these separate into six rootlets, each of which divides again, making a total of twelve; the number is 393B. The shades appearing on these bases will be discussed later.

41

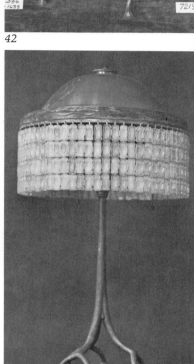

42

43

Striated Green Globe 44

The Striated Green Globe [44] is another good example of the smooth spherical shape. This shade is 10" wide, 5½" high and has a 4" aperture, measured from the outer edge of the lip. It is etched inside the lip with L. C. T.; opposite that, the number 4 appears. The shade is dichroic to a considerable degree. Unlit, it appears to be dark green, decorated with brown striations; around the center of the shade, and below the aperture, 2"-wide belts of iridescent purple may be seen. Illuminated from the inside, as in the illustration, the shade becomes light green and the striations remain brown; sixteen wavy lines run from the aperture to the border. The iridescent belts have turned into light green bands.

The base for this shade is shown in figure [28] and described in the accompanying text.

44

A similar Favrile shade is seen in lamp #341 from the Tiffany Album [45]; its global entity is intact, except for the unseen opening at its base, there to allow the introduction of an electric socket. The irregular striations remind one of the isobar lines on a weather map. The massive base crests to a giant wave carrying the globe.

45

46　　　　47

Feathered Purple Globe 46, 47

This globe is our last specimen of the truly spherical shades. Measuring 12″ at its base, it is 3″ across the flanged aperture and 6″ in height. Its coloration is highly dichroic. In reflected light [46] the shade appears to be dark purple, decorated with ten greenish-golden feathers, very delicately drawn. (Ten seems to have been a favorite divisor in the decoration of Favrile globes.) The feathers, each fringed on either side with thirty narrow vanes, rest on the lower border and run to just below the aperture.

Delicately etched dragonflies—one of Tiffany's favorite motifs—fly around and through the feathers. Nine in all, of various shapes, they range from ½″ to 2″ in length. Two can be seen vaguely in the illustration; one large dragonfly is on the right side of the central feather, a small one slightly lower and to the left.

In transmitted light, the dragonflies become less distinct; the feathers change to gold, and the dark purple background turns yellow; narrow blue stripes now appear between the feathers [47].

48

Both the base and shade of lamp #211 in the Tiffany Album [48] are composed of Favrile glass globes adorned with Art Nouveau leaf designs. The upper edge of the shade is scalloped. This is apparently an original oil lamp which has never been electrified.

MODIFIED SPHERES

Orange Spider Web 49

With this shade we arrive at a modification of the simple sphere [49]. Henceforth we will find that different shapes have been imposed upon its symmetrical smooth roundness without, however, materially altering the essentially globate appearance of the shade. The modification of this shade is minor and consists of ten heavy threads which radiate from aperture to border; they are slightly raised above the spherical surface. This elevation produces or accentuates a pronounced color change which, as we shall see, is typical of such raised areas.

The weblike appearance of the shade is increased by numerous threads of "spider silk" spiraling between the radial threads. Here again, a certain degree of dichroism exists. When the inside light is extinguished, the yellow-orange background of the shade changes to brown and the spider web assumes an iridescent silvery color.

The Orange Spider Web is 10″ wide, 5½″ high, has a flanged 2″ aperture and is marked *L. C. T. Favrile*.

49

Balanced Lamp 50

This shade is 7" wide, 4" high and has a flanged aperture 2¼" in diameter [50]. It is marked *L. C. T. Favrile*. The lower portion of the shade is globular, but the upper half consists of flattened areas between raised ridges. In reflected light, both the flat and curved sections appear to be the same dark green color, traversed with thin curved lines in a spiral pattern; a strong silver-blue iridescence is also present. In transmitted light, the flat portions of the shade refract differently and appear golden yellow, while the rounded ridges between them are a darker orange-brown; as always, in transmitted light the iridescence disappears.

This diversity of color, displayed when light passes through dissimilar curvatures in the same Favrile shade, is a delightful characteristic of the modified spherical shades, and probably a prime reason for their existence. The greater the divergence from the strictly uniform sphere, the more striking are the color surprises. We first observed this phenomenon in the raised spider legs of the Orange Spider Web shade, and we shall see it demonstrated even more dramatically in succeeding examples.

The most impressive feature of this base is the large round bronze balance connected to the stand by a stem-and-leaf design. It permits considerable latitude in raising and lowering the lamp. Another adjustment device near the socket permits the globe to swivel. The stand emerges from a 3"-high dome in the center of a 7" platform; the same raised leaf design that decorates the balance adorns the dome. It is described in Tiffany Studios' catalogues as "Balanced Lamp" and is numbered 415.

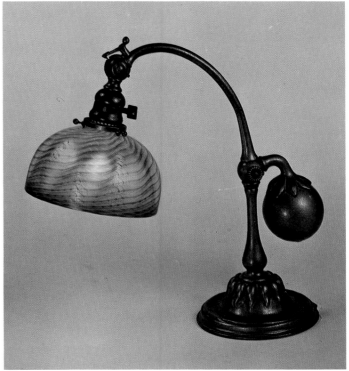

50

Low Nightlamp 51

This small shade is 10" wide, 4½" high and has a 2" aperture. The signature is *L. C. T. Favrile*, etched into the glass near the aperture [51].

The design resembles an arrangement of ferns, whose heavy midribs originate at the aperture and extend toward the lower edge; they are raised above the surface of the shade and are brown in color. Thinner, lighter brown veins angle out of each midrib. The fronds themselves are a brilliant golden-orange, enhanced by the dark striations of ribs and veins.

Because of the prominent midribs and the thinner, yet still protrusive veins, the surface of this shade is far from smooth. Faithful adherence to nature is evident in the minor irregularities of both ribs and veins. Here, too, the diversity of color coincides with the irregularities in the essentially spherical surface of the shade; the raised midribs and veins are darker in tone than the flat areas of the fronds.

The inner surface of this globe, as is the case with most Favriles, is white and smooth, except where the heaviest midribs cause a slight swelling.

The base is low, about 8" in diameter, and shaped like a round squat oil receptacle. The cap over the fill-hole has become the on-off switch for the lamp. The upper surface of the receptacle is decorated with meandering arabesques. Three gently curved arms, provided with small vertical stops at their ends, support the shade and hold it in place.

51

Student Lamps

Tiffany Studios produced an extensive line of student lamps, a great many of which have been preserved. Their popularity is probably due to their tasteful design, great lighting efficiency and ease of operation. A twist of the wrist raises and lowers the light source to any required level. In addition, the adjustable arm places the light directly over the object to be illuminated. Obviously the Student Lamp is a superior reading or desk lamp, made even better by the Favrile shade which further insures against glare. Originally designed as oil lamps, most have been electrified. Some still carry the impressed admonition "Close valve before filling."

The lamp shown in figure [52] has an adjustable arm, which carries the electric socket, and a round horizontal ring upon which the shade rests. The canister, a bronze cylinder, serves as the counterweight on the other side of the stem. Its surface is decorated with a number of elliptical and circular forms, made from minute twisted wires, soldered to the surface. Similar varisized circular forms adorn the top of the cap, the platform of the stand, the base supporting the electric socket and other areas of the stem. Each of these motifs has a small bead in its center. While not overly elaborate, the design is aesthetically pleasant.

52

The actual oil container, complete with valve, is inside the canister, ready to be filled. The original bronze tubings, which carry the fuel from canister to wick, are carefully preserved. If he wished, the industrious student could still burn the midnight oil.

The Favrile shade is 9½″ in diameter and spherical in its lower section. The upper portion of the shade is divided into ten triangular areas; almost flat in themselves, these are so angulated at their slightly raised corners as to flow smoothly into the circular circumference of the shade. As we have learned to expect, the color scheme reflects the surface irregularities. Yellow is predominant in the center of the flat triangular areas, while the raised edges between them are dark green with a bluish tinge.

In comparison, the Striated Green Globe, which we have seen in figure [44] as being smoothly rounded without raised segments, is uniformly dark green when unlit and becomes an equally even green-yellow when illuminated.

The discussion of student lamps would not be complete without mention of two particularly intriguing examples out of twenty-eight appearing in the Tiffany Album. The first features a basket-weave canister, combined with a filigree metal shade [53]. Twisted wire decoration is again in evidence. In the other [54], the canister is centered, with a leaded glass shade on either side. Obviously, the Favrile shade was not, as generally thought, the only type employed for student lamps.

53

54

Orange Globe on Teardrop 55

Here we see a Favrile shade on a Favrile base. The globe is 12" in diameter, 5" high and has a 2" flanged aperture, marked 16595 on the inside and 4248 on the upper edge [55].

Only the lower third of the globe is round; the flattened upper portion consists of eight convex and eight concave areas. These alternating areas are triangular, with the narrow angles at the aperture.

Shallow grooves are engraved over the protuberant "triangles," and continue to the lower rim of the shade (see second "triangle" from the right). In addition to these curved grooves, the globe is covered with thin wavy lines. A reticular pattern is thereby created in the shade, caused in part by linear embellishment and partly by the surface irregularities resulting from the grooves.

When lit from within, the surface concavities are light yellow, the convexities a dark orange. The inside of the globe is light green.

The base is composed of a three-legged tripod, which holds a Favrile vase in the shape of an inverted teardrop. The tripod's circular bronze band is decorated with wire applied in a scroll pattern. Three delicate arms extend from this band to support the shade.

The Favrile vase is 12" high, 8" at its greatest width and has a 5" flanged aperture, upon which the base of the light socket sits. The base also bears an applied wire design, similar in concept to that seen on the tripod stand.

Dark brown stripes divide the vase into sixteen longitudinal sections, each 1½" at its greatest width and tapering to a point at the tip of the teardrop. Coarse-finished, it is greenish-brown in reflected light, and also highly iridescent as can be seen at its upper surface in the light reflected from the globe. In transmitted light, the color becomes dark orange. The illumination of this teardrop Favrile base is an adaptation, as are the supporting arms.

55

56

An unusual combination of Favrile base, Favrile stem and Favrile shade in one lamp is illustrated in figure [56] taken from the Tiffany Album. The shade portion of the mushroomlike lamp appears to be about 12" wide and is completely closed at the top. It has a slightly uneven surface, with radial grooves near the center. The stem is lightly grooved and rests on a raised Favrile platform decorated with an undulating design.

57

Pineapple Lamp   57

A landmark desk lamp, the Pineapple, happily combines seven impressive Favrile shades with cascades of translucent glass pendants and a geometric pattern in its base [57]. It exemplifies a successful integration of base and shade.

The largest of the seven Favrile shades is 10" in diameter and occupies a central, slightly elevated, position; it is surrounded by six shades, identical in design but only 7" in diameter. All have 2" flanged apertures covered by tiny finials. Very similar to some of the Favrile shades described previously, each has ten raised areas, which might almost be called corners, radiating from the top center of the shade.

In transmitted light, these curved junctures of flat surfaces appear dark green, while the triangular portions between them are orange-yellow. In reflected light, the shades appear to be almost uniformly green. Oscillating bands add still more depth and dimension to the basic tone.

The Favrile globes rest on narrow bronze rings; twenty lavalieres, each consisting of four opaline glass jewels, hang from the rings of the six 7″ shades. Each jewel has on its inner surface an oval indentation from which tiny glass fibers radiate. These account for the widespread and surprisingly glare-free diffusion of the light thrown by the single bulb inside each shade.

In the base, rhomboid-shaped jewels of an iridescent greenish-orange hue uncannily duplicate the distinctive shape of pineapple scales. The glass gems are arranged in four vertical rows, with eight pieces embedded in each. Of several sizes, the largest (2½″ in length and width) are seen in the second row from the bottom, at the most bulbous circumference of the sphere. The shapes also vary from row to row. In the lowermost, they are horizontally elongated, thereby blending easily into the flat bronze platform; the pieces in the top tier are vertically extended, leading the eye upward along the ascending stem. Leaflike protrusions, from the bronze platform below and the fluted stem above, grasp the "pineapple" at both ends. The illumination of the base is an adaptation.

The Tiffany Album illustrates several different versions of this lamp: with from three to seven shades, on plain table bases and on floor bases. Figure [58] shows a floor lamp with five Favrile shades, numbered 387. Instead of glass jewel lavalieres, this shade employs closely grouped long glass prisms. Note the sharp studs on the Favrile shades. A Favrile shade with similar prisms is shown in figure [43].

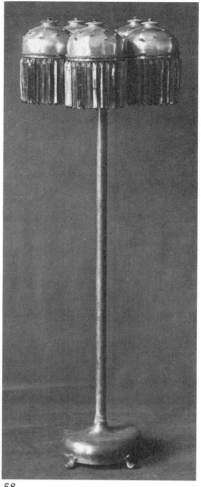

58

HANGING FAVRILE SHADES

Next we shall examine two small *Hanging Shades*, which represent interesting changes from the usual globular pattern.

Open-End Orb 59

This shade is 6½″ in both height and width [59]. Yellow-orange, it is decorated with six feathers outlined in green. The leaf spines are also green, and the barbs angling off these shafts are gold. In reflected light, the globe is covered with a faint purplish iridescence.

59

The Pear Shade 60

The second of these hanging shades is shown in figure [60]. The Pear Shade is 10½″ high and 8″ at its greatest width. Its background glass is light orange and transparent—too transparent in fact to conceal the illuminating bulb within, which therefore causes excessive glare. The shade is decorated with green leaves and yellow flowers, interconnected by light green stems.

60

Favrile Miniature Shades

IT MAY seem that we are deserting our small-to-large, simple-to-complex progression by turning to miniature shades after describing some fairly large globes. Most of these lamps, however, are made up of a number of the miniature shades embodied into elaborate supporting fixtures, the aggregate of which usually outshines the individual Favrile globes both in over-all size and in importance.

61

62

The "Aristocrat of the Garden" has maintained its distinguished reputation among the Favriles. A major prizewinner, this basic design was created by one of the most distinguished of Tiffany artists, Mrs. Curtis Freshel. All Lily lamps embody a cluster of miniature shades, in combinations of from three to twenty-four units, the most popular being three, ten, twelve and eighteen. Though far more common as table lamps, a floor model was also produced.

LILY LAMPS

Though fashioned in a great many sizes and shapes, these shades average 4" to 5" in height, 2" to 3" in width at the lower border and about ¾" at the aperture; this opening resembles a bottleneck and is designed to fit over a small candelabra socket. Only miniature bulbs can be used, and even these glare through the highly transparent shade, detracting from its delicate coloration. Some of the tiny shades are grooved, fluted or channeled and have undulating or scalloped edges. Others, resembling morning-glory blossoms, are smoothly bell-shaped with almost straight edges.

These ramifications of shape are matched by a color range which rivals that of the rainbow. Most are also highly iridescent. Many contain longitudinal striations of white, gray, pink, green, blue or purple. Some have one color near the aperture and another at the border. They are signed *L. C. T. Favrile.*

Three-Light Lily   61

In this lamp, the flower stems are comparatively short and the shades hang down to within 2" of the table [61]. A fourth stem ends in a hook which allows the small lamp to be carried about with ease. All three shades are dark gold.

The circular platform of the base is 5" in diameter. Its border is decorated with a leaf pattern, and a fluted design with radial ribs leads from its upper surface to the short main stem. The finish is gold doré, and the base plate is impressed with the Tiffany Studios signature and the number 320.

Eighteen-Light Lily   62

As a rule, Lily lamps are uniform in color. Varicolored shades on the same lamp, in gold, orange, blue, green and rose, are also most attractive [62]. The Lily shades hang from slim curved stems of varying lengths (15" to 20") which grow out of a platform about 5" high and 10" in diameter. The beautifully carved leaves covering the platform are – strangely enough – not the long narrow leaves of the garden lily, whose blossom the shade represents, but rather the round leaves of the water lily, which belongs to quite a different botanical group. The base of this lamp is equipped with a switch that controls the light bulbs, its knob being the replica of a lily leaf. The lamp is signed and numbered 1063.

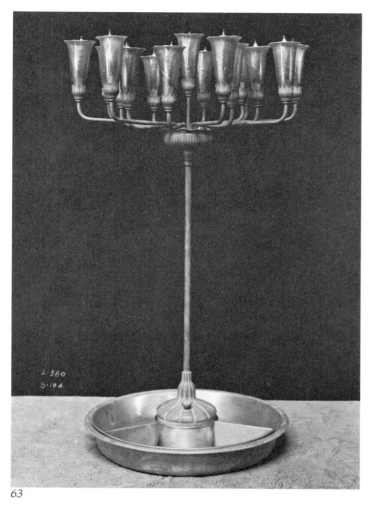

63

Several variations of the basic Lily lamp design were produced. Among the thirteen contained in the Tiffany Album are six styles with three lights, two with six, one with seven, one with ten, one with twelve and two with eighteen lights. Figure [63] shows a Lily lamp with fourteen shades which stand erect in a circular arrangement instead of depending from bent stems. The very thin main stem rises from a hollowed-out circular platform, which at one time may have served to catch candle drippings.

Floor Lily 64

The floor model carries twelve lilies; it is 4½' high and measures 18" at its greatest width [64]. The platform is the same as that used for the table lamp, except that it sits upon a slightly larger round bottom plate, 11" in diameter. The long lily stems twist and turn around each other as they wind upward. However, they do not unify into a single stem as on the Lily Stem table base, compare figure [261]. The finish is dark gold.

Each of the shades is signed, and the base is impressed with the Tiffany Studios signature and the number 685.

64

65

66

CHANDELIERS

Moorish Chandelier 65

In this ceiling fixture [65], illumination is furnished by six miniature shades. Each is about 5" high, 3½" wide at its bottom and has a flanged 2" top secured by three screws to the socket holder. The width is sufficient to take a medium-sized bulb in the standard Edison socket. Ten slightly raised ridges traverse each shade in a longitudinal direction and divide it into ten panels. In transmitted light, the panels are a medium to dark orange, while the ridges are light yellow to white, adding emphasis to the contours of this cluster.

From the bulbous end of a bronze shaft, three curved arms reach out to grip the main ring of the chandelier. The over-all distance from the ceiling canopy to the flower globe rims is 36"; it is 17" from the upper edge of the main ring to the bottom of the single-bulb shades.

The ring is 14" in diameter and consists of two metal rims, joined together by interlocking cirlces of tightly twisted wire. More wire ornamentation, reminiscent of that seen on the student lamps, see figure [52], embellishes the upper rim. The six shades hang from the lower rim on thin straight shafts, wound round with twisted wire. Thirty bronze chains, made of circular links and ending in bronze balls, also depend from the lower edge of the main ring, five of graduated length between each two shades; the middle one, being the longest, carries the biggest ball (2"), with the others proportionally smaller. The interplay of light on the curved shades, balls and chains adds still another dimension to the strong and showy Moorish design. The contrast in color between the orange shades and the bronze-work, finished in greenish patina, is especially pleasing.

Turtleback Chandelier 66

This ceiling fixture is very similar in feeling to the Moorish Chandelier, although it carries only three of the miniature shades [66]. These, however, are about an inch wider and so able to accommodate larger bulbs. The shades are round, smooth, yellow and ornamented with thin bands of eddying orange striations. The overall height of the chandelier is 36" from the bottom of the canopy to the bottom of the lowest hanging bronze balls.

Its main ring, 18" in diameter, is fastened to the ceiling by means of a shaft similar to that used for the Moorish fixture, but here we find five curved arms rather than three.

Ten large turtlebacks, set into the bronze ring in artfully wrought windowlike recesses, constitute the outstanding feature of this chandelier. Their green-blue iridescence, swirling with yellow specks, furnishes a sharp yet compatible contrast with the yellow-orange of the shades.

From the lower rim of the main ring hang twelve large multi-faceted balls on round-link chains; each face consists of a small piece of turtleback with leading between the facets. Their color is the same as that of the turtlebacks set into the main ring but, in the absence of transmitted light, appear darker. Between the turtleback balls, and suspended above them, hang smaller copper balls on chains; still higher is another row of even smaller balls on beaded chains. The decorative impact of these spheres—especially that of the turtleback balls—is greatly enhanced by the high positioning of the shades within their periphery. This causes multicolored reflections to re-bound from hundreds of iridescent facets. With each minute shift in the observer's viewpoint, another fascinating change occurs.

The illumination behind the turtlebacks set into the main ring is an adaptation.

Golden Ball Chandelier   67

Two kinds of Favrile shades—the globe and the minia-ture cluster—are combined in this fixture [67]. The globe is suspended slightly above the median point of the fixture, whose over-all height is 40". At 14" in diameter and 6" in height, it is rather large of its type. A small hole in its center serves to accommodate the supporting pipe.

The background of the shade is dark gold, enriched with multitudinous striations in light gold, and is equally intrigu-ing both in transmitted and reflected light.

The six miniature shades are somewhat unusual in that they are closed at the bottom. Each is 7½" high, 4" at its widest diameter and has a 2" slightly flanged aperture. The mark *L. C. T. Favrile* is engraved on each flange. Longitu-dinal rills divide each shade into ten slightly convex panels, which meet at the pear-shaped extrusion at bottom center. The long upper portions of these shades are transparent and almost colorless, with just a faint yellow-opalescent tint. Only the lower third and the knob are golden, decorated with serpentine striations and endowed with an exquisite iridescence of golden-bluish-purple hues.

Suspended from round tubings, the small shades hang from the outer rim of a most elaborate golden canopy, 30" wide, in which filigreed leaf designs alternate with fretwork geometrics. Each is flanked on either side by a gilded chain bearing three brass balls. Identical chains hang in loops be-tween each two shade supports. The fifty-four brass balls comprise the dominant feature of this unique chandelier, which, at least at first glance, may seem to outshine the miniature shades of more intrinsic worth.

The shades in this fixture are adaptations.

67

Hurricane Lamp 68

This rather odd Favrile represents one of the earliest specimens of its type [68]. Dating before 1896, when Favriles were first placed on the market, its origin closely approaches the time Tiffany obtained his patent on Favrile Glass in 1894 or may even have preceded it, as the lack of the registered signature indicates. It is undoubtedly the oldest piece in the collection. The lamp consists of a bottomless glass urn, a base and a crown, with an over-all height of 25".

The urn measures 13" in height and 12" at its widest portion, slightly above its center; from there it narrows to 6" at the top and to 5½" at the bottom opening. The basic color in the upper half is ecru, assuming a greenish-blue toward the lower end. A free-flowing design of slender, lily-type leaves spreads from the inferior to the superior edge; there it joins a pattern of shorter and heavier leaves which originate from the superior edge and run halfway down toward the bulge of the urn.

Both leaf forms are yellow-brown with reddish and green striations. Additional orange striations flow vertically between the converging long leaves while gray striations encircle horizontally the upper portion of the urn, crossing over the short leaves. There are five repeats of the design.

Certain breaks in the leaf forms, uneven outlines, irregularities in the striations, minor faults in the coloration and an unsmoothness of the glass surface seem to indicate that we are dealing here with the earliest stages of a craft which later reached the highest standard.

An ornate crown, 8" high, tops the urn. It is made of a delicate wire tracery, interspersed with beads of varying sizes, in Persian style. The lower portion, 9" in width, contains five elliptical jewels of ruby-red glass which conform to the five design repeats of the urn. The upper portion of the crown is a bell-shaped cupola with a tapering top, ending in a ball.

The base, made of the same wire filigree as the crown, cradles the urn in five leaflike supports; the leaf stems arise from a narrow metal ring, 9" in diameter. These stems as well as the ring are trimmed with strings of beads. Five pairs of tiny legs support the ring.

The illumination is an adaptation.

68

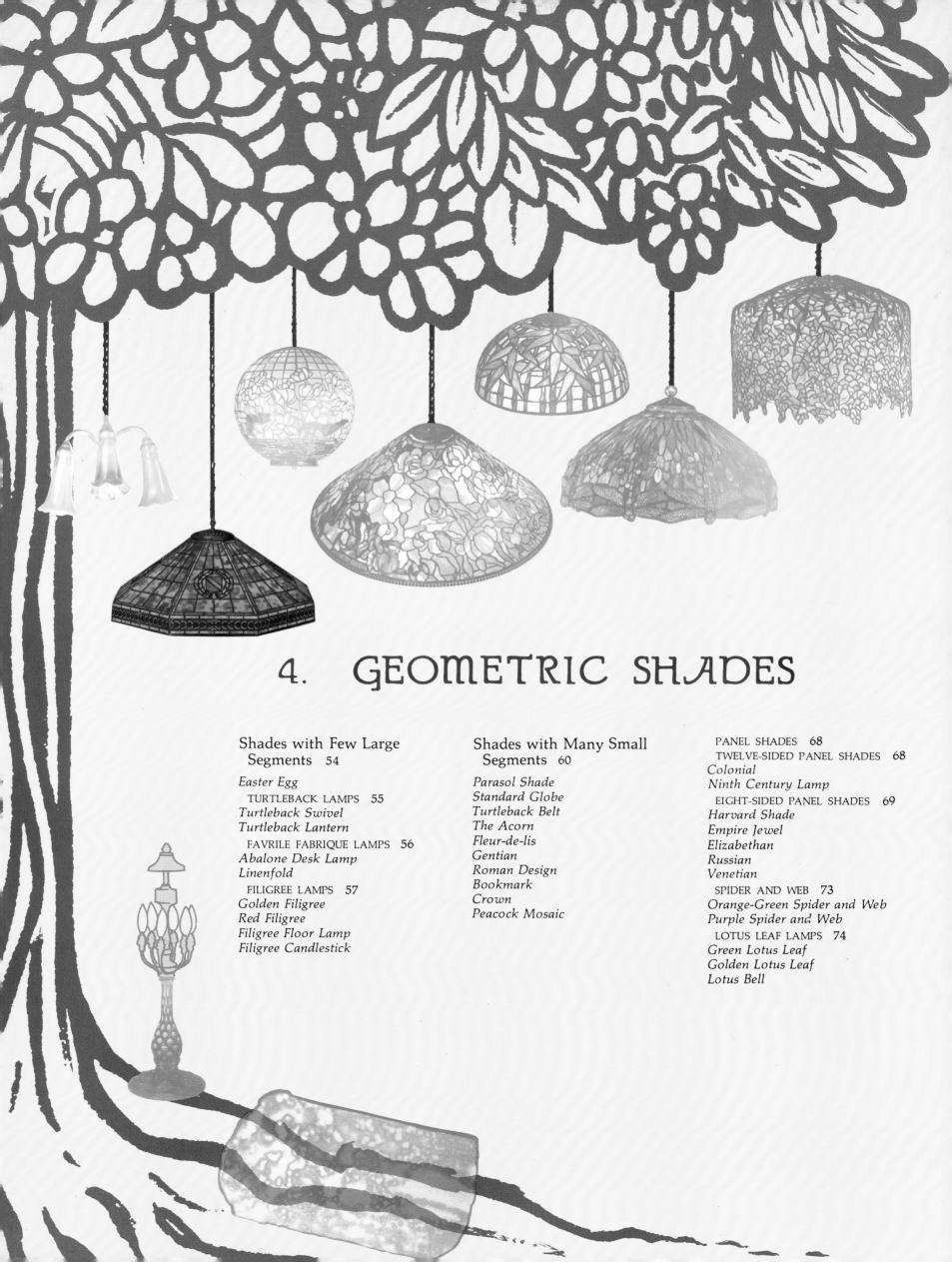

4. GEOMETRIC SHADES

PROCEEDING from the one-piece blown Favriles to the more intricate leaded shades, our first step takes us to the geometric designs which represent their simplest aspect. The shades are constructed of glass segments in such standard shapes as squares, rectangles, triangles, ovals, ellipses and rhomboids. In addition, their arrangement within each shade follows prescribed geometric patterns characterized by regularity, symmetry and repetition.

Under these conditions, the cutting and assembling of the glass pieces requires care and experience, but not an extraordinary amount of craftsmanship. Not even the selection of suitable colors involves the amount of artistic awareness required to create the naturalistic flower shades. At times, however, the juxtaposition of tints of the same color, and the adroit usage of striations and mottling, does add greatly to the ornamental value of a geometric shade.

Although some of the geometric designs are highly decorative and quite impressive because of their rich colors, the patterns themselves permit only a limited degree of originality and personal expression.

Unlike the Favriles, geometric shades are fabricated of more than one piece of glass. A basic distinction exists between one category of Geometrics, made up of a limited number of large-sized components, and a second classification in which shades consist of a large number of small pieces, the edges of which are covered with copper foil and directly leaded to each other. The latter constitutes the true Leaded Glass Shade.

Shades with Few Large Segments

IN THIS category, lead is not always used to bond adjoining pieces of glass together; sometimes the segments are set independently, other times fitted into metal channels which are leaded together.

Easter Egg   69

Hardly classifiable as a lampshade, yet serving as a light fixture, this ornamental oddity is 24" high and measures 18" in width, including decorative framework [69]. Its back and front exactly match, thus allowing it to be hung advantageously across an archway, where it can be viewed from both sides. While supplying moderate illumination for two otherwise dark rooms, it is at the same time an extremely interesting *objet d'art*. At first glance, the fixture appears to be a much magnified example of the jeweler's craft.

The 8" × 10" center globe consists of two 1" thick oval pieces of glass, highly convex on the outside, which are set into bronze bands hinged at the top. The illuminating bulb is inside, between the two concavities. The beautiful opalescent glass is opaque, with rough, irregular markings. It is surrounded by slender white and spherical green jewels, set into a network of twisted wire, forming elaborate Oriental filigrees. The hanging chains and the four pendants are of similar design, and also set with jewels. The fixture has been repaired.

The Easter Egg is a perfect transitional piece from the Favriles. Like the Favriles, it is unleaded, and though it consists of two pieces rather than one, both are identical and form a single unit. Discrepancies aside, it unquestionably belongs here, for the glass is not blown but poured.

In all probability, this shade was the only one of its kind.

TURTLEBACK LAMPS

In the following examples, the turtlebacks represent the principal elements of the lamp; in many other instances they serve as additional yet subsidiary features of attraction.

Turtleback Swivel 70

This small lamp, suitable for a side table or nightstand, is 9" in width and 14" high [70]. Basically, its head consists of two identical turtleback jewels. One forms the "front" and one the "back" of the shade; both are metal-rimmed and joined by triangular side pieces, also of bronze (not visible in the illustration). The turtlebacks are yellow-orange, and are characteristically round-cornered and rough-surfaced, with uneven humps and hollows; iridescent multihued swirls accentuate the irregularities. Hobnails form the main ornamentation of the metallic areas.

At its sides, the head of the lamp is hinged to two curved arms; joined at the main stem of the base, yet retaining their separate shapes, they descend to the circular platform. The latter is 5½" in diameter and stands on five small ball feet; its top is adorned with a leaf design, and sixteen green jewels are set around its periphery. The illumination of the jewels in the base is an adaptation.

Turtleback Swivel Lamps vary somewhat in size, color, style and decoration, some bases lacking jewels.

Another Swivel lamp appears in the Tiffany Album [71]. Made from (leaded) Turtlebacks set into a sphere, it has a large round opening; shell-like in design, it would serve especially well to light a painting.

Turtleback Lantern 72

Both the Easter Egg and the Turtleback Swivel consist of two single pieces of glass, each set into its own bronze frame. With the Turtleback Lantern, we confront for the first time a fixture which consists of several pieces of glass leaded into one unit.

The four-cornered, bronze-framed lantern is 8" wide and 12" high. Eight turtlebacks are set, two to a side, on each of its four sides. Four triangular pieces form the bottom of the lantern, and the top is open [72]. The bottom panel is hinged so that it may be opened to insert a bulb. Tiny triangular turtleback splinters, inset between the corners of the turtlebacks and the bronze frame, testify to the kind of finicky craftsmanship lavished on Tiffany lamps. From the top of each corner, a curved arm flows out of the frame and extends to a common center; at the junction of the four arms the lantern is fastened to a heavy supporting ring.

The color of the turtlebacks is yellow, tinged with orange and green. Again we find the typical surface irregularities which lend this lantern an air of rugged strength and real antiquity. Many viewers have taken an unusual fancy to this impressively simple piece, whose antecedents may have hung in the arched hall of an English castle or medieval cloister.

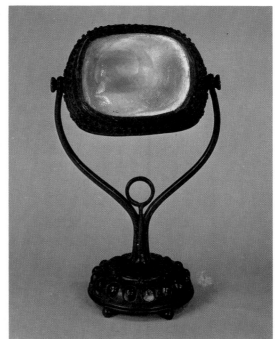

70

71

72

FAVRILE FABRIQUE SHADES

73

Abalone Desk Lamp 73

Part of the Abalone desk set, this lamp was made to match such other pieces as blotter, accessory box, calendar and desk pad [73]. Sixteen and one-half inches in over-all height, the shade itself is 5″ high, 10″ at its maximum diameter and has a 2″ aperture; it is impressed *Tiffany Studios New York 1928*.

The shade is composed of twelve panels of *Favrile Fabrique* 3″ high, which are bordered top and bottom by narrow horizontal slices of the same glass. In the vertical panels, the more or less regular ridges and grooves run vertically; in the horizontal panels, horizontally. Although the pleated texture is on the outer surface, the inner side is also rough.

The Abalone shade has a comparatively heavy lower metal border; its upper rim is pierced with seventy-two vertical slits, which play a double role as cooling device and decoration. Twelve small round pieces of abalone shell are set into the metal top and finial, both of which are furnished with still more airslits. The finish is light gold doré, which is only rarely used on shades.

Like the remainder of the desk set, both the four-sided stem and the eight-sided platform of the base are decorated with Moorish patterns, made of abalone shell set into incised bronze. The base is numbered 604.

Linenfold 74

This shade is 14″ in width, 6¾″ high and has a 6″ aperture [74]. Basically cone-shaped, it actually has sixteen sides. The entire center of each side is composed of a 3″-long panel of amber pleated glass, vertically rippled in a linenfold design. These oblongs are bounded top and bottom by thin strips of the same glass, with the ripples in this instance running horizontally.

The remainder of the shade is made up of two continuous metal strips, one below and one above the pleated panels; each strip is bent sixteen times to conform with the angle of the panels. The lower edge of the 2″-wide bottom strip is slightly lipped. The narrower upper metal strip ends in a wider scalloped lip at the aperture. As another exception to the rule, the shade of the Linenfold, like that of the Abalone Desk Lamp, is finished in gold doré rather than plain gold. Perhaps this can be accounted for by the large expanse of metal areas in these two shades. The shade is signed and numbered 1931.

The integrated base has a round 8½″ platform with a free-form lip; it is 23″ high, including the finial, and is signed and numbered 586. A tubular center stem is airily encased by long stylized leaves. Six leaves emerge from the middle of the main stem and curve outward and downward to the platform; six curve upward and cradle a serrated ball which rests on top of the base stem. The perforated finial has a flower knob. Like base and shade, it is finished in gold doré.

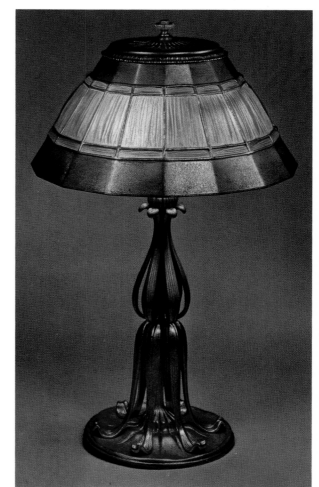

74

FILIGREE LAMPS

While metal filigree is interesting in its way and often succeeds in producing an attractive lamp, the technique is neither unique nor an outstanding example of metal craft. Of all the lamps in this volume, the filigree shades probably rank lowest on the scale of artistic excellence. It is said that they were made for competitive reasons at a time when Louis C. Tiffany had more or less retired from active management of the Studios.

Golden Filigree 75

This lamp is 20" high and carries a six-sided shade which is 15" wide between parallel panels and almost 18" between opposing corners; it is 6" high and has a 3" aperture [75].

The six lower panels form a horizontal apron about 5" deep; the upper panels are triangular in shape and slant upward toward the center of the shade. The glass in the panels varies from light yellow to dark gold and is covered with fine metal filigree in a design which incorporates stiffly stylized stems, leaves and flowers. Beaded metal strips decorate the edges and corners of the shade. All the metal is finished in gold.

The base, impressed with the Tiffany Studios signature and the number 631, consists of an eight-sided stem with a "waistline" about a third of the way up; from its maximum fullness in this grooved area, it tapers inward at both the shade and base ends. The stem radiates into an eight-sided platform. The base carries three sockets and is finished in light gold doré.

75

76

Red Filigree   76

This shade is 16" wide, has a 3" aperture and is completely unique in outline [76]. It is composed of eight sections best described as trapezoidal, whose long sides run from the lower border of the shade to the aperture. These sections are most uncommon in that they are curved both vertically and horizontally, such two-directional curvatures are very rarely found in sheets from the Corona Furnaces.

The glass is superior to that used in the Golden Filigree: it has a broader polychromatic scope ranging from red to yellow, orange and green; and also an infinitely more interesting texture, being both stippled and fibrillated, with added color in the fibrils. The shade is not numbered but an identical one in the Tiffany Album shows the number 1405.

Though heavier and thicker, the design of the metal filigree is similar to that seen in the last shade. The finish is green patina.

The base is a magnificent example of the glass-in-bronze group. This effect is produced by forcing Favrile glass through the openings in a reticular bronze pattern during the blowing process. The two rows of high-luster leaf-green extrusions consist of twelve units each. The globules in the upper row are elongated, as if to lead upward toward the slightly twisted bronze stem; the full-blown teardrops of the lower row seem to furnish a broader support at the lowermost part of the platform. Four spatulate feet raise the platform from the table surface. The stem, rising above the two rows of blown glass, carries the shade on three curved arms.

The base is finished in a medium shade of copper, and the stem is incised with three sets of darker grooves. From a small ring at the lower end of the stem, twelve even darker grooves radiate downward toward the reticular framework. The underside of the base is impressed with the Tiffany Studios signature and the number 21667. Other glass-in-bronze bases will be shown in subsequent chapters.

Filigree Floor Lamp   77

Entirely made of green glass, covered with the same metal filigree patterns that appears throughout this category, the base and
shade of this lamp are inseparably a single unit [77].

From floor to finial, the structure is 5½' high. The heavy platform is 16" square and 4½" high. On each side of its four sides two
slanting sections angle in from the platform to the stem; this stand
is 4½" square and consists of four sections, all the same length. The
fifth and topmost section of the stem widens out to carry the hexagonal shade, which measures 26" from side to parallel side and 28"
from corner to opposing corner.

Each panel of the shade is trapezoidal and is 10" wide on its
bottom border, slanting upward to the 5" aperture, at which point
it measures a little more than 2" across. An apron with a 2" depth
at each corner and a maximum 3" depth at its center depends from
each panel. All edges of the shade are beaded.

The glass is varied shades of green with scattered white patches;
its every surface is covered with metal filigree in a formalized leaf
pattern. All sections of the platform and stem as well as the shade are
illuminated from the inside. A twisted rope design made of wire
bounds every edge of the base.

Filigree Candlestick   78

Though properly belonging to table lamps, the Filigree Candle-
stick is illustrated here because it shares both color and filigree design
with the foregoing lamp [78].

An all-metal filigree shade with a geometric pattern is shown in
the Tiffany Album [200]; its border is edged by small balls which are
suspended from beaded chains at two alternate levels.

78

77

Shades with Many Small Segments

WITH THE next lamp we enter upon the most important subdivision of this chapter. As the name suggests, these shades are made of large numbers of small glass segments ranging, according to size and pattern, from several hundred to over a thousand. Clearly, the judicious combination of many pieces of glass can create effects impossible to achieve in any other manner.

Instead of following a sequence based upon shade sizes, we will in this category adhere to a more meaningful progression and start with shades which are homogenous in structure and color, then proceed to those which incorporate simple geometric patterns. The Tiffany Studios produced more shades in the multiple geometric category than in any other. That, of course, accounts for the fact that more of these are still in existence today.

79

The Parasol Shade 79

Presenting only the uppermost segment of a sphere, this gently curved shade is 24" in diameter. Despite its imposing width, it is merely 6" high and has an unusually small (2") aperture [79]. It is made entirely of quadrangular pieces of leaded glass, arranged in twelve horizontal rows (from lower border to aperture) and in sixty vertical rows (around the globe from left to right). Within each horizontal rectilinear row, all pieces are equal in size. In the vertical rows they gradually attenuate from 1½" wide at the bottom to ⅛" at the top. The bottom rim of the shade is made from a half-inch strip of bronze, which is unusually wide.

In shape and markings, the parasol shade also resembles a portion of the terrestrial globe, with the horizontal lead lines representing the latitudes, the vertical lines the longitudes and the aperture the pole. The orange glass is gently speckled with darker orange and traces of green and red; extensive pinhead mottling is also present. By reason of its simplicity, this shade has a naive charm and a special appeal. It is finished in light patina, is signed and bears the number 1520.

The base for this sphere is 26" tall, including the finial. Its round platform is 8½" in diameter and curves upward to join the stem at a height of 4½". Fluted with 60 radial ribs, it is fitted with a three-way switch which controls the six candelabra bulbs and stands on five ball-shaped legs. The slightly shaped stem, thicker at top and bottom than in the middle area, is fluted longitudinally. It displays the rather rare silver finish (restored), and is signed and numbered 28622. In the Tiffany Album its number is given as 370. The finial is of a special design, consisting of twenty-four radial ribs which merge into a delicate stem; five perforations are found in each of the grooves between the ribs.

In the Tiffany Album [80] the same shade, also numbered 1520, is exhibited on a base numbered 374 which has a ribbed platform and a slender stem, from which three upward curved arms stretch toward the shade support. The finial is identical.

Standard Globe 81

Though similar in style to the Parasol Shade and the same 24" in diameter, the larger Standard Globe is much deeper, measuring 10" in height from its aperture to the start of the apron, and 14" over-all [81]. The fact that the apron is not quite straight but to a slight degree continues the curvature of the shade makes it even more spherical in appearance. The 6" aperture indicates that the globe is designed for use with the large floor base.

The upper portion of the shade if formed of forty-eight vertical rows of quadrangular glass pieces which, however, do not line up horizontally. While we cannot therefore speak of seven horizontal rows, it will be sufficient to state that each vertical row is divided into seven sections. Two harmoniously interwoven designs separate the main body of the shade from the 4"-long apron.

The upper surface of the shade is orange with muted green and red mottling. In the interwoven designs, the glass is mottled with a darker green-gray, while the apron is rendered in rippled glass, textured on the outside, in orange and green with red striations.

81

Six leaded reinforcement wires, which run in a vertical direction from aperture to apron, are an important construction feature of this globe [82]. By their arrangement, they divide the shade into six sections, each containing eight vertical rows. Reinforcements of this nature are frequently employed in Tiffany shades, their differing routes evidently determined by the stresses to which the shade may be subjected. Undoubtedly these reinforcements are largely responsible for the remarkable resistance to breakage of these apparently fragile glass shades. Many of them have managed to endure almost unscathed or only slightly damaged for almost a century. The shade has the 4½" signature tag and is numbered 1516.

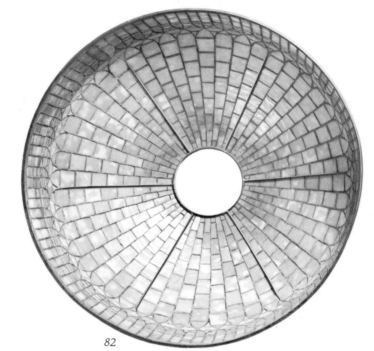

82

A globe shade, numbered 1501 in the Tiffany Album [83], demonstrates the painstaking care with which the leaded joints of one horizontal row are made to fall exactly at the center of the glass pieces in the adjoining row. This globe has no apron.

83

84

85

Turtleback Belt   84

In this shade we see the first major modification of the homogenous geometric shades so far discussed. This was accomplished by the introduction of a different glass in a different color [84]. The shade is 16" in width, 7" high and has a 3" aperture. It is signed and numbered 1494.

In the Turtleback Belt, the standard geometric arrangement of the globe is interrupted by a row of twenty turtlebacks which circle the circumference of the shade; typically rough in texture, they are green, touched with blue, and have a silvery iridescence. Below the belt, three rows of narrow longitudinally placed pieces of green mottled glass form the lower border of the globe. Above this belt, five horizontal rows of the same glass, the segments squarer and narrowing toward the aperture, constitute the main body of the shade. These upper rows are very attractively mottled with darker green speckles and spots; occurring unevenly throughout the shade, they look rather like clouds casting their shadows over a country meadow.

The quiet character of the shade is enlivened by the rugged texture, tonal variations and iridescence of the turtleback insertions. No other glassmaker has ever succeeded in producing such exquisite specimens.

The triangular platform of the base incorporates an interesting tripod effect, including a secondary level formed of three flattened leaves. From a third encircling ring, the fluted stem thins slightly toward the top, reaching a height of 24". It is finished in a light patina.

This base was purchased, although with a different shade, at the final closing sale of the Tiffany Studios' showroom on New York's Madison Avenue in June 1937.

The Tiffany Album depicts a similar shade, with fewer and larger turtleback pieces and one additional longitudinal row above the belt, on a Turtleback Base [85]. The square body of the base is made from four full-sized turtlebacks, and its frame stands on four turtle legs. The shade is carried on four arms which rise from the upper corners of the frame. Turtleback chips have been set into the small triangular spaces between the turtlebacks and the outer frame, just as in the Turtleback Lantern, see figure [72]. The base is numbered 227.

86

Acorn 86

This shade demonstrates the addition of a secondary design to the simple arrangement of geometric shapes [86]. Its largest diameter is 12", from which it tapers to an aperture a trifle over 4"; not designed for an aperture ring, the Acorn is meant to be supported by a three-armed base. It is signed with the ¾" tag.

The six horizontal and thirty vertical rows of quadrangular glass pieces are interrupted by a swath of stylized acorns, connected by an artfully contrived stem pattern and arranged in an alternating up-and-down sequence.

This is the first time we see a pattern evolved from a plant. In succeeding pages we shall encounter them with increasing frequency, and trace their gradual emergence from simple basic shapes to complex re-creations of natural forms.

The acorns are yellow in tone and extremely transparent; their partly stippled, partly fibrillated texture enhances their brilliance and causes them to stand out strikingly against the background of mottled bluish-green glass.

A similar but larger Acorn shade, number 1435, is shown in the Tiffany Album [87] on an unusual Favrile base. The glass body of the latter is enclosed within bronze straps which connect the acorn-decorated platform with the shade supports. The base is numbered 218.

Because its comparatively simple design was economical to produce, the Acorn achieved great popularity and was turned out in scores of sizes and shapes. Other formalized leaves, flowers and fruits were employed, as were diverse Moorish, Roman and Greek designs, to decorate geometric globes.

The Greek Key is used as a border design on an otherwise geometric globe in shade number 1444 in the Tiffany Album [88]. The base, whose stem consists of a classic column, carries out the Greek theme; it is numbered 199.

For a Moorish feeling, reference is made to the shade shown in figure [247]. In this, a strip of iridescent balls adds an Oriental note to the otherwise purely geometric globe; it is numbered 1508.

Another geometric shade—this with a simplified leaf motif—is shown in figure [42], which has already been studied in connection with the Root Base. Above the first four horizontal rows of precise rectangular pieces, we meet various rounded shapes which simulate leaves.

Despite this profusion of pattern, the geometric shades never approach the florals in concept, color or craftsmanship. Still, they filled such a deep decorative need that Tiffany competitors "flattered" him by sincere attempts at imitation.

87

88

89

Fleur-de-lis   89

The heraldic device of France's royal family is utilized to good effect in the Fleur-de-lis shade, which is 16" in diameter, 5½" high and is signed [89]. The catalogues refer to it as Trefoil; in the Tiffany Album it is numbered 1438. Its 5" aperture is fitted with a heavily beaded bronze band, which was not planned for use with an aperture ring; the shade must therefore be supported by arms.

The ten sections of the shade are marked off by flower stems carrying three-fold leaves, with an Iris motif centered between each two stems along the bottom edge of the globe. The flowers are of orange and yellow glass; the background pieces are a dark mottled green at the top and fade gradually into bland milkiness at the lower border.

The three-arm base, described in Tiffany catalogues as "Greek Model," and identified by the number 181 in the Tiffany Album, resembles a plain urn; it is embellished by four slightly curved legs, which stand on a squarish platform with a rounded protrusion at each corner. The urn has a rough texture and is finished in dark patina. More ornate urns of a similar type will be shown elsewhere.

Gentian   90

This shade is 18" in width and 6½" in height [90]. Though globular in its central portion, it assumes a chimneylike appearance toward the aperture and flares out at the bottom border. The finial, which in this case serves as a chimney cap, is 4" in diameter although the aperture measures only 3"; the extra-heavy two-piece rim of this opening requires a larger finial. The chimney is formed by four horizontal rows of fractured glass. Three are milky in tone and shot through with red, pink and green flakes; one narrower row is basically transparent, with more and brighter color embodied in it.

The main design begins just below the bottom chimney row. Sixteen floral stalks, each enclosed in a Gothic arch of highly transparent glass, curve over the sides of the shade, almost to the bronze rim marking the beginning of the apron. Their stylized green leaves and light blue flower petals are the only nonfractured glass to be seen in the shade.

The flaring apron consists of three rows, the top and bottom of which are made of rectangles of the same glass employed in the chimney rows. Between them, however, we find a very unorthodox but effective band of uncut green gems. This oddly contoured, strangely airy shade, made almost completely of shining fractured glass, is signed with the ¾" tag. Its number in the Tiffany Album is 1420.

The base is 22" high and carries a three-light cluster. Its integration with the shade is evidenced by the repetition of floral stalks and Gothic arches which appear both on platform and stem. The octagonal stem of openwork bronze tapers gently upward from a 9" round platform. The base is signed and numbered 2795; in the Tiffany Album it is listed with number 371.

90

91

Roman Design 91, 92

The globe which appears under that name in the Tiffany catalogue is a more advanced example of the geometric shade, both in shape and in pattern. Here, the spherical form has been flattened, creating a combination of shallow curves which gives this shade its extraordinary charm and grace. The Roman Design is 25" in diameter, 9" in height, has a 5" aperture and three reinforcement wires. It is signed with a 3½" tag and bears the number 1564.

The leaded pieces, instead of being predominantly rectangular as in the earlier globes, here consist largely of curvilinear forms [91]. In transmitted light they are orange-yellow, speckled with brown and intermingled with some almost white areas. A belt of ellipses and diamonds, bordered by narrow brown rectangles, encircles the globe at its center; these shapes are green on a yellow ground. A ring of long shallow half-ellipses, also green, surrounds the shade near its lower border; the rectilinear border row itself is composed of brown glass, mottled with orange.

In reflected light, the shade looks grayish-green, speckled with yellow. The sensitive mottling of orange and brown is now invisible, and the brown in the rows bordering the belt and at the lower border has also disappeared [92]. Because of this dichroic quality, a shade such as the Roman Design can serve to coordinate all the colors in a room or to emphasize and reinforce a single color. The dual personality of the dichroic shade makes it doubly intriguing. Subdued in daylight, it dominates the scene after dark.

92

93

Bookmark 93

Twenty-six inches in diameter, 14″ high and possessing a 6″ aperture, this shade is as large as any stained-glass example in the geometric category. The Bookmark incorporates more numerous design elements than any other discussed thus far [93]. It also has an unusually elaborate reinforcement structure, consisting of six vertical and two horizontal wires. One of the latter is near the aperture, the other close to the lower border; all eight wires connect.

The imposing apron, covering about a third of the globe's surface, contains eight circular motifs; each representing a colophon of master printers in the early periods of their craft. The colors within each design differ but all

share the same dark blue background. Geometric patterns in blending tones separate the six motifs. A similar configuration, minus the circles, makes up the wide upper border and also the four vertical bands which run between the two borders and divide the shade into four sections. Each of these sections is constructed of twenty-two thin rows of rectangular strips, interrupted at random by tiny round and square jewels, resembling a starlit sky. The shade is signed.

While this shade is still geometrical, repetitive and formal, it is far removed from the even and identical arrangement of leading pieces in the Parasol or the Globe.

The Crown 94

The Crown is a rare and quaint lamp which resembles its royal counterpart in that it too is adorned with bright jewels, symmetrically inset [94]. Its total height is 20″, and the diameter of the shade is 12″. The upper and lower edges of the Crown are defined by closely spaced white pearls, while the central area contains red, blue and yellow stones in diversified geometric patterns. The top of the shade consists of eight vertical and thirty-six horizontal rows, fabricated from golden-hued glass rectangles. A round yellow turtleback is embedded at the top center convergence point.

The tripod base is a bronze casting. Each support is composed of two disparate elements: a Sphinx with the winged body of a lion, sitting on stylized animal legs. Hooves rest on the triangular platform as if poised for flight. An intricately worked Oriental sword connects each winged creature with the bronze ring upon which the crown proper rests. The Sphinx was a favorite Tiffany motif.

It may be assumed that the Crown, like other one-of-a-kind lamps, represents either a special order or an experimental effort of the Tiffany Studios.

94

95

An equally odd oil lamp from the Tiffany Album [95] has an egg-shaped shade of open metal work over colored glass which appears to have been blown into the recesses. The cast-bronze base features large vertically arranged leaves. Numbered 143, it is a fine example of glass-in-bronze.

96

Peacock Mosaic 96

The Peacock Mosaic [96] is a ceiling fixture with the old-time charm of an oil lamp. A generous 38" in diameter, it is 10" high and tapers to an aperture of 5". As its name implies, this shade is made of exquisitely opalescent thin glass strips, inlaid on a copper backing. Their colors cover the full spectrum of the rainbow, whose only rival in nature is the peacock. The light of the (simulated) oil lamp illuminates the shade effectively and awakens its dormant iridescence to pulsating life.

The first of the three interlocking rows of glass, the one at the outer rim, contains ninty-six strips, ½" wide; the second is made up of forty-eight strips, 1" wide; the last, at the top, has twenty-four strips, 2" wide. Forty-eight peacock eyes, in green, orange, blue and gray, are inserted near the outer rim of the shade, and an equal number of triangular pieces forms the border row. In all, the shade contains 264 mosaic pieces. No other like it is known.

The lamp, finished in patina, provides a highly satisfactory source of light for a large area below.

PANEL SHADES

In this group, flat panels, circularly arranged, replace the smoothly rounded surfaces of the shades so far examined in the category of multiple small segments. The panel shades are divided into those which have twelve panels or sides and others which have eight.

TWELVE-SIDED PANEL SHADES will be discussed first because, due to the larger number of panels involved, their outline comes closer to the circular shape of a cone.

97

98

The Colonial 97, 98

This shade consists of four horizontal and twelve vertical rows of glass panels [97]; the large number of vertical rows permits the corners between the twelve sides to be fairly well rounded, since each need have only a 30° angle to complete the 360° overall circumference. Therefore, although multisided, the shade is superficially circular, representing the first step in the evolution from spherical forms to panel shades.

The dominant glass segments are quadrangular in shape and have rounded corners, with diamond patterns in between. At the lower border, the segments are long in the horizontal direction but narrow in the vertical. In ascending order, the segments become gradually shorter and wider until, in the top row, their vertical dimension exceeds the

horizontal. The shade's diameter is 16", its height 7" and its aperture fits a 3" ring. It is signed with the 4¾" tag and numbered 1594.

In translucent light, the color of the panels is a flaming golden-orange, mottled with rich reds. The dramatic mottling is strongest in the top row, becoming softer in its descent toward the bottom border. There is an abundance of mottles within mottles.

As can be seen by comparing the illustration with figure [98], this Panel Shade is a superlative example of dichroism. Illuminated, it throbs with life. In reflected light, a dim subdued greenish-yellow with muted orange mottles, it is so unobtrusive as to be almost unnoticeable in any surroundings; it may well deserve the name, Chameleon Shade.

The Ninth-Century Lamp 99

This panel shade also is twelve-sided [99]. Each panel measures close to 3" at the lower, angular, border and a little more than ½" at the rounded aperture; the width is 12½" between opposing sides, 13" between opposing corners. The height is a shallow 5½", the aperture 2¾". The shade has a short apron.

The apron and the divisions between panels are made from orange glass which is mottled with pink, red and green. In reflected light, the green and pink colorations assume greater prominence, with the orange subsiding. The panels

reveal an intricate form of Islamic interlaces in patterns which consist primarily of green rhomboids with blue centers; the rhomboids are outlined by thin strips of the same orange glass that forms the panel divisions. They are interrupted by small circles of light green. In the center of each side-panel is a circular design containing leaf clusters, executed in the same color as the surrounding rhomboids.

This extremely colorful shade contains, despite its small size, over a thousand sections of glass. It is finished in gold and signed.

99

The integrated base, 18" high, stands on a heavy, twelve-sided platform whose lower rim is decorated with twelve half-round jewels in a variety of colors. The platform is topped by a flat round disk which has eight jewels arranged in the center of circular patterns, with eight pearls set between them. From this disk, an eight-sided column extends upward, carrying another, similar disk at the top, with eight more jewels but without pearls. Above the top disk is placed a four-light cluster with sockets for candelabra bulbs. The base is equipped with a special 2¾" aperture ring. The low finial features a filigree of stylized blossoms. The base is signed and is impressed with the number 8821 which evidently pertains to the whole integrated lamp. It is finished in gold. The jewels have been replaced.

EIGHT-SIDED PANEL SHADES have more pronounced angles formed by their sides which further interferes with the circularity still noticeable in the two previous twelve-sided shades. We present five examples of this category.

Harvard Shade 100

Reputed to have been made for the library of Harvard University, this shade is one of the simpler specimens of the geometric type [100]. It is 20" wide between parallel panels, and 21½" between opposing corners. It is 8" high, has a 4" aperture, and is signed and numbered 1914. The side panels have a width of 8¼" at the lower border and taper to 2" at the aperture. They contain five horizontal and four vertical rows of quadrangular pieces. Alternate panels feature center motifs in the form of heraldic emblems. These depict various coats of arms in vibrant blues, reds and greens, surrounded by a stylized laurel wreath.

Each panel is edged with a thin strip of delicately striated glass. A 2" apron extends downward from the panels and is bordered top and bottom by a narrow horizontal strip of striated glass. A precise pattern of broken circles fills the center of the apron in a modification of the "strung coin" motif.

This shade also exhibits the striking dichroic feature. Pale gold when illuminated by outside light alone, it gleams with a vivid orange luster when lit, and mysterious greenish-gray mottles appear over the entire surface. It is signed and numbered 1593.

The base is 27" high and carries a four-socket cluster. It consists of a six-sided stem whose slightly rounded edges splay out onto a circular 7" platform, partially dividing it into six sections. The four low but wide feet are extrusions of the platform itself. The finish of this base is gold doré to match the gold shade, but the design was also made in bronze, copper and patina. Commonly referred to as "Stick Base," it is called the "Conventional Base" in the Tiffany catalogues. Impressed with the signature, it is numbered 581.

100

Empire Jewel   101

This panel shade [101] is more elaborate and also slightly larger than the foregoing, with a diameter of 20″ between parallel panels, and 22″ between opposing corners. Eight inches high, it has a 4″ aperture, and is signed and numbered 1593. The eight panels, identical in construction, are made up in the main of rectangular pieces of olive-green glass, intense in tone but of exceptional transparency; each is 9″ at the lower border and narrows to 2″ at the top.

One row of round white jewels (⅜″ in diameter) bounds each panel on all but the bottom border; there we find two rows of white jewels, separated by a row of colored glass triangles.

The center of each panel is embellished with a multi-colored oval design, constructed around a white 2″ oblong jewel. Each center design is rather tenuously connected with the lower border by one colored triangular jewel, of a different hue in each panel, and three tiny white jewels, only ⅛″ long; the extension to the upper border is in the form of a jewel-set cross. The panels are separated from each other by a 1″-wide strip of mottled white glass. A 1″ apron of the basic green oblong glass pieces completes the shade.

More than merely decorative, the Empire Jewel is an undisputed masterpiece of its kind. Rarely do we see such craftsmanship as that employed in the precise cutting and scrupulous assembly of its more than two thousand small slivers of glass.

101

102

Elizabethan Shade   102

Also referred to as the Church Lamp, the Elizabethan [102] is signed *Tiffany Studios N. Y. 1954* (note the abbreviation of New York, which is unusual on a signature tag). The size of this shade is identical with the Empire Jewel; that is, 22″ to 23½″ in width and 8″ in height with a 4″ aperture. The workmanship is especially worthy of comment, both because of the large number of leaded pieces involved and the intricacy of the winding and twisting shapes.

Each purplish-blue segment is composed of a double layer of glass; judging from its appearance in reflected light, it would seem that blue glass overlays purple. While the two double layers protrude only slightly beyond the outer surface of the shade, they extend ¼″ above the inner surface, rendering the inside of the Arabesque an astonishing vista of hills and valleys. Although this technique was often employed in Tiffany windows, one rarely encounters it in the construction of shades.

On the outside, the light bronze leaded lines are very delicate and thin; inside, they widen into ¼″ bands, the thickness required to bridge the gap from the one-layered to the double-layered glass areas. In some places, where jewels project, this shade is more than ½″ thick.

The eight sides, which are separated by 1"-wide strips of mottled violet glass, are identical in pattern. The typically arabesque design stems from a purplish-blue centered oval shape, surrounded by thin strips of mottled yellow and orange glass. A network of sinuous serpentine forms originates at the oval and spreads in every direction. Twenty-four assorted jewels add extra richness to each panel. In this fantasy of shape and color, each eye detects different images of flowers, figures and faces.

The apron, 1½" high, contains four large round red jewels and three rectangles of yellow-brown glass in each of its eight sections; set alternately, the gems rest on a background of dark blue and purple. Reinforcement wires — one for each panel — connect the lower border to the aperture.

The Elizabethan is the last one of the truly eight-sided panels. We now return to the examination of shades which belong to the family of cones, although the first example has a certain resemblance to the panel category.

Russian Shade 103

The Russian Lamp [103] is something of a hybrid; on one hand, it may claim a distant kinship with the panel shades on the strength of its flat insets, eight gabled and eight circular. On the other hand, it is vaguely related to the globes because of its smoothly rounded apron — curved not only in the horizontal, but also in the vertical direction. Its third and strongest family affiliation is, however with the cones in whose image their over-all appearance is fashioned.

The Russian Shade is 20" wide, 8" deep and has a 4" aperture; it is signed and numbered 1916. The insets, which are embedded in a weblike background pattern, are made up of mottled glass in a swirling multitude of colors. These center panels arouse more respect and admiration for the responsible artisans each time they are examined.

The fanciful interlaced design which makes up most of the shade's surface picks up the pale hues within each panel and adds emphatic red and purple accents. The lower border, which is similar in feeling, is set off top and bottom by a row of long ruddy-tinted rectangles. One of the two rectilinear rows which finish off the upper portion of the shade is of the same color; in the other, next to the aperture, the glass is royal blue. The leading of this shade is finished in gold.

The 23½"-high base, sometimes referred to as "The Four Virtues," is finished in gold doré. On the four-sided stem, the images of the four virtues — Charitas, Veritas, Fides and Puritas — stand out in low relief; each is identified on a shorter segment of the stem, below, separated by indentations. The round platform of the base bears four heraldic crests, and is slightly lifted from the table surface by four legs. The base is signed and numbered 567.

103

Venetian Lamp   104

This shade is close in feeling to its Russian predecessor because of the insets, but these are here not flat as in the latter, but rounded. This removes the last vestige of panel resemblance and places the Venetian definitely into the category of cones; it is 13″ wide, 6″ high and has a 3″ aperture. The combination of rounded and squared shapes is completely characteristic of the Byzantine style, often employed by Tiffany [104]. The lamp is part of the Venetian desk set.

as they approach the aperture.

This colorful and meticulously crafted shade, which contains well over a thousand tiny pieces, has an unusually heavy lower and upper rim but no other reinforcements. It is signed and numbered 515. The shade finish is gold.

The integrated base is 19″ high, and is completely covered with intricate Oriental decorations. Four tiers, two straight-

104

Both the border and aperture rows consist of golden glass segments; between them, the main body of the shade is made up of three horizontal and sixteen vertical rows of Orientally inspired mosaic motifs.

The first horizontal row consists of large ellipses, each of which contains two alternate leaf patterns, including a trefoil design. The leaves are green on a purplish-blue background, and two red berries may be seen in every other oval; each ellipse is rimmed with golden rectangles. In the second horizontal row, a squared cross alternates with a diamond design; both are rendered in green and red on a blue ground; golden circles serve to enclose the motifs. The third row marks a return to the oval in a reduced size; two alternating designs, green leaves on blue ground, are bordered in gold.

All the border rows are of a roughly stippled texture; the blue background is fibrillated.

Green diamond patterns with red centers fill the spaces between the oval and circular designs. These decrease in size

sided, two rounded, make up the 6″ round platform. The inch-high edge of the bottom tier bears twenty low-relief ferretlike figures; the animal is pictured in five different poses. Twenty-four trefoil designs rim the next round. The third tier contains sixteen interlaced motifs – the same number as used in the shade – with the electric switch inserted into one of the prominent perforations. Sixteen design repeats are also to be found in the fourth tier.

The center column of the stem consists of eight longitudinal sections covered with leaf designs like those of the shade; it rises from a 2″ disk, set with eight green half-round jewels. The stem, 5″ in length, is topped with a slightly smaller disk, set with four proportionally smaller jewels. Openwork ornaments distinguish the four-sided, topmost section of the stem. A fretwork design is repeated eight times on the almost flat finial.

The base carries a three-light cluster and is finished in gold doré. Like the shade, it is signed and is numbered 515.

SPIDER AND WEB

With these shades we approach a new subdivision, or perhaps it would be more accurate to say extension, of the geometric classification. Along with the familiar arrangement of rectangular leaded pieces in neat horizontal and vertical rows – in this instance, fifteen of the former and thirty of the latter – we find irregularities, carefully designed to convey the idea of a spider in his web. Thus it is the spider's rather heavy bronze legs that divide the shade into six panels.

However, in contrast with the many-sided shades previously discussed, these panels are not flat but curved. In addition to the separation of the geometric rows into six sections, differentiations also exist in the vertical plane. Unlike all the borders seen so far, the lower border of each panel is not straight but curves to such an extent that the panel measures a half-inch longer at its middle than at its side (8½″ and 8″ respectively).

This, then, is the first time we encounter the irregular lower border – one of the principal characteristics of the most famous and highly prized of all Tiffany lamps. Though still in a rudimentary stage, the Spider and Web represents a giant step toward naturalism.

The narrow glass pieces used to simulate the structure of the spider's web are irregularly shaped rather than rigidly uniform. Little more than ½″ in width, they decrease in length from 1½″ at the lower border to less than half that size at the top. In comparing this shade with an actual spider's web, we are, of course, exercising artistic license. Even the casual observer is aware of the fact that normal spiders have eight legs.

The Spider is 15″ in diameter, measured from the centers of opposing panels, and 14¼″ measured between parallel indentations. The 5½″-high shade takes a special 2″ finial, which represents the body of a spider, sitting in the center of the web it has spun.

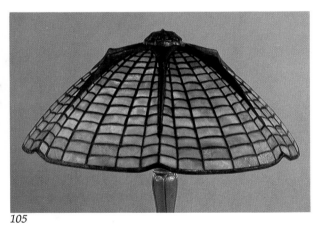

105

Orange-Green Spider and Web   105

This shade is executed in a combination of golden-orange and green, the latter predominant in its upper portion, the former in the lower half [105]. The diffusely mottled glass helps to create the illusion of the sun glittering through frail gossamer threads. It is signed and numbered 1424.

Purple Spider and Web   106

A more somber multichromatic effect is achieved in the sister shade [106]. Perhaps it is meant to depict an older web which has gathered dust and harbored death within it; a sense of sinister foreboding seems to issue from the small, dark shadows scattered throughout the spider's trap. This effect is created by the use of finely striated glass in purple, gray, green and gold, irregularly mixed with mottled pieces, and some of the best fibrillated glass to be found in any Tiffany shade. The shade is signed.

The shade is integrated with the Mushroom Base; the latter resembles an inverted mushroom whose umbrellalike cap has been deftly duplicated on the upper surface of the 8½″ circular platform. The grooved stem adds a final authoritative touch to this facsimile of a fungus. The base is 18″ high, has a three-light cluster and is finished in dark patina; it is numbered 337.

106

LOTUS LEAF LAMPS

The Lotus Leaf family grows, so to speak, on a bridge between the straight and static realm of geometrics and the active and exciting kingdom of flowers. The influence of both is clearly evident.

In the Lotus Leaf shades, we see crisply neat quadrangles in precise and orderly arrangements, but we also note a trend away, toward natural shapes. The veined pattern and erratic edges indicate that these designs were drawn from life.

Depending on which element is thought to outweigh the other, the Lotus family might either end this chapter or begin the next. Neither decision would be incorrect. With respect to the uneven lower borders, they would actually place these shades among the most advanced of the Tiffany Studios designs. Here again, however, one may argue that the border irregularities are too minor and still too uniform to meet the test.

107

Green Lotus Leaf   107

This shade is 25" in diameter, tapers down to an unexpectedly small 2" aperture, and, with a height of only 6½", is also exceptionally shallow [107]. The signature appears on a small tab attached to one of the main leaded ribs on the inside surface. Because of its resemblance to a certain type of Oriental hat, the Lotus is sometimes referred to as the Mandarin Shade.

The Green Lotus Leaf consists of a large number of glass quadrangles, set in such a way that they form ridges and grooves which run radially from the top center toward the periphery of the shade. The crests of the ridges represent the midribs of the leaf, the lead-edged grooves its veins.

Twenty-four midribs run from the center of each leaf to a point about halfway down the shade; here they split into forty-eight intermediary ribs, which split again near the border into ninety-six end ribs. Altogether there are more than 1300 pieces of leaded glass in this shade.

The Lotus is intrinsically green, but the tonal modulations are extremely sophisticated. The dark green near the aperture gradually gives way to a pale area in the middle of the shade. Darker and lighter triangular segments alternate from here to the bottom border, where the last tiny bits of glass are a grayish blue-green. All the glass contains well-defined striations, which are most pronounced in the darker segments. The variations in color, the grooving, the dissimilar striations, and the unevenness of the edge enhance the illusion that we are dealing here with a live plant leaf. Stippled and fibrillated glass is extensively used in this shade. Its aperture is covered by the Spider finial. In the Tiffany Album, the Lotus shade bears the number 1524.

The Lotus Leaf is often adjudged to be one of the most architecturally advanced Tiffany designs.

Except for its dark gold finish, the base is identical with the one shown in figure [79]. It also has the same 2" aperture ring and finial; it is signed and numbered 4485.

108

Golden Lotus Leaf 108

Figure [108] shows the sister shade to the Green Lotus, which is very similar in shape except for its slightly larger diameter and aperture (respectively 26″ and 3″). The gold color is darkened by orange around the aperture, lighter in the center of the shade, and assumes a slightly deeper tone again in its descent. The peripheral glass pieces are pearly white, with faint tinges of mauve and green. The border has a finely beaded rim.

The striations in the glass as well as its surface stipples and fibrillations are somewhat more pronounced than we have heretofore encountered, causing the shade to exhibit an extremely wide variety of light refractions. This shade had originally been sold to a French collector and came back to the United States just a few years ago. Lately, with the great demand for Tiffany lamps in America, many have been repatriated. At the same time, there is a constant flow of shades to museums in other countries.

Since Tiffany shades were, for many years, offered for sale on Rookwood pottery, the golden Lotus Leaf is shown on a Rookwood base.

109

Lotus Bell   109

The smallest member of the Lotus family is in the shape of a bell, 15½" in diameter, 7" high and has an aperture of only 1", the smallest on record [*109*]. The quadrangles of glass are arranged in a ridge-and-groove pattern, similar to that of the larger shades, except that only sixteen midribs spring from the top and branch into thirty-two in the center and sixty-four at the rim. The bell shape obtains for half the depth of the shade and, at its widest, measures only 6" across; from this diameter, it suddenly spreads to a dramatic 15½".

The glass is light green with a yellowish cast in the middle of the shade, darker green at the very top, and almost blue-green in the lower border area. Multidirectional striations, augmented by pinhead stipples and a fibrillated texture, greatly enrich the beauty of the illuminated shade. The latter is signed and numbered 422.

The Lotus Bell is set in its own 21"-high base. The platform, equipped with a switch, is raised off the table surface on four ball feet and is fluted, much like other bases already examined. Two bronze arms rise out of the platform and curve abruptly outward, away from each other, to form a harp shape. At their top juncture, a joint permits lateral movement of the shade. Because of the placement of the bulb in the upper portion of the bell, obviating glare yet allowing the light to spread through the flaring lower portion, the Lotus Bell makes an excellent desk lamp.

5. TRANSITION TO FLOWERS

THIS CHAPTER describes lamps which link two different areas of Tiffany art—the geometric and the natural. While these lamps still consist, basically or in part, of a rigid arrangement of squares; rectangles and other mathematically precise forms, they also incorporate more or less realistic representations of life.

The latter designs not only require greater artistry, but also involve more advanced craftsmanship in their execution. The exacting curves of leaves and blossoms, the delicacy of stems and branches and the multiplicity of surface textures involved in living organisms demand more skill than regular rows of uniform pieces.

Glass must be selected with infinitely more care when plant life is to be portrayed in natural color. It is, for example, not only the over-all color of a flower petal that must be correct; its internal tinge and tonality at each edge must match or blend with each adjoining piece. Sometimes, an entire sheet of multicolored glass may offer only a few usable areas.

In the shades representing this transition to flowers, we find that two main methods have been employed to superimpose botanical patterns upon basic geometric designs. In one, the flower design appears more or less confined to bands, rows, borders or belts, with all other areas remaining purely geometric. In the other, the plant material is distributed over the entire surface of the shade. From either of these types, particularly the latter, it is only a short step to the all-flower designs.

Flower Borders and Belts

IN THIS CATEGORY, advancement in the transition to flowered shades is measured by the number of geometric rows which have been replaced by plant life, either partially or completely.

Havemeyer Fixture 110

The first geometric-flower shade shown is a ceiling fixture, supposedly from the New York home of the Havemeyer family [110]. It is four feet across, and consists of four globes arranged in a square around a center globe. The four identical shades are each 14" in diameter and 8" deep. Bands of different geometric patterns, interspersed with rows of stylized flowers and leaves in blue and yellow make up their lower halves; their upper portions consist of thirty-two parallel strips of bluish glass. A 6"-wide band of realistically portrayed dark blue flowers with light blue leaves connects these globes with each other and with the purely geometric center globe, which is a replacement. The fixture had originally been piped for illumination by gas, and was subsequently electrified. In all probability, it was a special-order item.

Moorish-style wire filigree, with a fringe of copper balls, ornaments the top of each globe, and the same motif is repeated around the center circle.

Although the fixture is predominantly geometric in character, the addition of natural flowers and leaves marks the emergence of a new form.

111

Peony Flower Border   111

The peony, one of the most decorative of all flowers, was a Tiffany Studios favorite and inspired shades in the flowered globe category as well as in this group.

The Peony Flower Border [111] adorns a large globe, 24" in diameter and 12" in height, with a 6" aperture. It bears the 4" Tiffany Studios signature tag with the number 1574. The shade has thirty-six vertical and eighteen horizontal rows; five of the latter are completely covered by the floral border, which also intrudes upon the sixth. There are two wholly geometric rows below the design and ten above it. Instead of the wire rings found around the aperture in smaller shades, this opening is strengthened with a 1" metal rim. Six reinforcement wires run from the aperture, through the flower border, to the lower rim of the shade.

The peony blossoms are red, or red mottled with pink, and are made from undulating glass; the texture is on the inner surface of the shade. The dark red peony, left of center, is reversed from the expected position; turned away from the viewer, it shows how the stem connects with the base of the flower.

The peony centers are orange-yellow, the plant stems brownish-green. The foliage, made of stippled glass, runs the full gamut of greens, from shimmering emerald to a yellow striated grass-green, to a murky terre verte, shot through with pin-sized mottles.

The background glass is a virtually transparent yellowish-green, almost chartreuse, with opaque yellowish-gray specks. Infused with a seemingly endless variety of unmatched small, medium and large dark-green mottles, it endows the shade with a dramatic cloud quality.

The design is repeated three times, and each repeat contains four peonies. The geometric rows are color-harmonized with the flower border, achieving in deceptively simple style a wholly integrated work of art.

POINSETTIA FLOWER BORDERS

This flower, named for its developer, Mr. J. R. Poinsett, plays its most important role in the geometric-flower category, although it is also represented among the flowered globes. That these attractive, conservatively styled shades were quite popular in their time can be deduced from the fact that so many specimens have been preserved.

In such shades, the flowered band was placed so low that it may reasonably be referred to as a border design. It comprises almost half the shade, the other half being given over to two narrow geometric rows below and five geometric rows above the floral band. The lowest of the latter rows is encroached upon by the Poinsettia pattern, signifying the start of a wider flower distribution which would eventually lead to the elimination of the purely geometric areas. The next four rows are composed of squarish segments, which narrow toward the top. In the aperture row, the segments are rectilinear; this row is missing in the 14" example. There exists another rectilinear, partly interrupted, row which separates the geometric rows from the flower border.

112

Fourteen-Inch Poinsettia   112

The shade is 6½" high and has a 3" aperture [112]. The 4" signature tag *Tiffany Studios New York* is on the shade, together with design number 1556. The two bottom rows, each containing twenty-six pieces, are of mottled green glass with a faint orange tinge, and the same coloration is continued in the five rows above the border design. The intrusion of the flowers upon the fifth horizontal row (counting down from the aperture) is in evidence.

The flower border is dominated by the leaflike petals of the Poinsettia; indeed they *are* modified leaves, or bracts, and not a part of the flower at all. Similar to the bracts of the dogwood tree, their prime function is to protect the tender blossoms. The dogwood bracts, however, have assumed the shape of flower petals, while in the Poinsettia they have maintained their uniquely leafy look.

The artist has taken full advantage of the design opportunities this singular "flower" affords by selecting the most resplendent reds, intermingled with pink, for these petal-like leaves. The real flowers, small and inconspicuously contained within the "flower centers," are yellow and green, and are given somewhat greater importance by the use of a highly refractive undulating glass.

The true leaves are dark green and yellow-green, and the stems are of amply streaked greenish-brown glass. The design, containing five blossoms, is repeated three times. The small amount of background glass behind the Poinsettias is sunrise-orange, mottled with green, and synchronizes well with the yellow and reddish geometric rows.

Eighteen-Inch Poinsettia on Yellow 113

Besides its larger diameter, this shade is, at 7½", greater in height and has a wider (4") aperture than the 14" globe [113]. It carries the same large signature tag as the smaller shade, with the number 1558. Since the number and arrangement of the geometric rows is the same as in the 14" Poinsettia, the rectangular glass segments are necessarily larger, in order to cover the greater circumference. A major difference is the presence of four repeats of the flower design instead of three.

The "petal" colors range from pink to red to purple, scantily streaked with white. The stems are green, and the leaves range from light to dark green with occasional bluish overtones; they again intrude upon the adjoining geometric border row. The background glass and the geometric rows are essentially light green, infused with mauve for a softly mottled effect. Striations of the same hue are sparsely intermingled. The end result is a shade at once subdued and provocative. The shade is signed and numbered 440.

The base is rather novel, featuring four legs ending in claw-and-ball feet, connected by a wide, beaded band as they begin their outward curve. The main stem has a barklike surface and is adjustable in height from 25" to 32". Three 9" arms extend from it to support the shade.

113

Eighteen-Inch Poinsettia on Red 114

The design and measurements of this Poinsettia are the same as the Green, and it also bears the large Tiffany signature tag. The difference lies in the much more vibrant colors [114].

The long slender bracts are a dark, rich red, deepening into purple. The flowers proper (centered between the bracts) are executed in an orange-green, highly reflective rippled glass. The stems are greenish-yellow and the true leaves are bluish-green, with a trace of pink picked up from the red bracts nearby. The most singular part of the shade is the purplish-red section of the geometric area, whose tone appears to be taken from the strongly colored flowers; the tint is so intense that seemingly it would reflect that far away.

A green rippled aperture row matches a similar (interrupted) row around the center of the shade, which serves as the upper boundary of the flower border. A brown rippled row at the bottom of the flower design is suggestive of the soil from which such stems emerge. A purplish-green border row of rectangular glass pieces completes the shade.

114

DOGWOOD FLOWER BELTS

When the flowered band of a semi-geometric shade moves farther from the lower border, it can more properly be classified as a flower belt. Considering its placement near the center of the shade and the occasional extension of the flowers above and below, the belt is another advance toward the all-flower shade.

115

Sixteen-Inch Dogwood   115

A belt of blossoms a bit below the midpoint is the main feature of the shade, which is 16″ wide, 6½″ high and has a 3″ aperture [*115*]. There are three rectilinear rows of glass below the flower belt and six almost quadrangular rows above. As one can see, the belt is not strictly confined but has an irregular outline, encroaching on adjoining rows in both directions. Three of the twelve horizontal rows are completely filled by the flowers, which interrupt three more, leaving only two purely geometric rows below and four above. There are thirty-two vertical rows.

As in the Poinsettia, the "petals" of this flower pattern are, in actuality, modified leaves or bracts, whose function is to protect the unobtrusive true flowers–here seen as the yellow "centers." However, the bracts look exactly like scalloped flower petals, the only difference being that they are unusually heavy. The bracts are white, with quiet pink and green mottling, or whitish yellow or whitish pink. The branches are soft brown, the leaves medium to dark green with yellow striations; some are of bluish-green rippled glass. The design is repeated three times.

The co-existence of flowers with a large number of fully developed leaves is another example of a complete life cycle compressed into a single shade; in nature, the dogwood flowers appear early and are ordinarily lost before the leaves appear.

The geometric portions of the shade are executed in pale green glass, with a fine sprinkling of gray and yellow. Toward the aperture, a tinge of light blue appears in the green. The shade is signed and numbered 1554-8.

The base has a circular 8½″ platform which stands on four small upcurved feet; a double leaf pattern covers half its upper surface and curves over its rounded edge. Rootlike circular swirls fill the inner portion of the platform and wind upward around the main stem. The finish is dark bronze. In the Tiffany Album, this base is numbered 360.

Twenty-Inch Dogwood 116

This representative of the Dogwood Belts is more elaborate in design, in both its geometric and flower areas [116]. It is 20" wide, 8½" high, has a 5" aperture and is signed. Since it encompasses fifty-four vertical rows instead of the thirty-two in the 16" shade, the quadrangular pieces are much smaller despite the slightly increased size of the shade. The flower belt, however, is wider; starting above, and sometimes entering into, the third lower border row, it covers the area of at least six rows and, at intervals, invades a seventh; there are eight untouched rows above it.

In this shade, the artist has again taken the liberty of showing both flowers and leaves together, though this phenomenon is rarely seen in the living specimen. As in other Tiffany designs, the eye is allowed to roam beyond the restraints of time and space.

A most exquisite glass is used for the bracts which mimic flower petals. Some pieces are limpid and translucent with scattered pinhead mottling; others are cloudy and opaque, due to area mottling at the center of the petals, where in nature they are normally thicker, thus leaving the edges more transparent. The flower centers are made of yellow fibrillated glass, and the leaves are dark green with light gray striations. A few brown, grained stems complete the pattern, which is seen in three repeats.

Much more background glass is in evidence than in preceding flower borders and belts. Yellow-green in tone, with orange and pink spots, its uncommonly radiant quality is attributable to its odd texture: smooth on the outside, its inner surface is both knobby and undulating.

The rectangles of the geometric areas are whitish, with a glint of gray and yellow, striated with green. The striations, which are extra heavy and dark at both the lower border and at the aperture, thin out and lighten as they approach the flower belt. An extraordinary glass has been used for these otherwise unremarkable geometric rows: in the lower border rows it is both fibrillated and knobby on the inner surface; in the rows above the belt it is finely stippled on both sides.

The lower border is edged by an unusually heavy, half-inch-wide bronze rim. Four reinforcement wires on the inside connect the flower band with the aperture.

116

The shade rests on the Indian Base which has a round 9"-diameter platform whose outer rim is indented with squares and rectangles in linear patterns. It has no legs but stands flat on the table, the electric wire emanating from its side. The six-sided stem again has squares and rectangles, indented in the same straight Indian pattern as has the platform. The over-all height of the base is 27"; it is signed and numbered 528.

Twenty-Two-Inch Dogwood   117

The shade is basically a globe, with an almost straight-sided 4" apron and a secondary, more exaggerated globular swelling in the region of the aperture [117]. The shade is 22" wide, 8" high and has a 5" aperture; it bears the small (1⅛") signature tag.

decay; brown spots may be seen on the periphery of some petals, eating their way toward the vital centers.

The centers are of greenish-yellow striated glass. The few budding leaf formations, made of fibrillated glass, are bright emerald green, with yellow striations. The dogwood branches, which are quite heavy, are carefully executed in grained yellow-brown glass. The background is grayish-blue

117

In this combination of border and belt, the belt has been extended well beyond its previous limitations. The major portion of the shade is covered with blossoms, leaving only seven narrow horizontal rows which form the bulge below the aperture, one (interrupted) row at the start of the apron, and one at the bottom border.

From a strictly botanical standpoint, this would appear to be the best of the three dogwood shades shown, since it is almost completely covered with blossoms and has only a few young leaves. The heavy scalloped "petals" are of white mottled glass, lightly touched with gray and green tints. In painstaking tribute to nature—and with consummate craftsmanship—some of the blossoms give subtle evidence of

with streaks of white and yellow. Its high refraction quotient (see left side of apron) stems from the knobby texture of its inner surface.

The lower border is of green rippled glass, with another horizontal row of narrow rectangular pieces marking the start of the apron. The topmost geometric rows are very narrow, and made of alternating green and white glass segments. Four reinforcement wires run from the aperture to the center of the cone.

On account of the dominance of its floral pattern and the paucity of its remaining geometric rows, this globe has been given the most advanced position in the division dealing with flower borders and belts.

Scattered Flower Materials

IN THIS CATEGORY, progress of the transition is measured by the number of geometric rows which have been invaded by flowers or leaves as compared to those which have been permitted to remain intact.

Autumn Leaves 118

Though the background of this shade is most decidedly geometric, a leaf design is well distributed over its center portion, interrupting every one of the horizontal rows in this area [118]. Leaded stems further disrupt the rigid angularity, wrecking the precision of the pattern.

The globular Autumn Leaves shade is 22" in diameter and, at 12", is unusually deep. On it we find an oddly shaped finial—cylindrical, becoming conic—about 3" in width, but more than 7" high; it is an airy structure, woven of thin copper strips and crowned by a brass ball.

The thirty-two vertical rows of this shade descend to a deep apron, consisting of five horizontal rows of beautiful brownish-green mottled glass rectangles which have a stippled texture. Elaborately curved, the apron dips inward, then arcs out again to a lower border edged with beads. Six horizontal rows of mottled green glass surround the aperture. Both upper and lower borders contain thirty-two glass segments. At the bottom of the shade each of these pieces is 2" long, but at the aperture each has diminished to only ¼".

Between the total of eleven purely geometric rows, we see seven horizontal rows strewn with brilliant autumn leaves in highly refractive orange-red rippled glass. The glass used in the leaves is extremely heavy and protrudes noticeably above the surface of the shade. The leaves are irregular in shape and randomly positioned; from a distance, with their thin stems no longer discernible, they look as if they had fallen upon a green lawn. There are six repeats of the design.

118

A similar leaf design on a smaller geometric flower shade may be seen in the Tiffany Album [119]. Here the leaves are more smoothly oblong and more highly stylized, but they have the same long thin stems. A three-row apron, the middle row of which is rippled glass, begins directly below the leaves. Above the leaf area four geometric rows, terminating in a beaded rim, ring the aperture. The base, which was the oil font for the lamp, is covered with thin rows of mosaic, which harmonize with the lower border row of the shade. The shade is numbered 1445, the base, 149.

119

Flower Basket   120

This rather bizarre hanging shade is 8½″ high, 10½″ at its flaring edge and narrows to a midpoint width of approximately 6″ [120]. It is signed *Tiffany Studios New York*. The upper portion of the shade is decorated with pink and white apple blossoms, as well as foliage. They are distributed in an irregular fashion and in some areas occupy one, in others as many as seven, of the eleven horizontal rows. The lower part is mainly geometric, exquisitely worked in golden fractured glass with green, orange and blue slivers. It is highly iridescent.

As an adaptation, to eliminate the unsightly exposed wire originally employed, two thin wires, one positive, the other negative, are concealed inside two of the three supporting ball chains (one is visible in the center chain).

120

Water Lily Orb   121

The 14½″ spherical shape of this hanging shade is only interrupted by a 5½″ plate at its bottom [121]. The purely geometric area of the Water Lily Orb is largely unconfined and runs in the form of background glass unevenly through the flowered sections.

Unique in form and refreshing in concept, the shade consists of three disparate sections. The lowest depicts dark blue water from which the lilies rise; greenish-yellow leaves float on its surface, and in it we seek pink reflections from the blossoms and sunny highlights shimmering from the sky. The skillfully assembled glass segments consist of long, narrow slivers, representing waves.

The middle, and largest, section displays an abundance of pink flowers, tipped with rose, which are supported by fleshy stems and surrounded by green foliage. Two withered brown leaves are also in evidence. The third – purely geometric – section is limited to four horizontal rows.

121

Pansy   122

122

This shade is 16″ wide, 6½″ high, with a 4″ aperture. The design, which is too dispersed to be recognized as a border or a belt, is scattered over a large portion of the globe, leaving only the aperture row completely untouched by plant material [122]. However, the second and the third rows from the top are predominantly made up of rectangular pieces, as is the lower border row. Altogether, there exist eight horizontal and thirty-two vertical rows. The design has four repeats which are separated from each other by a grouping of geometric pieces. More than half the shade is purely floral.

In each repeat the pansies are executed in differing color schemes.

The familiar markings of the plant are accurately portrayed in flowers which combine orange with purple, white with yellow, yellow with blue and red with green. Even more authenticity is added by meticulous mottling which intensifies the color in the inner portion of the petals. Tonal variations are also provided by the employment of different types of textured glass: some petals are gently rippled, others undulated. The small flower centers are yellow, orange or red; the foliage is brilliant green, green with yellow or orange; only the long grayish-green stems are the same color throughout.

The background is a dull green, mottled with yellow, which ranges from dark tones in the lower portions to lighter hues higher up on the shade. The three rows beneath the aperture are almost completely white, with only a few greenish or yellowish areas in each piece of glass.

The shade carries the number 1448 according to the Tiffany Album.

WOODBINES

This plant, which belongs to the Honeysuckle family and is better known as Virginia Creeper, is represented by three shades, one of them 14", the others 16" wide. Featured are the vividly colored five-fold clusters of leaves in the absence of flowers. They occupy the lower portion of the shades which have no lower border row. Their upper portion is filled with geometric glass sections in characteristic shapes, namely half-hexagons in the aperture row, and oblong hexagons below. Highly translucent fractured glass is frequently employed in the geometric rows, as will be shown in two of the examples. It renders this area vividly transparent but necessitates the use of low-wattage light bulbs.

Fourteen-Inch Woodbine 123

The smallest shade of the family is 14" wide, 6" high, and has a 3" aperture [123]. The leaf clusters are almost miniature compared to the 16" Woodbine shades and rendered in a brilliant green striated with red and orange; they are concentrated in the lower part of the shade. The glass is fibrillated on both inner and outer surfaces, thereby increasing the radiance.

The background between the leaves and the hexagonal geometric rows above them is rendered in a most attractive type of fractured glass: its basic layer is filled with innumerable tiny bubbles into which have been embedded several layers of flakes, splinters and long slivers of secondary glass. This has created an astonishing variety of shapes and of colorations which encompass light and dark green, yellow, gold, orange, red and mauve in different stages of density and tonality. The shade is highly effective in reflected as well as in transmitted light. A 3" tag authenticates this Woodbine.

123

The shade is supported by the replica of a blown-glass base (similar to the one shown in figure [87]), but made from metal. There are five "bulges" which appear to be protruding between the "confining" metal straps. The latter continue upward into curved arms for the support of the shade. Inside the copper urn is the old oil receptacle, now electrified; on its bottom plate appears the signature, the Tiffany emblem, and the number 21218 impressed into the metal, as was standard procedure with oil lamps.

The copper urn, which is 9½" at its widest diameter, stands on a slightly larger platform, divided into five segments by extensions of the metal straps. It is 11" high to the ends of the support arms.

Woodbine on Green 124

The typical five-fold leaves of the plant appear in a variety of colors: some are pink with strong red striations, some white with purple mottling, others green with orange striations; the newcomers are orange with red streaks [124]. Heavily rippled glass, with the rippled surface on the inside, is used for all but the pink leaves. This accounts for the remarkable radiance of the shade. The background is green with yellow streaks, similar to the coloration of some leaves, and occasionally it is difficult to determine which a certain segment of glass represents. Branches or stems are not visible.

Between the aperture and the leaves, there are from two to three geometric rows which, in proportion, constitute a much smaller area than in the 14" sister shade. The grayish-blue half-hexagons of the aperture row fit into the second green-yellow row of elongated hexagons; the third row, green with yellow striations, is composed of larger hexagons, all of which are interrupted by leaves. The inner surfaces of these hexagonal segments are extensively fibrillated. The shade is signed; it is numbered 1468 in the Album.

124

Woodbine on Gold   125

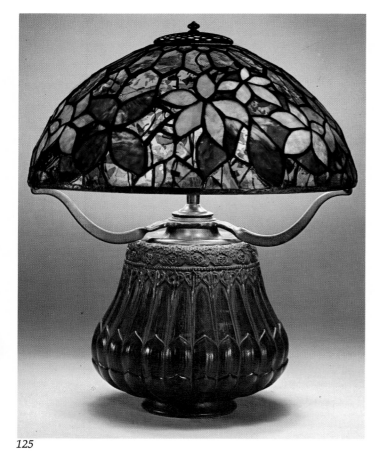

This shade has bright-green leaves with orange mottles and striations, and dark red leaves with blue and green striations [125]; all are constructed of glass smooth on the outside, but with more prominent undulations on its inner surface than can be seen in almost any other shade. The background, made in its entirety of fractured glass, is the most notable aspect of this shade. Its basic color is dark gold in which slivers of green and faint violet glass have been embedded. The pronounced dichroic quality of this glass causes the background to look lighter than the leaves when the lamp is lit, and much darker than the same leaves when the lamp is not illuminated. In reflected light, it also assumes a reddish tint. The metalwork is finished in bronze patina, and the shade has two signature tags: one 2", marked *Tiffany Studios*, and another, 1", marked *New York*.

The bronze base, in the shape of a squat vase, is 10½" at its widest diameter and 9" in height. It is impressed *Tiffany Studios, New York #27477* (in the Tiffany Album, it is numbered 142). Its surface is vertically incised to form twenty-four segments, each of which is divided in turn into three parts. The two bottom rows thus formed are shaped like nut shells; the archlike upper sections are adorned with garlands of flowers and leaves in bronze relief. Three bronze arms curve gracefully from the top of the urn to support the shade. This extremely docorative base is 19" in height, carries a three-socket cluster and is finished in dark copper tones.

125

Black-Eyed Susan   126

This shade, which is 16" wide, 7" high and has a 3" aperture, marks this subdivision's final milestone in the progression toward total flower designs [126]. The geometric rows are still visible but no longer dominant; their strength, which lay in their precision, has been destroyed by the superimposition of the flowers and foliage. Of eight horizontal rows, only the aperture row remains intact; all others have been invaded by vegetation; even the almost inviolate bottom row is here intruded upon by plant stems. There are thirty-two vertical and eight horizontal rows.

Some of the yellow-green stems are of considerable length and carry their flowers right up to the aperture row; other blossoms shoot off at different levels or droop down to overlay a large part of the shade. The delicate flower petals are a brilliant orange, which tapers off into yellow. Some blossoms are seen head-on, others in a side view.

The reddish-brown flower centers are made of heavy rippled glass. The foliage is emerald green, which furnishes both a strong contrast with the orange blossoms and a soft blend with the dull green, heavily mottled background glass of the quadrangular rows. The latter is a dark green at the lower edge and gradually fades to a light greenish-gray with pinpoint mottling at the aperture. The shade is signed but bears no number; one identical with this in the Tiffany Album is numbered 1447.

The main body of the base is shaped like an urn–an urn anchored by three thin bronze arms to a roughly surfaced 7" platform. Yellow-green turtlebacks, 1½" in height and less in width, form a belt around the base at its biggest diameter. Other urns of this type are decorated with green or blue turtlebacks. The inside illumination is an adaptation. The Tiffany Album number is 180.

126

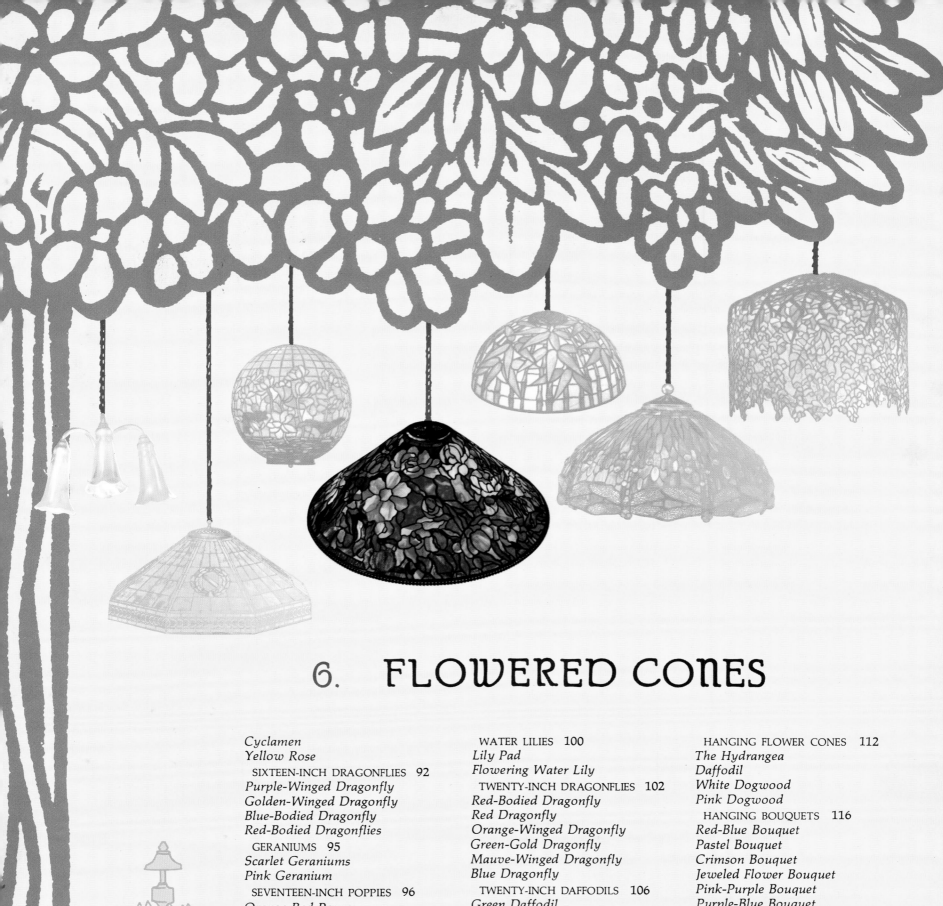

6. FLOWERED CONES

BECAUSE the cone-shaped shades form such an important division of Tiffany lamps, forty-eight examples will be shown. Next to the eight-sided panel shades, the cone is the simplest type of leaded shade from the standpoint of construction. In a horizontal cross-section it is rounded (circular), but vertically it is straight. This means that in soldering adjoining pieces of glass it was necessary to form a slight angle–but in one direction only, not two, as in forming globes. This worked to the advantage of the artisan and it also reduced internal and external strains so that a smaller number of internal reinforcement wires were needed in the cone shades than in the more complex globes.

From another standpoint, however, these shades present a problem; the cones –especially the larger ones–are not the easiest shades to display to complete advantage. In order to appreciate their rich design to the fullest, the eye of the beholder should be at a right angle to the surface of the shade. This means that it must be viewed from above.

The smaller cones may be set on low tables, nightstands, etc. It is more difficult to place the hanging cones which, at 28" in diameter and 10" in height, constitute some of the largest shades made by Tiffany. In a modern apartment, or even in the average private home, the dining room table is usually the only piece of furniture over which a cone can be properly suspended. In most other locations the shade must hang high enough to permit people to pass beneath it. When so hung, glaring faults are immediately evident. Not only are the electric bulbs exposed, but the flower design itself, viewed from an oblique angle, suffers serious distortion.

For this reason, the author suggests that such a shade be hung upside down, so to speak, with the aperture at the bottom, and sufficiently high for people to walk beneath, see figure [39]. Its beauty can thus be enjoyed at the proper perspective from almost any area within the room. In the great majority, the flowing lines of foliage and flowers appear quite natural, since most real plants bear random sprigs and blooms that reach in all directions. Only a few floral patterns with straight stems do not lend themselves to this treatment.

Insofar as possible, the cones will be discussed in a size sequence, starting with the smallest shade, measuring 16" in diameter, and ending with the largest, which is 30" in width. With only minor deviations, the shade height is correlative with the diametric dimensions, but the aperture measurements are less consistent; small shades originally designed as oil lamps with chimneys, and supported by arms, have larger apertures than similar shades supported by aperture rings.

Cyclamen 127

This shade is often referred to as Anemone. However, the four-petaled blossoms with their heart-shaped, pointed petals which are sharply reflexed against the stalks, indisputably establish their botanical identity as compared with the multipetaled Anemone, with its broad petals and spread-out blossoms. It is 16" wide at the start of the apron, 15" at its lower border, is 7" deep and has a 3" aperture [127]. A *Tiffany Studios* signature appears on a 2" tag.

The cone portion of the shade is effectively bordered by a row of green rippled glass at the aperture (which is encroached upon by flowers) and at the bottom where the apron begins. Another row, continuing the color and design of the cone, follows, and a final rectilinear row of green rippled glass finishes the apron and forms the lower edge of the shade. The three horizontal rows are all that remain of a geometric pattern. In all probability they have been retained for structural rather than artistic reasons.

The shade is meticulously constructed of a multitude of cunningly shaped and delicately colored segments of leaded glass. The design is repeated five times, though the repetition is difficult to detect because of the complexity of the pattern.

The oblong leaves, concentrated in the lower part of the shade, are light and dark green, fading occasionally into yellow; some are mottled with orange and gray, while others are made of rippled glass. Masses of fragile cyclamens rise from the foliage on long bluish stems. Pink with red striations, they are effectively set off by a background of light and dark blue.

127

128

Yellow Rose 128

This blossom-bedecked cone is 16" in diameter and narrows to about 15" at the bottom of the turned-in apron; it is 7" high and has a 3" aperture [128].

The buds in this shade are a self-mottled orange; as the blossoms open, the color becomes less intense, fading into mellow yellow for the mature flower. The roses are rendered in fibrillated glass. The leaves range from dark to emerald green, occasionally striated with brown, and are of a stippled texture. The rich blue background, strongly self-mottled, forms a pleasantly intense contrast.

In the three-row apron, the middle row of deep blue is sandwiched between lighter blue-green bands. At intervals, flowers and leaves infringe upon the apron.

The design, containing six roses and five buds, is repeated five times.

SIXTEEN-INCH DRAGONFLIES

Though fauna rather than flora, the Dragonflies are included in the flowered cones because they are life forms rather than geometric shapes. One may also cite the presence of vegetation in many of the Dragonfly shades.

The world-renowned Dragonfly design is incontestably the most popular of all those employed in Tiffany Lamps; no other has been used in such a wide variety of shades. It appears among the cones in both the 16″ and 20″ size, is well represented among the globes, and is outstanding in the category of shades with irregular lower borders.

The design provides the craftsman with unusual opportunities to show his skill and imagination. First there is the insect itself, which he can endow with varicolored bodies, eyes and wings. Then, since the shade is described by the Tiffany Studios as "Dragonfly and Water Design," he is free to create any sort of stream or pond he prefers along with every kind of atmosphere in which the insect flies. The mood may range from sunny peace to sad foreboding.

The maximum diameter of the Small Dragonfly is 16″, which lessens to 15½″ at the lower border because of the inward curvature of the apron. It is 6¾″ high and has a 3″ aperture. As a rule, it does not bear the Tiffany Studios signature, but its design number is established by the Tiffany Album as 1462.

Below the rectilinear aperture row (which is not always present), the shade has two rows composed of uneven, pointed oblongs, arranged vertically. The bodies of the seven dragonflies, one in each repeat, extend through the second oblong row to its juncture with the first. There are four small glass pieces between upper and lower wings, and two at each side of the insect's head. The three-row apron is incurved to such an extent that the last (border) row is only visible from below, not straight-on. Since the seven dragonflies, each with a wingspread of 9½″, must fit within the 50″ circumference of the shade, adjoining wings tips are extensively overlapped.

The overlapping areas, raised above the surface of the shade, thus give a striking three-dimensional quality to a conventional flat pattern. The wings are covered with an intricate metal filigree which simulates their natural veining. The insect's eyes are made from jewels or from flat glass.

129

Purple-Winged Dragonfly 129

In its over-all tonality, this is a rather subdued shade. The oblong glass segments below the aperture row are bluish-green, mottled with yellow and changing to greenish-blue in the second oblong row [*129*]. The insects' eyes are bright red jewels, the bodies blue, and the wings purple, striated with a brilliant blue. They blend with their immediate background, which is a mottled bluish-green streaked with white. The result is a pleasant, primarily monotone shade, suitable for a "busy" room where unobtrusive beauty is required.

The three-row curved apron is composed of green rippled glass, plain blue and olive-green rippled pieces. A top row of green rippled rectangles encircles the aperture.

130

Golden-Winged Dragonfly 130

In the upper elongated row of background glass shown in figure [130], some pieces are an almost solid leaf-green, others are green striated with yellow or blue. In the second row of oblongs, blue begins to dominate; between and below the wings, the blue becomes grayish in tone with a faint tint of mauve. In addition to the striations, much spot-mottling is in evidence; in the main, this consists of rounded specks, the same color as the glass segment, but somewhat darker and less transparent.

Yellow jewel eyes gleam out of darkish green bodies. The wings, a brilliant orange-yellow, are by far the most striking element of the design. In this shimmering base color, we can see some loosely defined green area-mottling which merges softly with the surrounding hues. These traces of green are the only color link between wings and background. In the apron's middle row and in the aperture row, orange-green glass combines the two major tonalities of the shade. The upper and lower apron rows are composed of the same grayish-blue glass used between and below the dragonfly wings.

The 24"-high base begins with a heavy round platform, 9" in diameter, supported by four small curved feet. Rounded knoblike projections, arranged in three concentric rows, cover the upper surface of the platform. The largest are in the outer row, the smallest near the stem. Wire designs, simulating stalks, run up the stand. Like the shade, the base is finished in dark bronze, and is signed on one of its feet; the number is 364.

Blue-Bodied Dragonfly 131

This is an even more colorful shade; except for the insect's wings and bodies, it is entirely made of rippled glass [131]. Thorax and abdomen are purplish-blue; the tails are green-blue and the heads as well as the unjeweled eyes are crimson red. The wings are a less vivid red, mottled with gray, blue and purple.

The base note of the rippled background glass is light blue, seen most purely in the upper oblong row. In the center of the shade, the blue is mixed with yellow and green, creating the aura of impending storm. This is enhanced by the seeming pulsation of the wavy surfaced glass segments. The same colors extend downward between the wings, into the three apron rows. There is no aperture row. The refraction of light from the rippled glass is extraordinary in its brilliance.

The urn base which has inserts of green-blue turtlebacks will be described under figure [190] when the design can be better seen on account of the lighter-colored glass inserts.

131

132

133

Red-Bodied Dragonflies   132, 133

The last representatives of this group are two examples which, if not shown next to each other, would be virtually impossible to tell apart [*132, 133*]. There is a definite reason for showing both these shades. On many occasions, we see lamps of the same design executed so differently that it is sometimes difficult to believe that they belong to the same category. This may be laid to the individuality of the artist and the originality of his concept. In this instance, we wish to show that the opposite is also true: two completely handcrafted objects can be almost identical.

In both shades the bodies of the dragonflies are a dark crimson; their eyes, made of half-round jewels, are the same color, and their wings are purple; the green rippled glass segments between them might represent a meadow or the still waters of a pond. Around the aperture we see a flaming sky, rendered in fiery yellow-orange rippled glass; the color diminishes in intensity as it descends, becoming ever more heavily striated with blue-green. The three apron rows, rippled like the rest of the background, consist of a blue-green top row invaded by the wings, a blue middle row and a lower orange-red row which forms the bottom edge of the shade and has a strong tonal affinity with the sky at the unencircled aperture.

134

A provocative base, numbered 140, is shown in the Tiffany Album with a 16" Dragonfly [*134*]. In the shape of a reed basket about 9" wide, its weave is uncannily captured in cast bronze. A cobra wound around the bottom of the basket forms what is probably one of the most fanciful of Tiffany platforms. Extending its head rather impudently, he seems to be saying, "I should be inside, but what are you going to do about it?"

This Dragonfly, made from rippled glass, bears the number 1462 and thereby identifies a type of shade which is usually neither signed nor numbered.

GERANIUMS

These herbs with their showy flowers and deeply lobed leaves were a notable source of inspiration for the Tiffany Cones. They are 16" wide, 7" deep and have an aperture which fits a 3" ring. The design is repeated five times.

Scarlet Geranium 135

Realistic large-lobed geranium leaves make up most of the main body of the cone [135]. The clearly definable older leaves, heavily mottled in yellowish-gold glass, fill the bottom half of the shade, with the newer leaves, bluish-green in tint, appearing toward the top. The stems are striated green, intermixed with yellow and mauve. A spectacular color contrast is created by the inclusion of scarlet flowers among and above the leaves; these are made from fibrillated glass. The background, consisting of fractured glass with flakes of orange and pink, establishes a sunny outdoor aura.

The Geranium is rimmed at the aperture by a row of blue rippled rectangles; below, a similar row forms the upper edge of a small apron. The middle row of the apron repeats fragments of the leaf design, and the third and last row of darkish green ripples curves inward, reducing the width of the shade from 16" to 15" at its lower border.

A signature tag is attached to the inside of the lower rim, without a number. The latter is supplied by an identical shade in the Tiffany Album as 1451, shown in figure [200].

The base, in the shape of a narrow bottle, is 25½" high. It consists of a framework of latticed bronze, into which green glass has been blown, forming a rhomboid pattern in the bulbous area and long ellipses on the slender neck. The bottle rests on four leaflike legs which splay outward onto an 8" platform; this is decorated with a wavelike design in high relief. The cone-shaped finial is an integral part of the base and is usually high; turning its knob activates a switch located just below. Four supports, with small decorative hoops between them, hold four individual upright sockets. The base is numbered D956. In the Tiffany Album, the number for this design appears as 338.

135

Pink Geranium 136

The *Pink Geranium* is 1" larger in diameter than the Scarlet, or 17" at its widest, suggesting a different construction form [136]. It also differs from it in coloration, although the flowers are constructed of the same kind of fibrillated glass. Here the leaves are a lighter green, mottled with larger patches of yellow and some blue; their inside surfaces have a stippled texture. The segmented stems are yellow striated with brown. The apron consists of two green rows, separated by a band composed of portions of the shade pattern.

In striking contrast to the Scarlet Geranium, the background of this shade—made of red and blue striated glass—imparts a sense of high drama rather than sunny serenity. A storm seems to be brewing behind the setting sun.

Three tags are soldered onto the leading around three sides of a large leaf, reading: *Tiffany, Studios* and *New York*.

136

SEVENTEEN-INCH POPPIES

The poppy decorates some of the most successful cones produced by the Tiffany Studios. These shades were made in two sizes: three of the 17"-wide cones, 7" in height and with 3" apertures, will be shown here; the 20" size will be discussed later.

Many Poppies are dichroic to a remarkable degree; even when unlit, they are among the most attractive of the Tiffany shades. The multitextured glass employed in these lamps also accounts for much of their effectiveness. Apart from these considerations, the naturally strong coloration of the flower supplied the Tiffany artists with almost unparalleled opportunities for vivid effects.

The metal filigree, applied to the inner or outer surfaces of the leaves and to the dream-inducing seed-pods of the plants, provides the poppies with a decorative "plus." The filigree also conveys the coarseness of the leaves and the realistic roughness of the capsules.

The design motif, made up of four flowers and three buds, is repeated three times. The seventeen-inch Poppies have a three-row converging apron which reduces the width of the bottom row to 16". They have no aperture row.

137

Orange-Red Poppy   137

The fibrillated-glass petals of this shade are a brilliant red, lightly streaked with pink and white [137]; the pods are orange-green and the leaves green with some orange striations; the buds are pink and green. Filigree covers the outside of both leaves and seed-pods; configurated glass has been used for the latter. The background is a turbulent orange, heavily mottled with green and striated with yellow.

An especially arresting feature of this Poppy is the extensive elevation of its overlapping leaves. Since the raised segments are almost half an inch above the surface, the shade in part acquires an added "depth" dimension. Each projection has a corresponding hollow on the inside of the shade.

The apron, which consists of two rows of blue glass with an orange one between, turns slightly inward. The shade is signed and numbered 1467.

The outstanding base features an interesting technique of glass-blown-into-bronze. It is made of green glass, blown through ribbons of pierced bronze, the whole crowned with a heavy-bodied bronze disk. Eight 3"-high glass bulges encircle the center. There are two more blown-glass rows, composed of diamond and crescent shapes, both above and below. The bulges are larger than those of the blown glass base in figure [135]. The base stands on five ball feet and harmonizes in color with the green glass of the shade. *Tiffany Studios, N. Y.* is the imprint. The electrification of the base is an adaptation.

A similar glass base, blown through a wire form, is identified as number 398 in the Tiffany Album [138]. In this, the protrusions are more numerous and are patterned in rhomboids as well as pointed ovals. The platform consists of a conglomerate of well-sculptured crabs. The globular Peony shade will be discussed later.

138

139

Red-Purple Poppy 139

Here, greenish-yellow leaves, made of undulating glass, surround flowers which range from pink delicately striated with white to dark red [139]. Their petals are made of fibrillated or granulated glass which enhances the flamboyant coloration. The buds and the seed-pods are green with red spots. Set against a background of purple mottled with blue, the plants appear to be moonlit under a midnight-blue sky. The typical three-row apron is of green and orange glass. Again, the overlapping of leaves is in evidence; while not as prominent, they are more plentiful than in the preceding shade.

Orange Poppy 140

This Poppy is more subdued than the Red-Purple [140]. Its petals are orange, mottled with yellow; some consist of rippled, some of knobby, glass. The flowers have purple centers, while the buds are still somewhat green. In this shade, the filigree of the leaves is applied to the underside of the glass, but on the surface in the case of the seed-pods. The background is a delicate bluish-green with some gray mottling. Upper and lower apron rows are rippled orange, with a row of green between them. The Orange Poppy is signed *Tiffany Studios New York 1467*.

140

EIGHTEEN-INCH CLEMATIS

The Clematis Cones, modeled after one of the most colorful climbing plants which support themselves on fences and trees, are made in 18" and 24" sizes. Examples of the former will be shown here, of the latter later on. It is worthy of note that there are no pattern repeats on either of the Clematis shades. Instead of duplicating a design several times over, the artist skillfully evolved one single comprehensive pattern. The 18" cones are 6" deep and have a 3" aperture.

141

Light Blue Clematis 141

The shade bears a tiny ½" signature tag inscribed *Tiffany Studios New York* [*141*]. This shade is delicately colored and can be used to advantage in a pastel decor.

About half the flowers, whose petals are made of fibrillated glass, are whitish to gray; the others are blue striated with white. Their centers are an exquisitely subtle orange. The leaves range from yellow-green to a deep bluish-green, with hardly noticeable stems. The background is a very tender blue, strongly striated with yellow and gray, which blends softly with the blue used in the blossoms. The shade is bounded by a green border at the top and by a one-row green glass apron around the lower rim.

The background glass is worthy of special mention because of its distinctive knobby texture; the knobs are roundish pea-sized elevations, ten to fifteen to the inch, which create a texture so pronounced that, although they are on the inside of the shade, they show through in transmitted light in certain areas.

The 9" rounded platform of the Clematis base sits on four short splayed feet. A pattern of twelve stylized leaves in low relief covers its upper surface and, via stylized leaf stalks, ascends the shaft. This was described by the Tiffany Studios as the "Foliated Design."

Three arms curve from the top of the stem and carry the shade. Illumination is provided by a three-socket cluster. The total height of the lamp is 24½"; height from base bottom to the arms is 18". The base is impressed with the Studio signature and numbered 11416. This may be a production, not a design, number since the latter is given in the Tiffany Album as 363.

Purple Clematis 142

Leaves as well as blossoms and background are here considerably more colorful [*142*]. The foliage is much more in evidence because component elements have been interchanged: additional leaves appear in this shade where background glass was employed in the other. Furthermore, an intense green makes these leaves stand out more prominently.

The dark blue blossoms, called "Blue Gems," are heavily mottled with purple in a strongly stippled glass which was carefully selected as to color and texture. The flower centers range from yellow to crimson red. The fractured-glass background, golden-orange with green, yellow and brown flakes, provides a powerful contrast. One row of rippled bluish-white glass rims the aperture; another whiter row forms the small apron. The Purple Clematis is more numerous than the Light Blue; it carries the same small ½" signature tag.

142

Arrowroot 143

This shade is 20" in diameter, 8¼" high, has a 4" aperture and carries the Studio signature [143]. In the Arrowroot, an oddly formed plant is treated in an unusual fashion. The roots, stripped to their essential shape, are strongly limned in shades of green shot through with white and yellow. But these roots—the source of tapioca—are not shown growing from the ground, although the adjacent brownish areas may well represent the soil. Furthermore, the roots are seen surrounded by the yellow-centered brilliant white flowers they helped to bring to bloom. The flower stems are indicated by the design of heavy, leaded lines descending from the aperture.

A blue-white sky in the top quarter of the shade adds another naturalistic note. Blue also serves to frame the aperture. The single-row apron at the lower edge represents a rectilinear strip of striated glass, green-yellow-blue in color.

The shade is an extremely effective formal rendering of this plant. Instead of attempting an exact imitation, the artist has succeeded in the more difficult endeavor of symbolically spreading before us the entire life cycle of the arrowroot. In the Tiffany Album, the shade bears number 1496.

The four-legged bronze base features an 8" platform decorated with six large stylized leaves, radiating from the base of the shaft, and six more which curve up over its outer circumference. Twelve stalks run up the stem of the base, ending with circular twists at three different levels. The height is 26", the finish dark bronze, like the shade. Its base plate is inscribed with the Tiffany Studios signature and the number 28612, but in the Tiffany Album it is coded 357.

143

144

In the Album, an Arrowroot shade is also shown on a base whose stem is covered with slender, pointed spears resembling marsh grass; the flat platform is composed of round water-lily leaves [144]. This base is numbered 225.

WATER LILIES

At least two basic Tiffany designs were inspired by the water lily, best loved of all aquatic plants; both were used exclusively in the cones. The less ostentatious of the two is the Lily Pad pattern, which may appear almost geometric to the casual observer. However, closer study will reveal the intricacy and true beauty of these leaf motifs. On the other hand, the splendor of the more spectacular Flowering Water Lily is immediately apparent.

145

Lily Pad   145

The shade is 20" in diameter, 7" high and has a 4" aperture; it is signed [145]. The design, which is repeated five times, is made up of about a dozen irregularly horizontal rows of floating leaves. These are depicted as they would be seen from afar and at an angle, for the pads—perfectly round in nature, with only a narrow slit in their surface—appear to be oval on the shade. The gradual diminution in size of the more distant pads proves the excellence of the artist's perspective. He has also been able to indicate the actual substance of the leaves by variations in tonality and leading.

The older leaves, on the periphery of the shade, are larger and darker in color than those nearer the top, so that the upper part of the shade is airier in feeling.

Yellow-green to blue-green in color, the glass of the pads contains both striations and mottles. Some leaves overlap, others float apart from one another. Between them, gently swirling waters create a sense of movement. Limpid in some areas, murky in others, the clarity of the water is indicated by the color of the background glass; from purest white it degrades to a speckled brownish-green. Round, closely set emerald-green jewels, strongly suggesting drops of water, edge the lower border of the cone.

The absence of a flower or even a bud makes this Lily Pad almost unique in the whole Tiffany line of flowered lamps. However, the ingenious treatment of leaves, stems and surrounding water compensates for the lack of a floral element.

The shade sits on one of the two examples in this volume of non-Tiffany bases—or perhaps one should say non-Tiffany Studio bases, since this one was made and signed by Tiffany & Co., the jewelry firm. It bears the number 15023 and was reportedly used in that emporium for the occasional display of Tiffany Studios shades. The beads in the platform match the beaded jewels in the shade.

The difference in approach is obvious, for here we see a conventional vase form adorned with equally conventional embossments. The Art Nouveau influence is absent and no attempt has been made at originality of any sort. Rising from an 8" platform, the base is 27" high and is finished in black with a faint tint of green.

Flowering Water Lily 146

This Lily shade is 20″ wide, 10″ high and has a 4″ aperture [146]. It is signed *Tiffany Studios New York 1490–6.* The cone shape is here slightly modified by a curvature at its greatest width. Instead of the straight or inward angled aprons previously described, a smoothly rounded apron distinguishes the Flowering Water Lily.

In this shade too, the designer's clever use of perspective is apparent in his handling of the lily pads. While the artist's working angle foreshortens all those at the lower edge, turning them into ovals and ellipses, their true roundness is revealed in the upper reaches of the shade. One, right off center, has an edge uplifted as if caught in a gust of wind. The pads are constructed of green glass, mottled with yellow and orange, and of bluish glass mottled with gray. The latter are knobby-textured.

The pattern also contains numerous large lilies, with pink-white petals and sprightly yellow centers supported by round reddish-brown stems. Flower buds are visible, and one thinks he sees a flash of crimson fish. All are laid against a background of the darkest, bluest water; near the top of the shade, it mellows into mauve; this glass is stippled on its inner surface. A lustrous band of green rippled glass, interrupted by an occasional bud, rims the aperture. A similar band—this one broken by both leaves and stems—encircles the shade almost at its bottom edge. The design, which is repeated three times, resumes below this row, and continues right down to the lower border.

Its depth of color, brilliance of design, and relative rarity combine to make this Flowering Water Lily one of the most impressive of all Tiffany lampshades, and fully entitled to the dash number awarded it.

146

A similarly engrossing lamp appears. as figure [147] taken from the Tiffany Album. It has a 16″ cone shade made of rippled glass which represents water and water plants; it features four large fish which extend over almost the whole shade from aperture to apron. They have a homogeneous body and large eyes. The Favrile base has the shape of an oil font and stands on a platform of lily pads.

147

TWENTY-INCH DRAGONFLIES

This is the second group of Dragonflies to be discussed. They differ from those in the first group in several major respects: as to size, their diameter is 20", their height 7" and their aperture 4"; Tiffany glass jewels are extensively used in their design; their aprons are not incurved and all three rows are plainly visible.

Of the great variety of jewels shown in the chapter on glass (see figure [23]), a few types were prodigally employed to add still more distinction to the Dragonfly. Twenty-one oval jewels were included in the background of each shade, three to each of its seven repeats. The largest jewels appear closest to the aperture, the smaller ones farther down the cone. In some instances, the jewels pick up and enhance the color of the background, in others, they furnish a contrast. The eyes are occasionally jeweled, most often in flat glass.

In both the 16" and 20" category, the dragonflies are of the same size. With an individual wingspread of approximately 8½", seven of them cover a circumference of about 60". Since the smaller cone is only 50" around, much overlapping of the wings is necessary. In the larger cone, which is 60" in circumference, no overlapping need occur. From the standpoint of size, the dragonfly seems better suited to the bigger shade.

Red-Bodied Dragonfly 148

Here the bodies of the insects are bright red, the wings yellow-green and the eyes green. Most of the background is dark red, becoming greenish in its upper third [148]. The effectiveness of the red, which is the color of glowing coals, is intensified by the texture of the glass. It is the rare configurated glass, extra thick, with ridges and knobs running in countless crisscrossing patterns; the ridges are as high as in rippled glass, but instead of parallel rows, they form a random and erratic network, which breaks up and refracts light in a most peculiar manner.

Moving toward the top of the shade, the red graduates into variegated greens; at the aperture, we see a band of solid green. At the other extreme, two green rows with a row of red between form the apron. A 4" signature tag is attached to the inside of the rim.

The shade is shown on a bronze base which looks old and well-worn. Its conical platform is grooved, but the ridges seem to have been rubbed down by long years of use; the reddish copper finish with dark bronze streaks completes the illusion of antiquity. The stem consists of two segmented sections, the smaller atop the larger. The base carries a three-socket cluster and is 26" in over-all height. A signature tag is impressed on the bottom plate together with the number 394.

149

Red Dragonfly 149

The color scheme of this Dragonfly [149] is similar to that employed in the last shade seen, though much subdued. The basic background tone is green, with yellow and bluish tints. A much diluted red, mixed with orange and mottled with gray, appears in the wings. The bodies are a bright red; the eyes are yellow and of filamented glass rather than half-round jewels.

Though lacking the configurated glass, this shade is also special in that the entire background is of rippled glass. The ripples run horizontally, which is rather unusual. Even the aperture row and the middle apron row are of dark rippled glass, but these ripples run in an up-and-down direction. The other two apron rows are constructed of smooth glass rectangles. Jewels, gray at the top and green midway between wing and aperture, add substance to the shade.

Because of its muted palette, the Red Dragonfly is more pleasant, if less showy, than its color-rich counterpart. It is signed.

The base, supported by four small splayed legs, has a 9" round platform, decorated with twelve highly stylized leaves in low relief. Twelve stalks run straight down the stem and end in circular wire twists at two alternate levels. The base carries a three-socket cluster and is finished in dark copper. It is signed and numbered 358; the number 11416 also appears.

Orange-Winged Dragonfly 150

A singular color scheme confronts us here, rarely employed in Tiffany shades [150]. Deep, shimmering blue-greens form the background of this shade, which is edged at the aperture by a bright blue border; two of the three rows in the apron are the same cerulean blue. Green and blue jewels add their own special luster. Even the insects' eyes and bodies share the same somewhat eerie scheme. In striking contrast, the wings and the center row of the apron are a self-mottled orange. The shade is signed and has been awarded dash number 1495–12.

The base, which depicts the "Four Virtues," is finished in bronze and numbered 567. It has been described previously along with figure [103], where it is seen in gold doré.

150

151

Green-Gold Dragonfly 151

This cone [151] displays a spectacular combination of colors employed on rare occasions by the Studios, or perhaps by one artist at the Studios. Another specimen utilizing this color scheme is shown below.

Hewing close to nature's own tones, the insect bodies are dark green; their eyes round blue jewels; their wings light green shading into yellow. The background in the lower part of the shade is made from mottled glass of unusual beauty, and ranges from light sky-blue tones to midnight hues which are almost impenetrable in their density. In addition to purple and orange speckles, the glass also has striations of the same color running through it.

Toward the top of the shade, the bluish purple resolves into orange, until—at the aperture—we see a single band of yellow, speckled with light and dark orange. The same colors are used in the middle row of the apron, whose upper and lower rows are bluish-purple. The twenty-one jewels gleam in darker shades of orange, emphasizing this color throughout the upper portion of the shade.

The shade and its Lily Stem Base, which is shown in figure [205], both bear the number 1495. The base is inscribed *Panama Philippine Exhibition of 1915*, where the lamp was an exhibit.

Mauve-Winged Dragonfly 152

The shade [152] is similar in many respects to the Green-Gold, displaying analogous tones of yellow, orange, purple and blue. The striations, mottles and cloudlike formations in the background glass create a feeling of unceasing movement. Their jeweled eyes a fiery red, their bodies glistening pink, seven purple-winged dragonflies float in this strange, seething sky.

A blue-purple apron simulates the water's surface, and the orange-tinted aperture row reflects the last rays of a setting sun. The shade is signed and numbered 1495.

152

Blue Dragonfly 153

The brilliant blue area of the background dominates the entire shade, overwhelming the scant sections which are strongly striated with mauve and the all-purple areas in the upper oblong row [153]. The blue-on-blue mottled insect bodies add to the impact, as do the light blue jewels.

The luminescence of the blue background glass is strengthened by its texture, which is both heavily fibrillated and deeply rilled on its inner surface. The mauve-purple glass is stippled. The wings of the dragonflies are aquamarine, and their flat glass eyes are deep orange. The aperture row and the top and bottom rows of the short apron are blue, striated with green, while the apron's middle row repeats the blue-mauve in the main body of the shade. The Blue Dragonfly is signed and numbered 1495–4.

The base is 25″ high and has a round 9½″ platform, which stands on four pad-shaped feet. On the rim and around the outer part of the platform surface we find thirty-two stylized leaves within an undulating loop design, interspersed by sixteen tiny flowers. Toward the center of the platform, a row of sixteen minute nodules line up with the leaf rows, and eight similar nodes surround the stem. Halfway up, the stem is further adorned with six oblong loops of the same basic design. The shade is signed and numbered 395.

A cone-shaped Dragonfly, similar in the general design to the 20″, but with more background glass, was also made in a 28″ diameter.

153

In this series, one is always impressed with the almost complete freedom the artist enjoyed. Unhampered by limitations imposed upon him in portraying certain plants and flowers, he could happily abandon himself to daring color schemes and textural contrasts. Using the Studios' most resplendent glass, he was thus able to obtain results more dazzling and dramatic than those observable in any other lamp. Many more beautiful examples of Dragonflies will be shown in future chapters.

TWENTY-INCH DAFFODILS

The daffodil belongs to the Narcissus family, which is well represented in the Tiffany line of lamps. It is also called the trumpet narcissus because of the trumpetlike cup centered among the flower petals. Three of the Daffodils belong here among the 20″ cones, another will be found among the 28″ cones and two more will be shown in the next chapter, describing globes. There we will also see a jonquil, which, belonging to the Narcissus family, is characterized by more rounded petals and much shallower cups.

The first examples of the Narcissus family are 20″ wide, 8″ high and have 4″ apertures. Each has a three-row apron. Long daffodil stems droop down, covering, together with their leaves, most of the cone surface, with blossoms appearing mainly in the area of the lower border. The design is repeated five times.

154

Green Daffodil 154

The shade is bounded by a bluish-green aperture row of rippled glass, and an apron whose upper and lower rows are of the same color and texture [154]. Some of the yellow-orange flowers are completely open, their petals already fading from rich orange into yellow; others are barely breaking from the bud. A few flowers penetrate the apron and are visible in its middle row, which is otherwise green. Exquisite green-gray mottling gives the flower petals a realistic look, most artfully portrayed in the large center cups.

The reedlike leaves, typical of this plant, are dark green, extensively mottled in light green, blue and yellow. The background is virtually the same bluish-green—almost as if the viewer were seeing through the interstices another patch of distant daffodils. The shade is signed and carries the number 1497.

Blue Daffodil 155

Although the same design as the Green, there is a considerable difference in the coloring [155]. The leaves show more blue and yellow mottling and the blossoms a paler orange. However, it is the light blue background that infuses this shade with a wholly different feeling. One seems to sense the presence of water; through the narrow openings between the leaves, one almost sees the reflection of a nearby stream. The apron and aperture rows emphasize the dominant blue color key of this cone.

The 28"-high base, finished in gold doré, is an odd squarish shape, and rather resembles a vase; each side displays a stylized Iris in low relief. The almost-flat platform is composed of four half-round extensions, so designed that the corners of the "vase" rise from their centers; intertwined leaves cover the upper surface.

155

Multicolored Daffodil 156

In comparison with the two preceding examples, this Daffodil [156] is extra-lively. While half the background glass of the shade is almost a single hue, the other half consists of rose, mauve, dark blue and orange segments. Gazing at one side of the shade, the viewer sees a green garden vista. Looking at the other side (shown in the illustration), all the tender colors of a setting summer sun are spread before him.

The flowers have deep orange centers, mottled with gray, and are made from fibrillated glass. The surrounding petals are bluish-white, mottled with light yellow; their inside surfaces are finely stippled. Stems and leaves are yellow-green and blue-green. The apron rows are basically yellow and green, with some blue, mauve, orange and rose tints on the lively side. The shade is signed and bears the number 2106, which is at variance with that of the other Daffodils, and probably a production, not a design number.

The 10" circular platform of the base is decorated with a flat leaf design on its rounded outer edge. On its upper surface, ridges, radiating inward from a beaded band, converge upon the stem. A stylized plant pattern covers the lower bulbous portion of the stem, encircling it in the form of a fluted band which winds its way toward the top. The base is signed and numbered 8619.

156

TWENTY-INCH POPPIES

In addition to the 17″ Poppies previously discussed, Tiffany's cone-shaped shades also include some very popular and effective 20″ specimens. The designs are similar, but the motif of the larger shade contains a greater number and variety of flowers and buds and is repeated four times instead of three. Lacelike bronze filigree is again found in the leaves (outside or in), and around the seed-pods (outside only). The three-dimensional overlapping of leaves, seen in the 17″ Poppies, does not always occur, and the three-row incurved apron is straight in the 20″ shades. An aperture row has been added, missing in the smaller Poppies. The cone is 8″ high and has a 4″ aperture.

The Poppies exemplify a type of Tiffany lamp which is extremely attractive even in reflected light.

157

158

Orange Poppy 157

This is a subdued shade, whose orange blossoms are cooled with mauve and yellow-white mottling [157]. The closed buds, a muted greenish-red in color, cluster toward the top of the cone. Some of the flower petals are made of rippled glass, textured on the inside.

The entire design blends gently into a bland orange background, mottled with greenish dots, whose serenity is scarcely disturbed by one or two azure blue accents. A broad band of light and dark green leaves forms the lower portion of the shade; their exquisite veining is depicted in filigree, applied to the back of the glass. The shade is signed and numbered 1531.

Yellow-Mauve Poppy 158

A more spectacular display of color is spread before us in the next example of the category [158]. Here the buds are green, speckled with orange. The blossoms are orange-yellow, with traces of pink introduced by means of fine mottles and striations. Against a background of deep purple, modulating into blue-purple and orange-purple, they arrest the most jaded eye.

The deft juxtaposition of dissimilar colors results in pleasing contrasts rather than painful clashes. Throughout the shade, traces of color serve as transitions from hot to cool and from dim to dazzling. Yellow in a green leaf, for example, is carried upward into a yellow blossom. The orange streak in a purple background segment leads toward an orange petal.

Blue rows of glass, with a purple row between, form the apron of this shade, and a single blue band of glass encircles the aperture.

Again, textured glass is extensively employed; rippled glass for the pods, fibrillated glass for the flower petals and stippled as well as fibrillated glass for the background.

Many of the leaves overlap or angle upward in such a manner that their abutting edges are as much as ½″ above the surface.

The shade is signed.

159

Red-Purple Poppy   159

Both color and glass in this shade are exceptional [159]. The blossoms are a deep coral red, with delicate shadings of white, gray and yellow; the buds are reddish-green mottled with yellow. The flamboyant background is basically a potent bluish-purple, strongly striated with every tonal modulation of the two colors, along with white, gray, rose and red. Bright red flower petals are encircled by purple glass or by blue glass with reddish undertones, which act as color bridges to unify the whole. The seed-pods are partly green, partly orange, and are covered with bronze filigree, which is also applied to the outside of the green leaves.

More than the usual amount of textured glass has been used in this shade, and all the texture is turned inward. The small buds penetrating the aperture are made of rippled glass—the larger buds are of configurated glass, the flowers of granular and fibrillated glass and the background segments are both fibrillated and densely stippled.

A blue band around the aperture and a blue and purple apron—these of smooth-surfaced glass—enclose this splendid creation by an inspired artist.

The base is the equal of the shade in quality, being one of the very best made by the Tiffany Studios. In authentic Art Nouveau style, its stem consists of sinuous spirals, rising from a round 10" platform. In the Studios catalogue it was called the "Design of Lily Stems" and is also known as the "Twisted Vine Base." Twenty-eight inches in height, it carries a four-socket cluster. The finish is green patina, and its bottom plate is impressed with the signature and the number 433.

Finished in gold doré, this base is shown in figure [261], where the stem can be seen more fully in a profile view, instead of foreshortened as in this illustration.

Orange-Red Poppy   *160, 161*

Even when viewed in reflected light only, this is a colorful lamp [*160*]. An exceptional contrast exists between its bluish-red blossoms, greenish background, mottled with gray and yellow, and green leaves. The green-orange aperture row and apron tie together and strengthen the tricolor scheme.

160

161

The comparison between the lit and the unlit shades dramatically demonstrates the amazing characteristics of Tiffany's dichroic glass. The most astonishing change takes place in the flower petals which, in reflected light, are bluish-red or purple with gray mottling, but in transmitted light turn into a pure and unadulterated red [*161*]. The buds which, unlit, are different tones of green, assume a reddish-orange hue. The greenish background, mottled with gray and yellow dots, flames into orange with russet spots. In the green leaves, the vein pattern becomes more evident. On the other hand, the gold finish and the outside filigree are more decorative in the unlit shade.

Undulating and knobby glass, textured on its inner surface, is used for the flower petals. Both inside and out, the leading of the shade is finished in gold; this blends happily with the golden background, and gives just enough substance to the filigree of the seed-pods. The green-yellow mottling of the poppy leaves furnishes a perfect backdrop for the filigree fretwork of their veins and capillaries; in this shade, the filigree is applied to their inside. Although the leaves do not actually overlap each other, their edges are occasionally raised above the surface of the background glass.

The shade is signed and numbered 1531.

Twenty-Four-Inch Clematis 162

This shade size – uncommon among the cones – constitutes an intermediate stage between the standard 20″ cones and the larger 28″ hanging cones. Its 24″ width is balanced by a 9″ depth and a 5″ aperture. This is just about the largest cone which can be displayed effectively on a floor lamp base; however, it may also be hung from the ceiling [162].

162

The design is an original entity without repeats, like the smaller Clematis cones seen before; it consists almost entirely of flowers in full bloom. The blue glass faithfully matches the natural color of the Clematis, and the verisimilitude is further enhanced by subtle variations of the blue, intensifying near the flower centers, and paling toward the petal points. The soothing blues are given needed emphasis with orange and yellow centers.

Strongly mottled green leaves appear to be sun-dappled, as in an actual garden, and a soft yellow, tinged with green, supplies a subdued but effective background. A single row of yellow-green rippled glass rims the shade at its aperture and lower edge; some leaves and flowers artfully impinge upon the bottom band.

The bronze beads encircling both upper and lower edges indicate that this cone may have been meant to hang since a beaded rim was frequently employed on shades intended for such use.

The finial features an iridescent gold ball, about an inch in diameter, at its center. We have seen this sort of Tiffany jewel occasionally used as ornamentation on both bases and shades.

HANGING FLOWER CONES

The large 28" cones, composed of intricate and colorful flower designs, are some of the most impressive of Tiffany shades. They were popular at the time they were made and remain so today. Their standard measurements are 28" in width, 11" in height and 5" across the aperture; most are strengthened by the addition of three to four reinforcement wires which, as in all flowered shades, run on top of leaded lines in a circuitous fashion.

A major disadvantage of the large cones has already been mentioned—the difficulty of finding places to suspend them so that they may be viewed without distortion. This factor becomes increasingly significant as the size of private homes continues to decrease. It is possible to use the large cone on the large floor base, but this requires a great deal of adaptation. Furthermore, the shade would still be much too high for good viewing.

For this reason, the author has suggested inverting these cones and hanging them from the ceiling. This, as already stated, will afford a properly angled view, no matter how extensive the design may be, from almost any part of the room. Properly hung and illuminated, the large cones are unbelievably effective.

Hydrangea   163

The most famous Hydrangeas will be found in the final chapter; among the large cones, this design is a distinct rarity [163].

The pattern of this shade consists of scores of large circular shapes, each of which is actually a cluster of twenty to thirty tightly knit tiny blossoms. The big "snowballs," as they are often called, are primarily white, with blue, green or pink tints which derive from their multiple components and sometimes give the glass a spotty aspect. Granular glass has been used for the white flowers, heavily undulating glass for the spotted.

The leaves are a vibrant green streaked with yellow, and some are executed in rippled glass. The background is gray-green, strongly streaked with blue, noticeably in sections where the blossoms have a bluish tint. Because of this color carry-over, the shade is especially harmonious.

In two or three places, well-defined dark areas show up sharply; a dense gray, heavily mottled with blue, and almost completely opaque, these may represent older, dried-up portions of the plant. (Such a section can be seen at the lower right of the illustration.) Green stems add a linear element to the design.

Both the upper margin (partly concealed by the finial) and the lower margin are beaded. Because no glass rows encircle the shade at either top or bottom, the flowers reach both rims without interruption. The 5" finial has a heavy bronze center knob.

This is the only large cone which is seen supported by a base; all others will be shown suspended from the ceiling. The shade is signed.

164

Daffodil

164

This flower was such a great Tiffany Studios success in other categories that it inevitably turned up among the large cones [164]. The design differs from that of the two 20" cones previously presented; here the stems run up instead of hanging down. Sharply delineated in shades of green and yellow, they terminate at different levels, thereby distributing the blossoms rather evenly throughout the entire shade.

The stems of the young flowers are still long, strong and straight, but the stalks leading to older blossoms are curved and bent, as if by age. The daffodils, made of undulating and rippled glass, are a lively orange with yellow tints. The rushlike leaves are almost indistinguishable from the stems in shape and color, except where their pointed ends can be seen.

Near the lower border, the background glass is heavily mottled green on green and yellow on green; ascending, it gradually absorbs gray striations, and ends, at the top of the shade, a light gray with yellow striations. An occasional blue tint enlivens the background. It would be hard to envision a more nearly perfect portrayal of a daffodil bed, as glimpsed from ground level. Looking up, one sees the taller blooms outlined against a halcyon spring sky.

At the bottom of the shade, two yellow-green rows enclose a thin center strip of yellow ripples; a ring of beads finishes off the lower edge. Two rows of rippled glass, one yellow, one green, and a beaded ring make up the upper border.

The shade hangs from three chains which engage hooks on the aperture rim. In the illustrations of hanging shades a flat finial has been placed over otherwise open apertures to reduce glare.

It is signed, has no reinforcement wires and is bent slightly out of shape.

165

White Dogwood   165

The design of this shade [165] depicts the upper reaches of a flowering
dogwood tree; the angle is such that the sky is visible through a network of
brown branches on which we see both leaves and blossoms. Here again, two
time periods have been merged to contain an entire life cycle in this magnificent shade.

The leaves are made from green and yellowish-green glass, with gray
and white striations. The four-petaled dogwood blossoms are remarkably
detailed, even to the curl of their scalloped edges. The flowers are a hyaline
white into which gray, light yellow and greenish tints have been introduced
by means of mottled and fractured glass. Some petals are constructed of
rippled glass, with the rills running from the yellow flower centers toward
the outside of the petals, the texture facing the viewer.

The design is a single entity and is not repeated.

The superb blue background includes every conceivable variation of
this color, from deepest marine to delicately striated and mottled white-
blue. A yellow-green rippled row borders the shade on both top and bottom.
Beaded rims provide the final finishing touch. The Tiffany Studios signature
is present.

166

Pink Dogwood 166

This shade has been photographed from a slightly higher angle than those already seen, and so shows more of the over-all pattern. Though quite different from the previous Dogwood, this design also covers the entire cone without repetition [166].

The scalloped petals are predominantly white, with pink at their peripheries; this blush of color is accomplished by expert mottling and the judicious use of fractured glass. Though fabricated of flat glass segments, the edges of the older flowers appear to curl. Glowing yellow leaves, constructed of undulating glass with green and red striations, add a welcome warmth to the cool color palette, and a skein of greenish branches ties all the scattered elements together.

The background glass ranges from orange and light purple on one side to greenish-blue and true blue on the other. The branches enter the pattern at the lower (beaded) border and break through the horizontal row of orange-green glass; a similar row rings the aperture. The shade is signed.

HANGING BOUQUETS

The Tiffany Studios produced a series of 28" hanging cones, each depicting an artist's concept of flowers rather than botanically correct stems, leaves, blossoms and buds. Gathered in the form of a bouquet, these impressionistic fantasies have, for obvious reasons, been referred to as "Renoirs." Free to create rather than conform, the Tiffany craftsmen "grew" dream gardens, in which exotic flowers flourished. Riotous blooms, unknown in nature, rest against equally unreal but equally rich and resplendent backgrounds.

Needless to say, these shades are among the most colorful and exciting ever produced, and their exquisitely textured glass endows them with superb radiance. Each of the color schemes employed is so dazzlingly different from every other that the eye is fooled into assuming that the exuberant, unrepeated designs also differ. However, a close inspection will show that all shades of this type are identical in design. For easy reference, they will therefore be identified by their predominant colors.

Red-Blue Bouquet 167

While a veritable rainbow of colors can be seen in this shade, the most striking are the reds and pinks of the petals against the blues of the background [167]. The red as well as the pink flower petals exhibit exquisite striations, combined with area mottling (see center flower), while the blue background displays spot mottling in a profusion of small specks of lighter blue, green and rose. The red and pink blossoms also have an unusual texture, since they are fibrillated on both outside and inside surfaces. The white blossoms are made of rippled glass. Others are of white and orange rippled glass, with some containing violet tones. All flower centers are orange. The buds are red, orange-pink and purple.

The stems are dark brown, and the long narrow leaves, made from configurated glass, are a brilliant green, streaked with small quantities of yellow and orange. A rippled blue border row encloses the cone at both top and bottom; the lower border is invaded at dozens of points by leaves and buds. Despite the profusion of colors, the shade is well balanced tonally; the mottling employed in much of the glass has a unifying effect which is further enhanced by its subtle texture variations. Three reinforcing wires are found inside this shade, as well as three tags: one (2") is marked *Tiffany Studios*, another (1") *New York*, a third (1") 603–12 (dash number).

167

168

Pastel Bouquet   168

A less emphatic color scheme is employed in the Pastel Shade [168], whose soft floral hues are set against an equally subdued sky. The gently glowing flower centers are a muted mottled orange. The blossoms themselves are, for the most part, quiet pinks and mauves. The light-blue background, made of glass with a small-knobbed textured surface, adds to the tranquility by dimming and diffusing light rays. A few red blossoms and several brilliant orange-green mottled leaves appear in the pattern and furnish needed highlights.

Of all the visible flowers, the most interesting is the fully open bloom facing the viewer; its petals, which derive a great deal of their beauty from the knobby texture of their glass, are a weird and wonderful collection of pinks, striated with several shades of blue.

The yellow-green leaves are of fractured glass: in the lower foreground, green slivers and flakes can be seen floating in a yellow ground, deftly portraying the deterioration of the older leaves. Other foliage is rendered in rippled glass, with the texture facing outward. A bluish-gray row of rectangular glass rims this shade at the aperture and bottom edge. The cone has three reinforcement wires; it is signed and dash-numbered 603–8.

169

Crimson Bouquet   169   Radiant red flowers dominate this shade; almost the same coloring is employed for both the unfolding buds and full-blown blossoms [*169*]. It is evident that the same sheet, or sheets, of crimson glass, endowed with an undulating texture on their outside surface, have been used for all the flowers, yet the artist has managed to create an astonishing variety of color effects. By the most painstaking selection and juxtaposition of speckled, mottled, veined and striated glass segments, he has duplicated every nuance seen in nature.

Most of the flower centers are yellow, mottled with orange, but some are made of fractured glass with green and pink flakes on gray ground. The leaves are executed in pale green and bluish-gray, with scarcely noticeable stems. A brilliant background of configurated glass flows around the flowers in coruscating tides of color. Orange-red with undertones of greenish-blue in the center of the shade, it abruptly becomes a deep ultramarine as the eye moves left; mottles of light blue and pink may also be detected. A green border row and a beaded edge finish off both top and bottom of this Bouquet cone.

One would expect that a blazing red, bordered by a brilliant blue, along with other assorted bright spots scattered over the scene, would add up to a glaring blare. Amazingly, however, this shade emerges as a triumph of color coordination.

It has been photographed from above to show as much of the surface as possible. It may have been the artist's intent to indicate a seasonal change by lightening the blossoms toward the back, where they pale from yellow to white. Here, too, the leaves are a lighter yellow-green, and the background softens to a misty blue splotched with pink. The Tiffany Studios have made several such attempts to include several seasons or life cycles within the framework of a single shade; some examples have already been shown, and others will follow.

The shade has no reinforcement wires, and it is signed.

170

Jeweled Flower Bouquet   170

At first glance, the eye is caught by the extravagant colors of the flowers in this cone [170]; the dark purple blossom near the aperture; the flaming red bloom with orange and brown mottling directly below; next to it, a bright yellow unfolding bud. Striking in themselves, these colors are given added impact by the unusual textures of the glass employed: undulating glass for the red-green petals, rippled glass for the pink petals, fibrillated glass for the red-blue petals.

However, despite the spectacular color, the most interesting feature of the shade probably resides in the prominent chunk of orange glass which forms the flower center of the yellow-white blossom at the far left of the illustration; it projects its irregular profile about ½" beyond the surface of the shade. A similar raised flower center, not quite as prominent, may be seen in the large full-blown flower in almost the exact center of the shade; it is composed of a large rough piece of yellow-green rippled glass. These three-dimensional flower centers, while common in nature, are rare in Tiffany shades; the dramatic employment of glass chunks, which look like uncut jewels, is comparable to the use made of drapery glass in Magnolia shades.

The leaves are most carefully crafted, partly in yellowish fractured glass set with green, orange, and reddish-brown flakes; partly in undulating glass of a basically green color, with striations of yellow and blue. The bottom border, into which the design often wanders, is of grayish-blue ripple; the row around the aperture is the same color, but in untextured glass. The shade is signed.

Pink-Purple Bouquet   171

As clearly illustrated in figure [171], the name of this shade derives
from its dominant colors. The pinks deserve special attention because of the
fine craftsmanship evident in their execution. The barely open bud at lower
right center shows red striations running through primarily pink petals; at
the lower left, a full-blown flower displays a deeper red with white patches;

171

the petals of the flower closest to the aperture have almost-white centers
with the pinkish red appearing only on their margins. The purple bud in the
center of the shade is of particular interest because of its color; purple glass,
being rare, is zealously sought by serious collectors.

The glass used for the petals of the two fully open flowers in the upper
area of the shade is noteworthy both for the beauty of its rippled texture and
the quality of its color. The bloom at the left deserves a closer examination:
in its grooves we can see secondary tones of light blue, with the crest of the
ripples remaining a pinkish gray; such close coordination of texture and
color is not easily accomplished or often seen.

The flower centers are rippled yellow, spotted with green, brown and
red. Light green leaves and stems complete the floral pattern. The blue background begins with light blue ripples, which seem to surge up from the lower
border and increase in density and darkness as they approach the aperture.
The shade is banded at both top and bottom by a single rectilinear row of
deep orange ripples.

Purple-Blue Bouquet   172

In the Bouquet seen in figure [172] the emphasis is again on the much-admired purples and blues. Although the cone includes a few excellent pink blossoms in rippled glass and white blossoms in highly refractive pebbled glass, its great strength stems from the profuse employment of the radiant "royal" colors. Against a fantastic, ever-changing, but mainly blue, back-

172

ground – mottled with purple, pink, orange and green – we find soft mauve buds and blossoms, brilliantly mottled with deeper lilac, lavender and violet; the range extends all the way to a wine-dark purple, and the effect is most impressive.

The leaves provide a necessary balance in bright tones of orange-green and yellow-green; some are made from highly reflective undulating or rippled glass. The flower centers are various hues of orange, spotted with pink and red. Some are of rippled, others of fractured, glass. On top and bottom, earthy green borders of rippled glass establish firm boundaries for this purple-blue flight of fancy. The Bouquet has reinforcement wires running from the aperture ring halfway down the shade; it is signed.

HANGING TRELLIS CONES

Several types of Trellis shades were produced by Tiffany Studios. One of them belongs most definitely to the category of cones in that it is perfectly round, with the lattice-work merely simulated within its confines. Other, more realistic trellis structures are many-sided, with the struts forming the angles between the sides. Similar to the panel shades, but much larger, these trellises are, strictly speaking, not cones. However, they resemble them closer than any other shade form and will therefore be discussed here. Some simulated trellises appear also among the globes, but the most lifelike representatives are found in the chapter dealing with irregular lower borders.

The ROUNDED TRELLIS SHADES, representing true cones, will be shown first and described by means of four examples. They will be followed by a discussion of the many-sided or, more exactly, twelve-sided trellises.

173

Hollyhock on Gold   173

The trellis seen here is an extremely simple one, since the hollyhock customarily climbs on strings or wires instead of wooden supports [173]. These wires are indicated by heavy lead lines, largely covered by the plants and only visible between and above them as they stretch upward toward the aperture. In so doing, they form a geometric pattern on the upper portion of the shade, where the vertical supports are crossed by horizontal strings or wires. The latter may have been added for effect, since they are not needed in growing this plant.

The glass flowers are masterful reproductions of the living blooms. Variegated as in the average garden, some are red, some pink, while still others have pink-and-white petals, blush-colored near the center, snowy around the edges. All have yellow centers. In faithful imitation of Mother Nature's own, the green glass buds swarm up the wires, seeking out the sun. One bud, near the lower border, toward the left, is just about to burst forth; we can plainly see the first sliver of pink. Large green-orange leaves, oddly shaped and handsomely striated, spread over the lower portion of the cone. The background glass dominates the lower portion of the shade with a radiant sun-orange glow and acquires a decided green tinge as it nears the aperture.

The tone is circumscribed at its lower beaded edge by an unusually wide border band in green fractured glass with orange-brown flakes; leaves intrude upon it at intervals. There is no aperture row, but the bronze aperture rim bears a scalloped design.

The shade is signed and has dash number 625–1.

174

Hollyhock on Blue-Gray 174

In a Trellis identical in size and design with its sister shade, the craftsman has—solely through the use of color—created a completely different
mood [174]. It is primarily the background glass which sets the two shades
so far apart; here it is somber and hazy rather than glowing and vibrant.
The almost transparent glass is faintly blue, streaked with delicate greens,
pinks and purples, as if mist and drizzly rain had spread over the landscape.
Near the lower border, the background darkens into grayish blue, mottled
with some more of the menacing greens and browns.

The pink blossoms are streaked with white, the red with green. In the
white flowers at the right of the color plate, the care and artistry lavished
on this cone are most clearly evident. Note the natural blush of red at the
inner corner of each petal, near the flower center. Inevitably, a good deal
of time was spent—and glass sheets used up—in finding and matching these
few segments.

The buds twining up the trellis are two tones of green. The leaves are
green with reddish-brown striations; many penetrate the lower border row,
which is green striated with orange. The shade has a beaded bottom border
and a scalloped aperture rim. It is signed and numbered 625–5.

Nasturtium   175

Apparently the showy nasturtium was a great source of inspiration to Tiffany Studios artists, who used it in several of their most memorable shades. The Nasturtium Trellis [175] will be described here; Nasturtium globes, in two sizes, will be shown and discussed in the next chapter and a final example appears among the irregular lower borders.

The five petals of the nasturtium are spirally arranged and form a funnel-like shape. In this cone, the flowers appear in shades of yellow, orange or red, as they often do in nature. Several of the petals are most remarkable in that they have raised spinelike ridges, brought about by the use of low-relief drapery glass. One of these glass segments, mauve-red in color, may be seen in almost the exact center of the shade; another drapery glass petal is visible in the orange flower in the upper left, above the middle lattice, abutting a green leaf. Other blossoms are made from undulating and from rippled glass. Throughout, the flower centers are similar in color to the petals. In the forefront of the shade, as shown, tints of red predominate; on the unseen side, more of the orange and yellow are present.

The large leaves are, in their way, almost as beautiful as the flowers. Justice has been done them by the employment of a medium green glass, marvelously mottled with darker green, blue, orange and gray. Even their very natural veining has been successfully simulated by the painstaking selection of striated and speckled glass.

However, they lack the characteristic lobulated shape of living nasturtium leaves, with their many indentations, and look instead like the leaves of the pond lily. (Judging from the frequency of their appearance in unrelated plants, the latter must have had a special attraction for the Tiffany Studios.) The fleshy yellow-green plant stems wind at random around the half-hidden vertical and horizontal supports of a sturdy wood trellis.

A startling color note is introduced in the bluish-purple background glass, which is both striated and mottled with mauve and green; because of its luminosity, increased by its undulating texture, it provides a vivid yet not-overly florid contrast. As if modified by reflections from the red flowers, the potent dark blues at the bottom of the shade blend into purple tones around the blooms. (Some of the glass shows the symptoms of heat fracture, multitudinous fine cracks which are probably due to too strong bulbs having been too close to the glass; see bottom left.)

The upper and lower borders, both mauve-gray, form part of the trellis, together with a third band which encircles the shade slightly below its center and five intersecting vertical struts. The 3½″ signature tag reads *Tiffany Studios New York 602–3.*

175

176

Grape 176

In this cone, the clearly defined trellis consists of eleven vertical and three horizontal lattices, heavily laden with clusters of grapes and many of their unmistakable leaves [176]. The two large leaves in the lower right quadrant are especially remarkable; made of drapery glass, their folds and wrinkles stand out in amazingly realistic high relief. Subsidiary ripples and striations, in combination with the most meticulous shading, almost bring these tough, textured leaves to life. Drapery glass was rarely used in a Tiffany lamp shade, and never to better effect than in this brilliantly conceived and executed trellis cone.

The balance of the shade is equal to the leaves in creativity and craftsmanship. At an early stage, the grapes are greenish-blue or light pink (at left), then acquire a tinge of darker blue or red; ripened, they are dark red and deep purple (at right), ready to be picked. The leaves undergo the same metamorphosis; first small and yellow green, they grow larger in size and deeper in tone, until they reach full maturity and beyond. The rusty leaf resting on the center lattice is clearly past its prime.

From top to bottom, the background also varies. Perhaps the oranges and pinks in the lower portion of the shade reflect unseen flowers and grass; the blue in the upper portion is almost certainly the sky, visible through open spaces of the arbor.

Both the top and bottom borders form a portion of the trellis, with possibly two more horizontal rows between; only one is visible, but the spacing would seem to indicate the presence of another, completely covered by the plants. The trellis adds an interesting linear element to the lush design. There are three reinforcement wires and three signature tags: a 1½" tag, *Tiffany Studios*; a 1" tag, *New York*; and a ¾" tag, *608–10*.

TWELVE-SIDED TRELLIS shades are really only once removed from cones. With twelve flat sides, they are not smoothly round as any proper cone must be; however, since the angularity at the twelve junctures is so very slight—only 30°—they are, in essential shape, closer to cones than to any other category. Both shades are 30" in width, 12" in height and have 8" apertures, which require special rims and finials. There are four repeats of the design. Six reinforcement wires are used in each shade. The grid consists of three horizontal rows and twelve vertical supports; the latter also form the boundaries of the twelve sides.

Twelve-Sided Grape Trellis on Green 177

The slats in this shade are grained in striated brown glass; they simulate chestnut wood of good quality, which has been carefully carpentered [177].

The predominant color of the cone is the shimmering yellow green of the background, made of a light green fractured glass, inlaid with dark green, yellow and orange fragments. These help to induce an illusion of air in motion. The green of the background is reinforced by the coloration of the large leaves; their fibrillated texture adds still more strength to the light and dark greens, spotted with blue and yellow.

Sizable clusters of red, blue and purple grapes, textured in stippled glass, glow against this background. The red grapes are minutely mottled with dark purple dots in their very center. The purple grapes have blue striations at their edges and the blue are streaked with purple.

Stems and tendrils in striated reddish-gray glass twist around the trellis to attach the plant. The shade is signed.

Twelve-Sided Grape Trellis on Blue 178

This twelve-sided trellis is of precisely the same design as the sister shade, but the background is basically blue, modified by grayish-white, rose and a little purple [178]. This glass is of rare beauty, which derives from the infinite refinements of its mottling and striation. The stippled-glass grapes are magenta, bright and dark blue, and deep plum purple. Some leaves are luridly mottled with yellow; others are made of green fractured glass, containing yellow, brown and orange fragments.

The trellis supports are more gray than brown; made of fibrillated glass, they are reminiscent of old maple wood in color and graining. Stems and tendrils of the grapevine wind over and under the lattices. A Tiffany Studios signature appears on this shade.

178

7. FLOWERED GLOBES

I N SHAPE, the globes are much more complex than the cones. Instead of being curved in only one direction – the horizontal – the shades in this category are curved in both the horizontal and vertical planes. Aesthetically, this produces a more pleasing shape. It is also superior from the artistic standpoint, since the globular surface permits a more natural rendering of three-dimensional objects like trees and flowers. Technically, greater craftsmanship is required to produce a globe since it is more difficult to lead flat pieces of glass in such a way as to form a surface that curves in two directions.

On the other hand, the proper placement of globes in a room is a much easier matter than the disposition of cones. Since the surface of a globe has a considerable vertical component, the design of the shade, especially its lower aspect, can be more readily seen from the side.

However, the upper portions of large globes are still poorly visible, especially on high floor bases. This becomes a serious handicap in instances where they carry the best part of the flower design, while the high apron, always in full view, shows mainly stems and stalks. The reverse hanging of globes, as suggested for cones, is under these circumstances an effective method of showing them to their best advantage. The high and medium-high photographic views of globes in the illustrations demonstrate the superiority of these angles over the conventional profile views.

179

Small Dogwood   179

This lamp and base constitute an integrated unit [179] – integrated because the unusually small 12" leaded shade (the smallest shown in this book) fits the equally unusual 12" circumferential rim of the base, which in turn rests on four arms. The shade is 5½" high and has a 3½" aperture, which is not designed to fit an aperture ring; it is signed. In the Tiffany Album, a similar globe is numbered 1417, shown in figure [201].

An over-all pattern of pink-and-white dogwood blossoms covers the globe. These blooms exhibit the scalloped edges so typical of dogwood petals; extraordinary craftsmanship is evident in the way in which a darker tone of pink, almost red, is made to appear on their outer edges. Dark green leaves with yellow striations are seen between the flowers. The background, of ornate fractured glass, is milky-transparent and contains orange, red and green slivers. The shade has neither a bottom nor an aperture row.

The 7" round platform of the base stands on four ball-shaped feet. Its upper surface is decorated with six coiled wire designs, 2" in diameter; the end of each wire runs up the heavy stem and ends in another smaller coil at the bulging head of the stem. This is a miniature version of a design used on other bases, including Tiffany floor lamps which bear twelve of the same wire twists in a larger version. Three curved arms support a circumferential ring on which the shade rests. The height of the base, with shade, is 20½"; it is finished in gold.

Fourteen-Inch Tulip   180

Tulip globes were made in three sizes; the larger, 16" and 22", will be discussed later. This specimen of the smallest size is 14" wide, 6½" high, has an aperture of 3" and is signed [180].

The blossoms in this design are somewhat stylized, and, in most instances, only three of their six petals are shown. Some of the mottled orange glass employed is rippled on its outer surface; a number of the yellow blooms are constructed of glass which is stippled.

The stems are speckled light and dark green. Foliage is present in vast profusion; the leaves are dark green with light green and orange specks, or light green with dark green specks, and very life-like in appearance. The background is of light and dark purple glass, streaked with green and blue. The design, which contains six tulips, is repeated three times. Here again no boundary rows of glass are present, either at the lower border or at the aperture. The shade is signed and numbered 166.

The Small Yellow Tulip is shown on an important base, featuring the glass-in-bronze technique, using green blown glass. It is similar to one seen previously in figure [76], except that the bronze network is much more intricate; consequently, many more of the green glass protruberances appear.

The shape of the base is that of a narrow bottle with an extended neck. On the neck, the protruberances are oblong, in harmony with its slender length. At the rounded belly of the bottle, the glass pieces are rhomboid. The bottle-shape ends in four leaf-patterned "legs" which rest upon a low, 7" circular platform, decorated with a wavy design. The high finial carries a knob which operates the light switch.

The shade is illuminated by six candelabra-type sockets, see figure [25c], which are held by six bronze arms curving out of the upper part of the stem. The finish is dark bronze. It is signed and numbered 338.

The base is similar to the one shown in figure [135]; though that has only four arms and sockets, it includes four ornamental hooks between the arms, which are omitted in this specimen.

180

181

A rare shade, 14½" in size and made entirely of round, glossy pebbles set in flower forms, is identified as number 1459 in the Tiffany Album [181]. Known as the "Pebble Shade," it is supported by four curved arms extending outward from an ornamental metallic "cap" which covers the upper portion of the Favrile base (numbered 214). The feet of the base are round iridescent glass jewels.

MINIATURE DRAGONFLIES

The Miniature Dragonflies, smallest examples of this successful motif, are 14" in diameter, 5½" high and have 2" apertures. The six spread-winged insects, smaller than their counterparts in the 16" cones, cover the 44" circumference of their small shade without overlapping. A fine bronze filigree, applied over their wings, simulates the venous structure. The bodies are slightly askew and the wings droop a bit, which may indicate that the insects are at rest. In all other shades of this design, the dragonflies are stretched straight out, in flight position.

The glass segments of the background are arranged in three more or less horizontal rows, the upper and the middle row consisting of narrow oblong pieces, the lowest one containing rather long and wide pieces. They are leafshaped and rather large for so small a shade; actually, they are longer and wider than comparable pieces in the larger Dragonflies. Each of the six repeats of the design contains from five to six jewels, two large and three or four smaller ones, the highest jewel being occasionally replaced by flat glass. A rather undefined lower border row and a more definite aperture row complete the design. No jewels are used in the eyes of the dragonflies.

This shade is integrated with the Mushroom Base which has been discussed with the Spider and Web (page 71). The finial, representing the Spider's body, is actually more attuned to the latter shade; yet its twelve ribs conform harmoniously with the six repeats of the dragonfly design.

182

Green Dragonfly on Orange 182

The green wings, mottled with yellow, spring from lighter green bodies [182]; the eyes are the same shade as the thorax. The background glass is a glowing gold, with small roundish mottles of orange.

The horizontal row at the lower border consists of irregular segments of orange-gold. The more conventional aperture row is made of green-gold glass rectangles. The two large and five smaller round yellow-and-red jewels adorning each section blend with the orange mottles as if they were three-dimensional outgrowths.

The shade is finished in gold; it carries the large (4") signature tag and is numbered 1585.

The Mushroom Base is finished in gold doré and impressed with the Tiffany Studios signature and the number 337.

Blue Dragonfly on Gold 183

It bears three separate tags: one 2" long, inscribed *Tiffany Studios*; another 1¼", marked *New York* and a third, ¾", carrying the number 1585 [183].

The wings of these insects are blue, with green and yellow mottling; their bodies and their eyes are green. The background is made from a highly dichroic glass, which, in reflected light, looks green with gray mottles; in transmitted light, it is yellow with green mottles. The green mottles deepen in tonal intensity toward the top; toward the bottom, the shade grows increasingly yellow. The bottom row, accordingly, is almost pure yellow, with just a touch of green, while the aperture row is green with merely a hint of yellow. The six semi-spherical jewels are orange and yellow.

183

184

Dragonfly with Red Jewels 184

This Shade is identified with a 4" tag, marked *Tiffany Studios New York*, and a ¾" tag, bearing the number 1585.

The dragonflies have purplish-blue bodies, and varicolored wings in many shades of blue, purple, red, green and orange [184]. The dark green background, as well as the border and aperture rows, are strongly striated with light and dark orange; the background glass is of a fibrillated texture. Six ruby-red jewels add a fiery note to the somber color scheme.

The shade is supported by the Mosaic Dragonfly Base, which is similar in shape to the Mushroom Base. The 8" round platform is covered with tiny pieces of greenish-blue mosaic, spotted with orange. Three dragonflies in high relief rest upon the mosaic plat-form. A barklike pattern of fine-spun bronze wires rims the outer edge of the platform, and also rings the stem of the base. From this encircling design, the wires spiral up the stem; mosaic glitters be-tween the spiraling wire bands. One of the most successful Tiffany bases, it provides the perfect complement to the Dragonfly shade design.

Red Dragonfly 185

Here, both the bodies and eyes of the insects are ruby-red; their wings are red with a smattering of yellow and green [185]. The dragonfly bodies are executed in undulating glass. The background at the bottom of the shade is green knobby glass with orange stria-tions; in the upper area, it is blue-green, changing to blue-purple at the top. Reddish striations penetrate the green and the blue glass, unifying the rest of the globe with the red dragonflies. The aperture row is pale yellow with a tinge of green. The five jewels are orange, green and blue. Instead of the sixth jewel, above the blue one, there is a round piece of cream-colored glass. The stunning impact of this shade stems from the blazing purples and blues so boldly employed.

The shade is signed and numbered 356–1. Evidently, it was given the base number by mistake since the shade number for this category is 1585. In the Tiffany Album, an identical lamp has the number 1585 on the shade, 356 on the base. However, there can be no doubt that the dash number is not a mistake.

The bird's-eye view of the base affords a good look at the mosaic-paved platform, with one complete dragonfly, along with a good half of the wire-bark border. The base is impressed *Tiffany Studios New York 356*.

185

186

A larger and more elaborate spherical mosaic base, marked 147, is illustrated in the Tiffany Album [186], in conjunction with a 16" Dragonfly cone, numbered 1462. It appears to be as high as the shade, that is, 6¾". Several of the insects appear in low relief on its mosaic-covered circumference, together with some flowers and leaves.

Sixteen-Inch Bamboo   187

The bamboo also inspired shades in a number of different sizes, all of them globes. The smallest will be shown here, and the 22″ size later in this chapter. This globe is 16″ in diameter, 7″ in height and has an aperture of 3″ [187]. It is fully signed and bears the number 1448.

The underlying pattern is composed of the bamboo's cylindrical, sectioned stems; brownish in color, they seem to be growing alongside a horizontal wire trellis. The long tapering leaves are made of green fibrillated glass with yellow mottling. The glass used is slightly rounded rather than completely flat, since each leaf covers considerable distance and must conform to the curvature of the globe. This is one of very few lamps in which the Tiffany Studios used curved glass. The shade is also unusual in containing only two repeats.

The background glass is whitish, semi-opaque and mottled with more opaque spots of the same milky-white. On the lower portion of the shade, the segments appear to be almost geometric; they are not, however, since their sides are formed partly by the irregular, jointed stalks, partly by the leaves, and, at top and bottom, by the uneven run of the trellis wires.

Despite the lack of colorful flowers, or perhaps, because of it, the shade achieves a peculiar purity as well as an exotic quality.

The Bamboo globe is shown on its own integrated base and with its special finial, both fashioned in Art Nouveau style; the base consists of a sectioned main stem, supported by eight slimmer reedlike stalks each of which divides into five rootlets. These rise from a round 9¾″ platform. The finial is made of sixteen reeds radiating from the center to the periphery where each divides into two rootlets. The center knob depicts a multitude of seeds.

187

SIXTEEN-INCH DAFFODILS

In the chapter on flowered cones, we discussed, besides a 28" Daffodil shade, several of the 20" examples of the Narcissi, and explained that none of them may properly be called "Jonquils"; only the Jonquil-Daffodil, later to be shown in this chapter, is entitled to that name because it alone has the requisite short roundish flower cups, surrounded by six petals. Because of their giant flower cups, both of the 16" specimens that follow belong to the Daffodil branch of the Narcissus family; these distinctive cup formations have also earned them the title of Trumpet Narcissus.

188

Long-Stemmed Daffodil   188

This shade is 16" wide, 7" high and has a 3" aperture [188]; it is signed *Tiffany Studios New York*. The daffodils are supported by extremely long stems; two in each repeat reach almost to the aperture, and the third is set near the middle of the shade. There are three repeats.

The flowers are orange-yellow; the large size of their center cups is especially evident in the daffodil facing directly forward and the one at center right. The stems are light-green, striated with yellow, and the segmented leaves, some bent by their own weight, are a dark green. The background glass in the lower part of the shade is green with yellow mottles; in the upper portion, it has lightened to white. As in many of the smaller flowered globes, there are no bottom or aperture rows. This shade is shown in the Tiffany Album, identified as number 1449.

The simple base begins with a 7" circular platform, flat at its periphery and rising to a slightly elevated center. A six-sided stem with smoothly rounded edges ascends from this center to an over-all height of 23", narrowing as it approaches the top. The finish is patina on dark bronze.

Spreading Daffodil   189

Completely covered with blossoms, some thirty flowers may be counted on the comparatively small 16" shade [189]; it is signed and bears the number 1448. Although it also contains three repeats, in other respects the Spreading Daffodil is very unlike the Long-Stemmed Daffodil. Not only are the blossoms more numerous but, in this instance, they are distributed over practically the entire surface of the shade. The petals are yellow and the cups a beautifully mottled deep orange; the depth of each cup is indicated by a darker orange spot in its center. The large cups definitely establish these flowers as Trumpet Narcissus or true daffodils.

The comparatively thin stems are greenish-yellow, and the pointed leaves are an agreeable blue-green spotted with yellow. The background is dichroic; when the lamp is unlit, it appears to be orange with blue speckles, but turns yellow-purple, with the speckles barely visible, in transmitted light. Blue and purple highlights appear in some areas as if small vistas between flowers and leaves permitted a glimpse of adjoining plants.

The shade is ringed by three rows of rectilinear segments. One, of the dichroic background glass, encircles the aperture. The other two—one at the bottom border, the other 2" above it—are mottled blue and give the effect of an apron.

189

190

Small Apple Blossom

190

This signed 16" shade is 7" in height and has a 3" aperture [190]. White and pink five-petaled flowers, centered with bright yellow and accompanied by reddish buds, form the liveliest part of the pattern. The surrounding foliage is green, mottled with yellow, and at first glance may be difficult to distinguish from the background glass. The latter is several shades of blue, some bits of which are mottled with deeper blue, others with gray and orange. A row of long grass-green rectangles completes the lower border.

The urn-shaped base was made to contain oil, and still has its original receptacle. Evenly spaced around the surface of the urn, we find four heavy bronze stems in high relief, each carrying three green and yellow turtleback "leaves." The 7¼" circular platform, from which the stems emanate, has additional stemlike ornamentation on its upper surface. The shade is supported by three arms, curving out of the upper portion of the urn.

In reflected light, the green and yellow turtlebacks display a dazzling blue and purple iridescence. In transmitted light, their colors harmonize with the basic color of the shade. The old-fashioned urn shape and the uncommon turtleback inserts add up to one of the most inventive bases designed for small shades. The finish is bronze, with touches of patina. The illumination is an adaptation. The base is signed with a monogram of the letter S within a larger T.

Rambling Rose

191

This Rambling Rose shade is a quaintly appealing rarity. It is 16" wide, 7" high and has a 3" aperture; a ¾" signature tag is attached [191].

Several noteworthy features are embodied in this small shade. For one, the flower design covers its entire area, without repeats. The roses climb at random, massed in one place, entirely absent in another. Yellow, speckled with opaque gray or pink, they all have orange centers.

The small leaves of the golden rambler are rendered in a whitish, somewhat translucent fractured glass, which incorporates large splinters and flakes of green glass. The artist may have been inspired to this extraordinary portrayal by close observation of the natural leaves; in this climber, they are not only tiny, but tightly curled into even smaller dimensions.

The background glass is remarkable in that it is both mottled and rippled. Essentially sky-blue, it is modified with yellow and green; the rippled surface is on the outside, giving rise to remarkable scintillation.

Still another singularity is the employment of a second type of background glass. Fractured and milkily translucent, it has been infused with reddish-brown flakes and splinters. This glass is double-thick and so juts well above the surface. Since it is most in evidence along four vertical lines, it may signal the presence of unseen wooden pickets underneath the blanket of blooms. In the illustration, several segments of this glass, one below the other, can be seen directly below the aperture, in the exact center of the shade. A row of green-yellow mottled glass encircles the aperture, and another rings the bottom edge of the shade. The finish is bronze.

191

SIXTEEN~AND EIGHTEEN~INCH TULIPS

The 14" Tulip has been dealt with earlier in this chapter. Two 16" Tulips and one 18" will now be discussed. Although the 18" shade is slightly out of size sequence, it seems preferable to treat the three Tulips as a group.

192

Sunset Tulip   192

This shade is 16" wide, 7" high and has, for a 16" globe, an uncommonly wide 4" aperture; it is signed [192]. The design is the same as that of the 14" Yellow Tulip, see figure [180], the only difference being that all the glass pieces are slightly larger in this shade because of its greater size.

The blossoms are orange-yellow, pink and red, all generously self-mottled, with many of the petals made of rippled glass. The slender flower stems, constructed of granular glass, are light green and speckled. A darker green, sometimes tinged with yellow, is used for all the foliage.

Basically rose, the background segments are irregularly streaked with green and orange, which affords a certain degree of contrast while at the same time blending with both the blossoms and the leaves. There are no border or aperture rows.

The urn-shaped base, containing the original oil receptacle, is similar to the one described in conjunction with figure [126], except that the turtlebacks are yellow instead of green.

193

Tulip on Blue   193

A different design pertains to the sister shade which is also 16" in diameter and 7" high, but has a 3" aperture [193]; it carries a 3" tag, inscribed *Tiffany Studios N. Y. 1906*. The yellow-mottled pink and red blooms are realistically rendered, rather than stylized as in the Tulips so far seen. In many of the flowers, all six petals are visible. These tulips are so constructed that some of their petals actually overlap, as in nature; where this occurs, the blossom seems to spring out of the background. The petals are fabricated of knobby glass or are stippled.

The foliage is light and dark green mottled with yellow; the flower stems are also green, but more uniform. The background of blue mottled glass, fibrillated in texture, affords a splendid contrast with the red flowers. Both the bottom border row and aperture row are citron yellow. Two lead lines encircle the shade about one and two inches above the border row; they may represent the remains of an over-all geometric background. Possibly they are a substitute for the nonexistent reinforcement wires.

The base, shaped like a flower vase, is similar to, though plainer than, the one shown in figure [125]. Eight inches at its greatest width and 10" in height, it is embossed with thirty-two cactuslike leaves and carries a two-socket cluster. Eight tree stumps form its 7½" scalloped platform. The 19"-high base is finished in a mottled brown. Only the platform is cast bronze. The Tiffany Album lists its number as 189.

194

Tulip with Apron   194

As the last representative of this pattern, and somewhat prematurely in view of its more than 16" size, we now turn to a globe which has the largest apron we have so far observed [194]. At its widest, it is 18" in diameter, 9" in height and 4" across the aperture; the signature is *Tiffany Studios N. Y. 1596*. The 4" apron is essentially vertical, scarcely angling out at all. Each of the shade's three repeats contains thirteen tulips.

As in the Tulip on Blue Ground, all six petals of some flowers may be seen; here, too, they are ingeniously overlapped in such a way as to add the dimension of depth.

The flowers range from light orange, streaked with dark orange and reds, to dark reds, streaked with light red and orange; the red petals are constructed of stippled glass. The stems are grayish-green, and the leaves vary from dark green to blue-green. In the apron, the horizontally streaked earthy brown background, in which the stems and leaves originate, is suggestive of good garden soil. High on the shade, the background glass is the light pink-violet of a late afternoon sky.

Three geometric rows encircle the globe: one (green) at the lower edge; one (blue-gray) at the beginning of the apron; the last (blue-gray) at the aperture. We also see a number of lead lines circumscribing the shade above and below the apron row, and others below the aperture row; they are broken at irregular intervals by leaves or blossoms. Since the shade has no reinforcement wires, these solder lines may have been employed for additional strength.

THE PEACOCKS

The peacock was one of Tiffany's favorite motifs. The large Peacock Mosaic has already been shown among the geometric shades and here we present three of the Peacock globes, in two different dimensions.

195

Small Peacock   195

The shade is 16" in diameter, 7" in height and has an 3" aperture [195].

Massed peacock feathers create the pattern of the shade, which is more parabolic than spherical. Each of the eight design repeats contains two of the distinctive peacock "eyes," one above and slightly to the right of the other. The swirl of feathers is executed in green, yellow, orange, red and brown. The purple-centered eyes within this setting are thinly ringed with green, and then encircled by a broader band of translucent gold glass. There is no horizontal border row at the lower edge of this globe, and very little, if any, background glass. (Those green segments at the lower border probably represent the less flamboyant "eyeless" feathers.) The triangular greenish pieces at the aperture may be the remains of a geometric row or simply part of the feather pattern.

The carefully planned irregularity of its surface calls for extra-close scrutinizing of this shade. Some segments are elevated, either because they were cut from thicker glass or because they were soldered at a higher level than the pieces surrounding them. The peacock eyes are also elevated.

The surface is made more uneven by extremely heavy and intentionally raised lead lines, which start at the aperture and run down. These simulate the quills of the peacock feathers, from which subsidiary barbs branch off at an angle. The shade has been repaired.

The platform of the base is 9" in diameter, and almost 2" thick; four spatulate feet raise it above the taple top. It is decorated with a two-row formal flower design, from which wire stems rise in a precise coil pattern, halfway up the shaft of the base. Three curved arms support the shade. The base is 21¼" high and is finished in bronze. In addition to the signature, it is impressed with the number 365.

Blue Peacock with Apron   196

At the upper edge of the apron–its widest point–this globe is 18½" across. At the bottom of the slightly concave apron, it measures 18" in diameter. The shade is 8" high and has a 4" aperture [196]. On the large 4½" signature tag attached to the lower border, the inscription reads *Tiffany Studios New York* 1472–6.

The design, in its essentials, is not unlike that of the Small Peacock. However, its color scheme is infinitely more original and exciting, which undoubtedly accounts for its having been accorded the dash number. Although its color scheme is breathtaking, the Small Peacock portrays the typical feather tones more truly.

196

The twenty peacock eyes are again arranged in two staggered rows; their centers, purplish-blue in color, are surrounded by a narrow green rim, which in turn is set within a broader belt of gold.

On the upper part of the globe, the feathers are deep purple-blue with glorious striations of red. In the center, some of the feathers gradually shift to blue, then, around the upper row of eyes, to bluish-green mottled with orange. Around the lower row of eyes, the predominant color is pink with a tint of blue.

A thin horizontal row of golden-orange glass interrupts, but fails to contain, the feathers; cut off again by a second row of mottled green glass, they re-emerge within the apron. Here they meet blue, orange-red and orange-green feather tips, rising from the lower border row of mottled green; the latter is identical with the upper apron row. A row of dark purple rectangles rings the aperture. Throughout the globe, the purplish-blue glass is fibrillated, emitting a soft glimmer.

The quills are very heavy and project even more prominently than those in the Small Peacock. They are also less random in their course: each runs unwaveringly to one of the peacock eyes. Their barbs extend laterally, in systematic style, forming an intricate network over the entire globe.

This shade was also made in other colors and textures; one, fashioned entirely of rippled glass, is shown in the Tiffany Album and bears the same number, 1472. The author has seen a completely rose-colored shade of this design in an excellent state of preservation.

The Peacock with Apron is supported by the integrated Peacock Base, whose 12" scalloped platform is decorated with a raised design, consisting of six peacock feathers, each with a mosaic "eye" at its center. The six long quills run upward and, in so doing, enclose a green-marbled-with-yellow glass amphora, which makes up the main body of the base. Although it is made of six separate glass sections, it gives the vase a glass-in-bronze effect, the metal being represented by the six feathers. The illumination of the base is an adaptation. Its number in the Tiffany Album is 224.

At the top of the vase, the quills meet with a heavy bronze lid, completely covered with a stylized pattern of tiny plumage. From this, three curved arms rise to support the shade.

Crimson Peacock with Apron 197

The shade has the same dimensions, general shape and design as the preceding one except that it is a trifle higher [197]. This results from the existence of two aperture rows (instead of one), the first one being almost vertical, the second gradually leading into the globular structure; it looks like the inception of a chimney form.

There is a considerable difference in the color scheme of the two globes. Here the feathers above the upper row of peacock eyes are a purplish crimson with striations of blue, green and gold. The eyes themselves are blue-green, made of a finely stippled glass. They are set within a narrow rim of glass which is green on top and blue on the sides. Beyond this rim is a broader border of gold with orange mottles. Some of the crimson feathers extend into the area between the two rows of eyes, where they are met by others which have a green coloration and striations of orange and brown. Near the start of the apron, the crimson feathers, now of a softer hue and modified by orange and brown, spread out, enclosing the green plumage. Undulating and fibrillated glass enhances the brilliance of the feathers.

A rectilinear horizontal row, rendered in greenish-white and mottled with orange, starts the apron but permits some reddish-brown feathers to break through, and the same is true of another horizontal row of greenish-white rectangles. A similar third row forms the lower border. Between the two latter, there are irregular feather tufts in light green.

The base is of the same size and amphora shape as in the sister shade, but the six bulging sections are made of bronze instead of glass. They display a knobby texture simulating tiny feathers. The platform again has six bluish-green peacock eyes embedded in its surface.

EIGHTEEN-INCH PEONIES

The Peony, sometimes called "Glory of the Garden," inspired many Tiffany shades. At hand are two specimens of the intermediate size; the 22" globes will be met later.

Spring Peony   198

This shade is 18" wide, 7½" high and has a 4" aperture [198]; it carries three tags: *Tiffany Studios*, *New York* and *1475*. The shade is not altogether spherical, but drops off into an apron and also curves in its upper portion to form a smaller secondary rotundity.

The peonies are portrayed in self-striated reds and pinks, specked with green; their centers are a bright orange-green, fashioned of glass whose fibrillated surface makes it highly refractive. Several buds, in the same colors, may be seen at the beginning of the apron and at the aperture. The foliage, made of pebbled glass, is emerald-green, streaked with orange. Both blossoms and light green stems penetrate the two geometric apron rows. In each of the three repeats, the floral colors differ greatly.

At the top of the shade the background is almost white, with milky spots; nearer the bottom a faint glint of green appears. Four extremely light rippled rows ring the shade; one is at its lower edge, one at the midpoint of the apron, one at the beginning of the apron and one at the aperture. These imbue the Spring Peony with a feeling of airiness, further enhanced by even sprightlier hues on the unseen side of the shade.

198

Summer Peony   199

Quite a contrary impression is gained from its sister shade, which is of the same size and design, but of darker hue [199]. While its blossoms are also red and pink, with fine self-mottling, some appear beyond their prime; the splotchy mottles of yellow and brown and the corrugations of the rippled glass give them a wilted look. The flower centers are deep orange. Here, the leaves are also more mature and of a deeper green, with scattered yellow speckles. The fibrillated-glass background is a cyanotic blue, with glints of green and mauve softening the stringency. The four rectilinear rows are milky white, mottled with blue, green and orange.

The shade is signed with the same number, 1475. A similar shade with a somewhat shorter two-row apron has been shown in figure [138]; it is numbered 1533.

This glass-in-bronze base, a unique example of its type, consists of eight vertical glass bulges, each 8½" high and 2½" wide. Milky white, with a faint blue-green tinge, they were blown as a unit through bronze wire strands of two alternating designs.

199

At the top, these metal matrices lead to a wire-decorated neck from whose throat three curved arms emerge. The four legs of the base are 3" balls of glass, overlaid with wires in a coil pattern. The base measures 12" at its widest diameter, and, from table level to the tips of its three curved arms, is 16½" high. The over-all height of the lamp is 25". The base is damaged; its illumination is an adaptation.

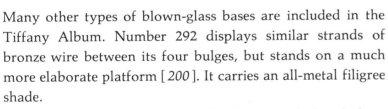

200

201

Many other types of blown-glass bases are included in the Tiffany Album. Number 292 displays similar strands of bronze wire between its four bulges, but stands on a much more elaborate platform [200]. It carries an all-metal filigree shade.

Base number 217 consists of eight vertical glass bulges, separated by thick undecorated wires, which rise from a platform of curved leaves [201]; three arms carry a 12" Dogwood shade which is similar to the one shown in figure [179].

Another blown-glass base from the Album, numbered 219, has ten vertical bulges with the same type of plain wire dividers [202]; it stands on a platform of flat curly-edged leaves and carries the Geranium shade previously shown in figure [135].

202

NINETEEN- AND TWENTY-INCH NASTURTIUMS

A 28" Nasturtium hanging shade has already been described in the chapter on cones. Two intermediate sizes will be shown here; another Nasturtium shade, 22" in diameter, will shortly be discussed and the last one, an 18" specimen, will appear among the Irregular Lower Borders.

Nineteen-Inch Nasturtium 203

The widest circumference of this shade is 19", but the measurement at its lower rim is only 18". A mere 7" in height, the shade is unusually shallow for its width; its aperture is 4" [203]. Two signature tags are attached, one, 1½" long, marked *Tiffany Studios*, the other, 1" long, *New York*.

The five-petaled blossoms proliferate in the lower part of the shade, and many color modifications may be observed. Originally yellow, the nasturtium has been horticulturally developed in a host of varied hues, a number of which are portrayed here. In this one shade, we find flowers in very minutely self-mottled orange, pink, scarlet red and yellow, as well as some, not caught by the camera, in orange-green rippled glass. The pattern is a single entity, without repeats.

A large quantity of foliage covers the upper portion of the shade; as in nature, the overdevelopment of leaves has here suppressed the growth of flowers. The green leaves are strongly striated, mainly with orange, but now and again with reddish and bluish tints; some are heavily mottled with yellow or gray. The large mottled leaves are made of knobby glass. Indeed, the knobs coincide so closely with the mottles that color and texture actually complement each other.

In shaping the nasturtium leaves, the artisan abandoned nature. Though their size is proportionally correct, their

203

outline lacks the lobed indentations of the living plant. Apparently a pond lily leaf has once again been substituted.

With so many leaves to cope with, the craftsman attempted to create a three-dimensional quality by lifting the edges of adjoining glass pieces. Though difficult to capture on film, the success of his effort is best seen in the upper left third and in the lower right center of the globe. There is no background glass that may definitely be distinguished from the leaves. A geometric row of mottled yellow-green finishes off the lower border; no aperture row is present.

Due to the magnificence of its coloring, this shade is very showy without being in the least blatant.

Twenty-Inch Nasturtium 204

Though referred to for convenience as being 20" wide, the shade is actually 20½" across at its widest point and has a 4" aperture [204]. Only 7½" in height, this signed globe is even shallower in proportion to its width than the preceding one.

204

The design is similar to that of the 18" Nasturtium, except that the foliage is more profuse; in some places an uninterrupted cascade of leaves runs from the aperture all the way to the lower border. Two such formations are visible in the illustration, one in the center of the globe, the other close to the left border. There are two more on the hidden side of the shade. The overlapping of the green-orange leaves is not as well portrayed as in the 18" Nasturtium.

As in other shades of this design, the pattern is unrepeated. The blossoms between the extensive leaf formations are executed in lighter tones of yellow, pink and orange. A few pink flowers, streaked with white, are made of rippled glass and can be clearly seen on the right of the illustration; all the rest, with the exception of the red blooms, are of such a strongly undulating texture that they seem to throw off sparks. An inward-curving row of orange-green rippled glass encircles the shade at its bottom border.

ՈⱭRCISSI

Jonquil-Daffodil 205

Because the combination of two flowers in one design is infrequently encountered in Tiffany shades, this globe is especially arresting [205]. The shade is 20" in diameter, 8" high and has a 5" aperture. It is signed *Tiffany Studios, New York 1917.*

The lower border is composed of two rows of yellow-mottled green glass rectangles; the uncommonly wide bottom band abuts on another only half its width. Above the latter we find a 3" swath consisting of forty-eight jonquils arranged in three rows of sixteen each. Their blossoms are wide open and face almost directly forward. In each row there are four repeats and every one of the four flowers in a repeat are of a different shape. Altogether there are twelve dissimilar flower shapes comprising the design.

The largest flowers are in the center row and all six of their milk-white petals may be seen; they are fabricated from a transparent glass which has some opaque spots. The orange, spotted with yellow, flower centers are only slightly raised, proving these to be true jonquils. The sixteen lowermost jonquils have only five petals, which contain yellow and pink tints; their downward-pointing petals penetrate the upper of the horizontal bands. At the top of the swath, the jonquils appear somewhat irregular. Quite a few green stalks are visible and some green foliage, mottled with yellow.

On the upper 6" of the shade's surface–divided from the jonquils by another narrow geometric row–the primary design consists of Trumpet Narcissi, or true daffodils, arranged in two staggered rows. Their elongated cups (the trumpets) most clearly differentiate them from the jonquils below. This motif is also repeated four times, with each segment consisting of four daffodils, two above and two below, whose shapes are again different from each other. The giant trumpets of the daffodils in the lower row penetrate the rectilinear band and encroach on the jonquil zone.

The narcissi are yellow, mottled with dark orange. The straight-edged narrow leaves, pointed at the end, cover almost the entire background and are executed in green and blue-green textured glass, with fine-grained stipples on the inner surface. The stalks supporting the upper row of narcissi originate in the jonquil swath and serve as demarcation lines between the four repeats. Instead of the more usual quadrangles, the aperture row consists mainly of downward-pointing triangular pieces of orange glass, spotted with green. A few slivers of similarly colored glass make up the tiny amount of visible background.

The numerous repeats of two related but dissimilar designs, plus the division of the globe into two distinct

205

girdles, gives this shade a very stylized look, reminiscent in a way of the repetitive formality of the geometrics.

The base is a variation of the Lily Stem design, also called the Twisted Vine Base, as shown in figure [159]. Five of the many vines which twine upward around the stem veer outward from it toward the top, each at a different angle, to support the 20" circumferential rim on which the shade rests. The base is 18½" high to the rim, 28½" in total height and is finished in patina. It is impressed with *Tiffany Studios New York 5230.* A fine example of the naturalistic application of Art Nouveau, it ranks among their choicest bases.

Daffodil on Blue   206

Another rare Narcissus shade is represented by this globe which measures 21" at its widest circumference, at the start of the 2" apron, then tapers inward, reducing the width at the lower border to 20" [206]. The height is 9" and the aperture 5".

The flowers appear in two alternating groups: in one they are standing upright, with the blossoms unfolding in the top portion of the shade; in the other the stalks are bending down and the blossoms are close to the apron. This results in a well-spread coverage of the shade with flowers and also permits the daffodil stems and leaves to be displayed in full view in some areas. There are four repeats of the design. The flowers display an extra-large center cup, which is typical of the trumpet narcissus or daffodil. They are made of yellow and orange glass, attractively mottled with darker tones of the same colors. Each trumpet exhibits a carefully placed two-tone mottle. The glass is of a fibrillated texture and exudes a diffuse glow.

The stems are yellow-green, dotted with tiny grayish pinpoints. The leaves range from soft olive greens to brilliant verdant tones and are rendered in configurated glass.

The highly sophisticated background is purplish in the lower parts of the shade, with an area-mottling of blue and orange, and also with spot mottles of the same color. It provides a dramatic contrast to the yellow daffodils which is pleasantly softened by the effect of the variegated mottles. Toward the upper portions of the shade, the bluish tones in the background glass begin to dominate until light blue becomes the basic color, with the mottles appearing in purple and yellow-orange. This coloration is most evident in the geometric row adjoining the aperture row, consisting of sixteen large squarish pieces of glass, invaded by only four flower petals.

The aperture row itself, made up of twenty-four small glass segments, is grayish-blue, speckled with light gray. Four other horizontal rows, made of the same glass, traverse the globe: one immediately below the large squarish pieces; one two inches above the apron row; the apron row itself; and the lower border row. The two rows closest to the center of the shade are frequently interrupted by plant material. Despite these five circumferential rows, no perception of a geometric design pervades the shade.

The Daffodil is signed and numbered 1212; it is finished in gold.

206

Multiple Dragonflies 207

This extraordinary hanging shade, probably a special-order item, is 21" in diameter, 8¾" deep and has no aperture, its opening being filled by a turtleback [207]. It is signed and numbered 433.

Two types of Dragonflies have been discussed among the cones, and another among the globes; the largest of this design will be described in the chapter dealing with shades having irregular lower borders. However, the concept of the Multiple Dragonflies is entirely different from any of these others. As a change, it is refreshing to find them flying freely through the sky instead of hovering timidly in a restricted area at the edge of the shade.

Scores of gauze-winged dragonflies flit over this globe against an upper background of blue and a very much larger lower zone of golden yellow. The two colors of the background are separated by a horizontal leadline, and the division is further emphasized by the insertion of numerous blue jewels directly above this leaded "skyline."

Three of the four rows of these gossamer insects contain sixteen dragonflies each; the only exception is the lower-most row, which is made up of only twelve. As is readily apparent, the insects diminish in size as the globe curves inward. There are three repeats of the design.

The dragonfly wings are interpreted in shades of blue and green, with orange mottling; their bodies are a darker blue mixed with purple and, sparsely, with red spots; some eyes are green, some orange and all are of flat glass.

In addition to the aforementioned line of jewels, other jewels in three different sizes, but of the same semi-spherical shape and light blue color, are scattered about the surface of the shade. A row of jewels encircles what would normally be the aperture, but the expected opening is filled with a bluish-green turtleback. At the upper border of this hanging globe, a horizontal row of green-blue rippled glass adjoins a heavy bronze ring: holes in this ring permit the attachment of suspension chains.

In differentiation from the four other types of Dragonflies made by the Studios, all of which are supported by table or floor bases, this shade definitely represents a ceiling fixture due to the absence of an aperature.

207

Double Poinsettia   208

208

The smaller Poinsettia shades have flowered belts in combination with geometric rows and have been described in the chapter dealing with the transition to flowers.

The Double Poinsettia has five horizontal and eight vertical geometric rows, which portray a trellis [208]. Although the rest of the shade is almost completely covered with organic growth, these rows, in combination with eight repeats of the design, give this globe a highly stylized appearance. The effect is heightened by the formal and repetitive stalk-and-leaf pattern above the flowered sections.

Although these geometric vestiges are present, the placement of the Double Poinsettia in this chapter is justified by the amount of existing plant material and the extensive penetration of the geometric rows by vegetation.

This poinsettia shade is 22" wide, 8" high and has a 5" aperture; it carries the long 4" tag inscribed *Tiffany Studios New York 1551.*

The flowers grow on an octagonal trellis, with each of the eight sections embracing one stem, three blossoms and twenty-two leaves: two blossoms are side by side, with a larger bloom centered above them. The petals are white striated with pink, pink striated with red and red striated with crimson. The flower centers are greenish-yellow, and the foliage is green mottled with yellow and darker green.

Again we encounter the technique of overlapping; the edges of the inner, uppermost rows of petals are raised above the level of the lower outer rows. Several flower centers are also raised, and some leaves are made to lay atop the trellis slats. The latter are rendered in a spotted bluish-gray undulating glass with orange highlights.

The background is a softly glowing blue, spotted with red; the latter is so cunningly applied that it appears to be the result of reflection. A great deal more background glass is visible in the upper, foliated portion of the shade than in the lower flower-filled area.

Inside the shade, reinforcement wires run along four of the vertical trellis rows, from the aperture strip to the bottom rim. Along their route, they are exceptionally well soldered, not only to the trellis rows but to each adjacent leaded joint.

The Organic Root Base, one of Tiffany's most successful Art Nouveau designs, stands on four legs, with a diagonal spread of 15" between opposing legs. The root fibers which form the legs end in elaborately convoluted feet and extend upward to establish a platform some 2" above the tabletop and hence continue on their upward climb. Like their counterparts in nature, which are designed to carry nourishment from earth to tree, these climbing fibers symbolize the path of life itself.

The total height of the base is 27½", and the patina finish matches that of the shade. The signature reads *Tiffany Studios New York 442.*

Twenty-Two-Inch Bamboo   209

The small Bamboo lamp has been shown in figure [186]. This intermediate size is 10" high and has a 5" aperture. Tiffany Studios also produced a 26" size in this exotic reed suitable for the large floor base.

As compared with the 16" sister shade, the 22" Bamboo is not only larger but has an entirely different design [209]. Actually, there is not a great deal of increase in the size of the leaves themselves, but there are almost twice as many leaf clusters; these form three more or less distinct rows: lower, middle and upper. Some clusters also contain a greater number of leaves, the majority five, but a few as many as six. There are four repeats, compared with two in the smaller shade. Forty-four reeds instead of thirty bear the leaves, but their thickness has not been increased.

The color of the foliage varies from light to dark green, with striations and mottles of yellow, orange and brown. The latter predominates in some leaves to such an extent that it appears as their principal tone. Some fibrillated glass is again in evidence, as in the sister shade, but most interesting is the otherwise rare hammered glass. It has already been mentioned that some of the large bamboo leaves, extending over a large spherical section of the globe, are made from curved glass.

The highly translucent background glass with the faintest light gray striations has an interesting external and internal structure. Besides being fibrillated, it contains a myriad of the tiniest bubbles which gives a new dimension to the appearance of this unusual shade.

The globe is shown on one of the best Tiffany Studios bases, reputedly the most expensive one: the Leaf and Arc. In highly imaginative Art Nouveau style, it appears to symbolize the growth of a tree by introducing the three elements upon which its life depends: The roots which carry food from the soil are seen in the forked, interconnected arcs. The leaves which effect the plant's metabolism are shown growing out of the arcs. The air with its sunrays, moisture and chemicals is indicated by the recesses surrounding the leaves.

There are ten horizontal rows of leaves and arcs, each containing twelve units.

The over-all height of the base is 32½". Its platform, 11" in diameter, is composed of twelve huge leaves hanging downward and is supported by twelve legs. It carries a six-light cluster operated by a double-action switch. The base is finished in dark copper, signed and numbered 542.

209

210

Apple Blossom with Bronze Apron   210

This shade is set within a bronze fixture consisting of a collar, or apron, and eight ribs [210]. The open-work apron is made up of forty-eight overlapping circles, garlandlike in design; however, a close inspection will show that only alternate circles touch the lower edge of the shade itself. The eight arched ribs, which meet at the top center of the shade, are attached to the apron; their lower ends, flanged and leaflike, extend an inch below its beaded bottom border. The ribs are numbered from 1 to 8 on the underside of the flanges.

The shade is 22" in diameter and 8½" in height; one of the few intact hemispheres produced by the Tiffany Studios, it is unbroken by an aperture. To compensate for its absence, a 5" strip has been soldered to the inside of the shade, near its top, so that it can rest on any base with a 5" aperture ring. The Apple Blossom with Bronze Apron is finished in dark bronze and fully signed.

The metal ribs divide the shade into eight sections, and there are four repeats of each of the two designs, so that adjoining sections vary and alternating sections match. In the illustration, the left and right sections are identically patterned while the center section is quite different.

The blossoms throughout are pink, streaked with white and orange. The flower centers are a spotted yellow-orange. The oval-shaped leaves, typical of this tree, are executed in mottled tones of light and dark green, with a mere smattering of orange. The branches are beautifully portrayed in dark brown, modulated with lighter tones of the same color. Due, perhaps, to the comparative paucity of blossoms and foliage, the branches are particularly well depicted. The background in the lower part of the shade is a transparent golden hue, marked by darker orange patches; toward the top, it fades to a creamy white with yellow markings.

Like a few other shades that have been shown, this one is so unique that it may be considered a special-order item; no other of its type is known.

TWENTY-TWO-INCH TULIPS

This most popular of all bulb-grown flowers motivated the creation of many magnificent shades; though varied in size and shape, all belong to the globe category. While the poppy, the rose, the daffodil, the dogwood and the grapevine—to say nothing of the dragonflies— appear in both cones and globes, the tulip is strictly a globe flower, at least as far as regular production shades are concerned.

The 14", 16" and 18" shades have already been examined; now we arrive at the largest tulips. Characterized by a 4" apron, these are 22" in diameter, 9" high and have 5" apertures. Obviously, the shades are not truly spherical because of the decreased curvature at their aprons. Less apparent in the illustrations but of more interest, we find that each of these "globes" has a secondary curvature in the area of the aperture; this convexity swells 2" above the basic shape of the shade.

Yellow Tulip with Apron 211

The 4" apron of the shade has a lower border row of blue-on-blue mottled glass. Directly above it, the brown and green striated area is indicative of the flower bed in which the bulbs are planted [211]. Blue-green stalks and broad pointed leaves grow through the apron and into the main portion of the shade; only a few, however, pierce through the upper blue-mottled boundary row of the apron on the outside.

The globular area of the shade is almost completely covered with tulips in yellow speckled with white, yellow spattered with orange and orange flecked with reddish-brown. Where it is not mottled, the glass is highly transparent, with a delicately stippled or fibrillated underside; this combination of a basic glass type and a carefully selected texture successfully conveys the satiny sheen of the tulip petals.

Considerable overlapping may be seen, with the topmost tulip petals raised above the surface of the others. In some instances, all six petals are visible; more often, because of the angle or stage of bloom, only two or three are in evidence. The converging of the flowers toward the center, accompanied by a proportional diminution in size, is carefully portrayed.

In the body of the shade, the stalks are a light bluish-green, and the leaves several tones of mottled green. The cerulean blue and very transparent background glass (which looks almost whitish in the illustration) furnishes precisely the right contrast to the tulips. Around the aperture we find a row of blue-green mottled rectangles. There are three repeats in the design.

Inside, four reinforcement wires run from the aperture rim to the apron, where another reinforcement encircles the interior of the shade. From this, other wire connections are made to the lower rim. The reinforcement wires carefully follow the outlines of flowers and leaves, and are soldered to all the leaded seams they cross. A horizontal lead line also appears on the outside of the shade, about an inch below the upper rectilinear apron row; in addition, there exist other fragmentary lead lines, possibly reinforcements. The shade is signed.

211

Red Tulip with Apron   212

The photograph was taken from above in order to show the flower arrangement to its best advantage [212]. This illustration explains, better than words, the cautionary notes already sounded on the subject of lamp placement. Set too high, we limit ourselves to a profile view of the shade, which, in this instance, would be adequate only for the apron but would fail to reveal the top section of the shade where the excellence of the design lies. The photograph for the preceding color plate [211] was also taken from above, but at a lesser angle. A straight profile view would be most disappointing. The best view is obtained when the eye can see the most important area of the shade straight on, at a 90° angle, the same way as one looks at a painting.

The striking color scheme derives from the varying growth stages observed as the eye travels from the periphery toward the center, from the outside of the tulip bed (apron) toward the inside (aperture). Along this path, the blossoms range from light and dark pink with red mottling to crimson and deep red heavily infused with purple. Overlapping petals are again present.

The stems are light green, and the foliage, concentrated around the area of the apron, is dark green, mottled with blue, white and, less often, orange; this foliage glass has a pebbled texture. The background is a highly transparent green, streaked with orange. The three horizontal rows of geometric segments are of rippled green.

The shade is signed on a 4″ tag and carries the number 1548.

212

TWENTY-TWO-INCH PEONIES

Three Peonies have already been shown: the first combined a border design with geometric rows; two others were met with earlier in this chapter.

The large Peony globes are 22" in diameter at their bottom border, but their greatest width (23") occurs about 2" up from that edge, at the start of the apron. It is there that the apron turns inward. The shades in this group are 9" high and have 5" apertures. There are three repeats of the design, each repeat encompassing seven blossoms and four buds.

At best, these shades can only be called modified globes. First, there is the almost cylindrical apron; after an initial curvature extending about 6" above the apron (measured along the glass), the surface flattens out for about 5", forming almost a conical profile for this section of the shade; 2" from the aperture, the globular shape again reasserts itself. This conglomerate globe-cone-globe contour makes it imperative that the Peony be viewed from above; this in turn requires that the lamp be placed on a low table rather than a floor base. At too great a height, the rounded lower portion of the shade will show up well but the upper blossoms will be hardly visible and badly distorted.

Pink Peony   213

213

Many large flowers are distributed throughout the entire area of the shade, from aperture to apron [213]. Most of the blooms and buds are pink, streaked with white, including all those on the side of the shade not seen in the photograph; only a few are red, mottled with orange and deep garnet red. The stems are a mottled green, and the foliage is bluish-green with splotches of gray. Some of the peony bracts, those specialized protective leaves around the flower buds, are very deftly depicted in a light but lustrous blue-green.

The background glass is exceptionally beautiful: of a pebbled texture and highly transparent, it is a lambent gold, streaked with yellow and green, and spotted with orange.

The narrow apron is bounded by two horizontal rows of gray-mottled blue glass; contained between them, we see stem and leaf segments and some background glass. A similar row encircles the aperture.

The shade is signed and carries the number 1509.

214

White Peony   214

Despite the sameness of design, this globe differs dramatically from the preceding one in coloration [214]. In this specimen, the blossoms and buds are white tinted with green, and the flower centers span the entire yellow-orange range. Foliage and stems are a mixture of light and dark green, speckled with orange. The background is especially felicitous in tender tones of purple, spotted and striated with blue, and sparsely employed streaks of orange; tending to be on the dark side at the bottom of the shade, the background lightens as it nears the aperture. The border row, the apron rows and the aperture row are all constructed of the same rippled green glass, interspersed with an occasional orange segment.

The shade is signed.

Peony on Gold   215

This shade is signed and bears the number 1509. Blossoms and buds are dark pink and light red, streaked with grayish-white; their centers are yellow-green [215]. Stems and leaves range from pale bluish-green to deep pea-green, with yellow mottling.

The background glass is a golden yellow, with orange mottling and a sprinkling of green striations or dots. The three rectilinear rows are light green with orange mottles. When the shade is lit, the effect is that of sparkling sunshine. This is due, to a large part, to the use of undulating glass for the red petals, and stippled glass for the background.

The heavy, round platform of the base is 11" in diameter and stands on six small feet that turn upward where they touch the table. Twelve leaves, each attached to its own stem, are impressed around and over the outer edge of the platform; the design is similar to that found on the fluted floor base. The twelve stems converge toward the center and continue up the stand, lending it a channeled look. The base is impressed with the studio signature and the number 307.

Capable of extending from 28" to 35" in height, this is one of the tallest of the Tiffany table bases. Its finish is brass, probably not original, but resulting from the removal of another finish by improper cleansing methods.

215

216

Peony on Blue 216

This photograph, taken from high above the shade, affords the most inclusive view of the entire pattern [216]. The simplest way to discern the three repeats of the design is to start with the large blossoms at the top of the shade, two of whose petals are amputated by the aperture; from these reference points, the eye can readily find the rest of the pattern components, and the place where each appears again.

In this globe, the blossoms are red, streaked with grayish-white, and orange, extensively mottled with red; a solitary mauve-pink flower occupies a prominent place in the foreground. All the peony petals are fabricated of unevenly textured fibrillated glass, which transmits light in such a way as to make the flowers gleam and glisten.

The peony centers are yellow or orange, both spotted with red. Stems and leaves are dark green, with gray and blue tints. The protective bracts are best seen around the bud which impinges on the aperture at right center. The three horizontal rows are made of green and orange rippled glass.

The most impressive element of the shade is the exciting background, made of cerulean and midnight-blue self-mottled glass, streaked with purple. In sharp contrast with the sunny countenance of the previous peony, this shade looks somber and forbidding. It is signed with a ¾" Tiffany Studios tag.

Trumpet Vine   217

One of our highest-climbing (30') creepers, the standard trumpet vine would, in view of its size, seem an unlikely candidate for a lamp design; it has, however, been made to work amazingly well within the space limitations of this shade. The less lofty but larger-flowered Chinese variety, known as the giant trumpet, will be found in the chapter dealing with irregular upper and lower borders.

This globe is 9" high and has a 5" aperture; 22" wide at its lower edge, it measures 23" at its widest circumference, about 2½" above the bottom border [217]. A small ¾" tag bears the Tiffany Studios signature.

Like the Large Tulips, this Trumpet Vine is not truly spherical. The incurving lower border is one obvious deviation. There is also a secondary, more extreme, curvature imposed upon the upper third of the shade, resulting in a pronounced swelling. This additional rotundity rises from the main globe about 4" below the aperture and looks like part of a smaller globe fused onto the larger one. To the best of our knowledge, the precise shape of this shade has never been duplicated. More bulbous in its secondary bow than the Large Tulips, it lacks the intermediate flat, conic zone of the Peonies. The two curvatures flow smoothly into each other.

217

The swelling contours of this globe afford a better view of the floral pattern on its upper portion; without this curvature, the design could only be fully appreciated from above.

A crownlike embellishment, consisting of eight bronze flanges each about 1½" wide and high, is attached to the aperture strip of this globe. Six reinforcement wires run from this strip about halfway down the shade, following the route of existing lead lines.

The flowers (called bugles because of their trumpet shape) are partially fabricated of strongly textured undulating glass. They show the tender green of newly born buds, the orange, red and purple of mature blooms. The mottling of colors is superbly handled, especially of red into orange and orange into red; the exquisite craftsmanship can best be observed in the orange bugles, slightly to the left of center, where the placement of reddish mottles in the center of each flower petal was accomplished with meticulous care; within these red mottles there are secondary orange specks. Similar markings and the same degree of skill are evident in other flowers and leaves. In addition to this spot-mottling, a fine pinpoint dotting of gray adds immeasurably to the natural appearance of many of the petals. Some petals are elevated from the surface because they are constructed of double-thick glass; others, fabricated from glass of conventional thickness, are actually raised at their edges.

The heavy stems of the vine are light green; they support both the masses of bugles which make up most of the lower part of the shade and the profusion of leaves which fill its upper portion. The foliage is a medley of many shades of green, generously mottled with blue and orange. Some of the leaves are also made of extra-thick glass.

The background is fashioned from a richly hued blue glass, extensively striated with purple, which serves as an equally effective counterpoint color for both the green foliage and the orange flowers. The globe contains four pattern repeats.

The border and aperture rows are composed of brown and green glass which is both mottled and rippled. By running lengthwise, the ripples somewhat reduce the harshness of the geometric edge.

The circular, flat platform of the base is 10½" in diameter and is ringed with thirty-three bluish-purple iridescent balls. Four legs on leaf pads rise from it at a slight inward slant and converge in a thick knob to form the head of the stem. This knob is encircled by eight of the same iridescent balls, and another is centered within the finial.

The base is 28½" high and is finished in the same dark bronze as the shade. It is impressed with the Tiffany Studios signature and the number 10922. Because of its rarity and the fascination of the iridescent balls, the base is valued highly.

Twenty-Three-Inch Nasturtium   218

A hanging cone of this design has been seen among the cones and two smaller Nasturtium globes are pictured earlier in this chapter.

The large globe [218] under discussion is the same spherical shape as the latter two, but is modified by an incurved apron and a secondary, more pronounced curvature in its uppermost area. The shade is 9″ in height and has a 5″ aperture; 22″ at its lower edge, it distends to 23″ slightly above the border, at the start of the apron. It is signed with a 3½″ tag reading *Tiffany Studios New York 1506–2*.

Blossoms–some with as many as six petals–are strewn over the entire surface of the shade; their colors include yellow mottled with orange, orange mottled with red, red streaked with orange, and pink streaked with white. This rainbow riot is made even more brilliant by the use of rippled glass for the pink and red blossoms and undulating glass for the orange. All textured surfaces face inward.

The heavy stems are brownish-green at the bottom of the globe and become a lighter yellowish-green as they ascend. The foliage is made from undulating glass; in this instance, the textured surface faces out. Some of the green leaves are mottled with darker green and orange, others are streaked with white and yellow. Botanically their shape is incorrect, since they lack the characteristic angularity and indentations of the nasturtium leaf, but look instead like the leaves of the water lily.

The background glass is a translucent pink, mottled with green and orange, and has a finely filamented surface; unusually pronounced in this instance, these hairlike ridges are created during the manufacturing process and form an integral part of the glass, not a subsequent application.

The apron and border rows consist of green rectangles mottled with reddish brown; the earthy quality of the color may indicate closeness to the soil. The design pierces the apron row in several places and continues below it. There is no aperture row.

The 10″ platform of the base slopes upward into a heavy stem. Sixteen strips of mosaic inlay, green at the bottom and gradually becoming red, begin on the platform and run partway up the stem. From its comparatively narrow middle portion, the stem widens into a large bulbous top, which is almost as great in diameter as the platform. Eight green turtlebacks are set into its sides, and sixteen small replicas are modeled on the upper surface of the bronze bulge. From just below the sculptured turtlebacks, four curved arms stretch outward to receive the 22″ rim of the shade.

The lamp is 34″ high. The base, which rises 28″ to the bulb cluster and 22″ to the bottom edge of the shade, is regarded as one of the finest of Tiffany Studios creations in the area of pure craftsmanship; rarely have metal, glass and mosaic techniques been combined with such superlative success. In the Tiffany Album it carries the number 355.

218

219

Rose Bush

Though probably the best-known and best-loved of all flowers, the rose was rather neglected by the Studios; while prototypes were occasionally constructed, apparently the pattern was never produced on a regular basis. The cone-shaped Yellow Rose, the rare Rambling Rose shown earlier in this chapter, together with this equally rare Rose Bush, are our only examples of this flower.

The photograph of this hanging globe was taken from below in order to provide a more comprehensive and detailed view [219]. Its diameter is 24", its height 8", its aperture 5"; it is signed and numbered 1915. The shape is exceptional in that the shade gently recurves outward at its border. It is similar in this respect to the Chimney Dome of figure [90] and the Roman Design shade of figure [91], but here the reverse curvature is more pronounced.

The roses are yellow, spotted with orange, green and gray, and orange spotted with red; some mauve tints may also be seen. A few of the petals are made from undulating glass, which adds to their effulgence. In the larger flowers, we find the three-dimensional overlapping of petals, previously described in connection with Tulips, Poppies and Peonies.

The leaves, of fibrillated glass, are emerald green, streaked with dark green and yellow, and forest green, spotted with gray, yellow and dark green. The flower stems are a dark gray-green; those bearing buds are a lighter gray-green.

The background glass is light blue, with mottles of darker blue and violet. Against the green leaves and the blue background, the brilliant orange roses stand out in stark relief. The horizontal rows at the border and aperture are light green, mottled with darker green and blue.

Gourd 220

Although this plant would appear to provide unusual design opportunities, owing to the curious contours of its fruit, clearly the Gourd was not a Tiffany Studios staple; the shade shown was probably a special-order item [*220*]. Artistic license is again invoked in order that blossoms may be depicted simultaneously with fruits, and fruits of several differing plants portrayed within a single pattern.

The shade is 24″ in diameter, 11″ high and has a 5″ aperture. It is signed with the 4″ tag and is numbered 1522. Extremely high in proportion to its width, it is elliptical rather than spherical, curving evenly and ever so gradually from aperture to border. This results in both an aesthetically attractive shape and a form ideal for observation from the side; because the whole design is in full view, one need not set it low in order to enjoy it completely, as is the case with many globes and even more cones.

Since the Gourd is a trailing or climbing plant, it is appropriately shown on a trellis. Three horizontal struts are visible, one at the lower border, one about 4″ above that and one at the aperture; the fourth strut, which should logically appear 4″ below the aperture, is either missing or covered up. Nine vertical struts complete the lattice. All the supports are made from orange glass, streaked and mottled with green; at several points thick black tendrils have attached themselves to the trellis.

The design is repeated three times. Among other motifs, each repeat contains three small white flowers made of milky opaque glass, spotted with translucent areas and having faint yellow mottles at their centers. The leaves are various shades of green, mottled as well as striated with yellow, orange and blue. Some are cut from rippled glass with the textured surface facing out (see leaf penetrating lower border at shade center). Others are constructed of granular or knobby glass, with the texture facing inward (green leaf on left, at crossing of last vertical strut with second horizontal).

Four gourds—two broad and squat, two long and slender—appear in each repeat. Their glass is an agreeable mixture of yellow, white and orange, irregularly speckled in excellent imitation of the natural fruit. The undulations of this glass further emphasize the roughness of the rind, already indicated by the extensive mottling. The background, a dazzling blue judiciously streaked with green and purple, sets off the gourds to great advantage.

Three reinforcement wires run from the aperture ring about three quarters down the shade.

This Gourd was previously seen on the Spanish Base, for which it was designed, see figure [*34*]. Although this floor base has no extension, the height of the shade is adjustable up or down the stem by means of a special sliding ring. The stand is topped with a special Art Nouveau finial whose knob represents plant leaves and fruits. The finish is bronze.

220

221

222

Fruit Shade   221, 222

The dimensions of the Fruit Shade are: diameter 24",
height 9¼", aperture 5"; it is signed with three tags: *Tiffany
Studios, New York* and *1519*. There is no repeat of the design.
Two factors make this shade outstanding: one is the fruit
pattern, since fruit is infrequently portrayed in Tiffany
shades; the other is the seasonal transition depicted along the
circumference of the globe.

Many of the more advanced Tiffany shades show a
single plant in different stages of development. To illustrate:
if there are three repeats in the design, the first may depict
budding blossoms and leaves; the second, mature flowers
and foliage; the third, overblown, drooping or dying vegetation. In some instances, as has elsewhere been advanced, this
represents an impressionistic interpretation of nature; in
others, natural botanical conditions. In no case, however,
have these stages been displayed in such striking fashion as
in the Fruit Shade.

In the early-spring segment of this globe, illustrated in
figure [221], the fruits and leaves are observably immature.
The almost colorless grapes are constructed of fractured
glass, merely sprinkled with green and orange. The apples
are green pebbled glass, which is both mottled and striated;
the oranges are spotted yellow-green. The pallid leaves are
speckled light on darker green, with glints of gray and
mauve; a few leaves are executed in translucent green rippled
glass, textured surface toward the viewer (note large double
leaf just left to center, near lower border). The background
of light gray with a touch of purple conveys a sense of misty
April air.

A gradual color transition guides the eye to the other
side of the shade, shown in figure [222], where the growing
season is obviously at its height. The grapes are luscious reds
and purples, ripe and ready to eat; the apples, magnificently
rendered in mottled glass, are red, with a bit of reddish-
yellow and green; the oranges are, of course, orange, spotted
with touches of green and yellow. The leaves are a darker,
almost dense, green and yellow; brown spots indicate that
some of them will soon be shed. The blue background,
dappled with purple, depicts a heavy-hanging late summer
sky. While the colors of the glass have changed, the textures
employed in the various plant elements have remained the
same.

Both the lower border and the aperture are encircled by
a blue-green row of rippled glass. A thinner row of elongated
yellow-brown speckled rectangles abuts on each blue-green
row. These rows are also influenced by the transitional color
change, being light on the side of spring, deep and colorful
in the summer.

More than a mere source of light, this shade is the em-
bodiment of nature's annual miracle of seasons, depicting
the rebirth of life in the most dramatic period of the year.

The base is one of the Tiffany Studios' early ceramic vases, finished on the outside in copper. Long-stemmed flowers and foliage, delicately modeled in low relief, are arrayed around the lower and middle areas of the vase. Longer stems carry tight buds all the way to the upper rim.

The platform is 6" in diameter; immediately above it, the base bulges to its maximum width of 10". The vase is 17" high and is finished in copper; the lamp's total height is 29½". The signature is etched in script and reads *L. C. Tiffany, Favrile Pottery*. The number is not legible.

223

Twenty-Six Inch Poinsettia   223

Several of the smaller Poinsettias have been covered under transition to flowers and the Double Poinsettia was examined earlier in this chapter. While these Poinsettia shades were produced in quantity, the globe under discussion is quite rare. It is, however, shown in the Tiffany Album, where it is designated number 1528. The execution is also rather special, since the flowers and leaves tend to be stylized rather than realistic.

The shade [223] is 26" wide, 11" high and 6" across the aperture. It is signed with three tags: *Tiffany Studios, New York* and *1528*. Four reinforcements run from the aperture ring to the lower border.

There are three repeats of the design. Flowers cover most of the shade surface, and the leaves are mainly to be seen in the lower section. As explained in describing earlier Poinsettias, the small blue and green formations which seem to be flower centers are actually the flowers themselves; the large petal-like red bracts surrounding them are really modified leaves.

The colors of the latter include pinkish red, streaked with white; deep orange, streaked with red; and deep red, streaked with purple. This wondrously hued striated glass has a knobby texture which imparts a mysterious glow. The

formalized leaves are made from speckled glass in yellow-green, and in bluish-green, both with orange spots; the very straight stems are rendered in green-brown plain glass.

In the lower part of the globe the background is a glossy warm gold, speckled with orange and highly transparent. When illuminated, the sun actually appears to be shining through. In addition to large orange specks, the glass is full of semi-opaque pinhead dots. Toward the upper part of the shade the background lightens, and the large orange speckles are completely replaced by the minute dots. On their inner surfaces, these extraordinary segments of glass have an undulating texture that lends a strong refractive quality to the light, similar to, yet more diffused than rippled glass.

While there are no horizontal geometric rows in this shade, either at the lower border or at the aperture, echoes of them remain; at both these locations we find a horizontal leaded line running around the entire periphery. These lines are interrupted by plant formations, but their existence is never in doubt. Near the lower border, two more leaded lines appear at intervals of about an inch above the first, but these are discontinuous. With less impairment of the natural flow of a flower design, these leaded lines probably serve the same structural function as rigid geometric rows.

ORIENTAL POPPIES

Two categories of small Poppies (16″ and 20″) have already been met among the cones. The Oriental Poppy, which we deal with now, is not only the largest specimen of this design, but, with the exception of the Magnolia, is also the largest of all the globes; a perennial, the oriental poppy grows three feet tall. In the execution of these expansive shades, more, however, was involved than mere size. Few would dispute their designation as masterpieces – among Tiffany's finest.

The shades are 26″ in diameter, 13″ in height and have 6″ apertures; the latter indicates that they were designed for use with the large floor base. The upper halves of these globes are spherically curved, but for some 6½″, measured from the bottom up, their profiles are almost flat. The pattern is repeated three times.

Because of their large size, the Poppies are heavily reinforced with four to six vertical wires; these run from aperture to lower border. Although this shade design is identified by the number 1597, one of them, the Red Oriental Poppy, is inexplicably numbered 1902.

Oriental Poppy on Gold   224

This is the only one of the three to be shown here which has a strictly defined apron; a boundary row of bluish-green rectangles, striated with orange, separates it from the main body of the shade [224]. Two inches below, another row of the same glass encircles the apron; a third, slightly wider, forms its bottom border.

The greater part of the apron is composed of stems and leaves, though parts of poppies also appear in it. The stems are orange-green. The winglike leaves are made of fractured glass whose basis is a pale green inset with flakes of darker green and orange. In the lower portions of the apron, the brown umber background glass suggests soil.

Above the apron, the shade is crammed with blossoms delineated in every stage of development and seen from every conceivable angle. From closed buds to fully open flowers, they are depicted head-on, hanging down, facing up and in back view.

In color, the poppies range from pink with white and yellow striations, through crimson red, to red with purplish mottles and striations. The majority of petals are made from softly gleaming undulating glass; most often the textured surface is turned inward, but in some segments it faces out. The purplish-red blossoms are made of the rare configurated glass.

The oddly eyelike flower centers consist of a dark purple "iris," surrounded by a narrow band of orange, striated with green.

The most arresting aspect of the shade is its fractured glass background. The basic glass above the apron is orange, brightening to glittering gold at the aperture; flakes of henna and a sprinkling of green enrich the essential color. The very rough textured surface is turned inward. This background glass has a remarkable dichroic quality; in reflected light, it becomes dark blue with brown spots. The masterfully executed shade is signed and numbered 1597.

224

Yellow Oriental Poppy 225

Although of exactly the same shape as the preceding globe, there are no apron rows in this shade and its flower design is altogether different; it actually has fewer flowers but they are somewhat larger and cover the shade more completely [225]. It is signed and bears the number 1597.

The shade is composed almost entirely of blossoms; some are pure yellow, but most have orange mottling, especially on the outer edges of their petals. The flower centers are purple with green accents. Many of the poppies face outward, affording a full view; others are turned away, displaying the undersides of their petals, as well as their well-developed protective bracts (see bottom flower, center right). A few flowers face the sun.

Many of the petals are made of coarsely stippled glass. A number of new buds, showing a bit of their blazing red interiors, are most clearly visible in the upper portion of the shade, although they are scattered throughout. The well-defined stems are greenish-tan. The yellow-green leaves have been fabricated of a granular glass which counterfeits the hairy foliage to perfection. In several areas, a three-dimensional effect is obtained by overlapping flower petals.

A light and transparent fractured glass, containing multitudes of blue and red and green flakes and splinters, makes up the background; between the poppies one

225

seems to catch a glimpse of grass or sky or blossoms in adjoining beds.

A geometric row completes the lower border; while there is no real row at the aperture, we find in its place a large number of fairly regular fractured glass segments. The shade exudes an extremely pleasant aura.

Red Oriental Poppy 226

Although the design is the same, the color scheme is greatly at variance with that of the Yellow Oriental Poppy, being so much darker as to seem almost funereal [226]. The blossoms are blood-red, mottled with darker red and gray, and the glass used is textured on the inside; some segments are stippled, others bear shallow ripples. The flower centers are purple with blue tints. The yellow-green and blue-green of the foliage is dappled with lighter and darker tones. The orange background glass is both spotted and striated in greens, blues and purples. A yellow-green horizontal row encircles the lower border.

The shade is signed and numbered 1902. It also has been shown on a base in figure [37].

226

MAGNOLIA

This famous shade is the largest of the globes and is further distinguished by the fact that it is the only design in which drapery glass was used in substantial quantities. Aside from an occasional leaf in other shades, this heavy texture was restricted to Tiffany windows, since no other flower has petals large and fleshy enough to justify the employment of this particularly thick glass. While the leaves and petals of the younger plants are still rendered in the less heavy rippled and knobby glass, drapery glass forms the midribs of petals and leaves in the more mature specimens. Even if we were to disregard the huge size of the Magnolia and the inclusion of this rare glass, the shade would be outstanding because of the excellence of its floral pattern. It is of dramatic simplicity, composed almost exclusively of blossoms, branches and background.

These globes are 28" wide, 14" high and have 6" apertures. Each has a horizontal row around its lower edge, but none at its aperture. There are three repeats of the design. Six vertical reinforcement wires run from the aperture ring to the bottom border. This shade is equally at home on a large floor base or suspended from the ceiling.

Magnolia on Mauve 227

This appears to be the least mature of the specimens shown, therefore less need was felt for drapery glass in the construction of this shade [227]. The desired effects were achieved by the use of other less theatrical but equally interesting glass types. One which was liberally employed is covered with scores of pea-sized knobs on its inside surface. Though its heavy texture can best be seen in the large open blossom at the left center of the shade, the majority of the whitish petals are fabricated from the same sort of knobby glass which has also been used for the orange-yellow flower centers. The knobs are inside the shade, but they show through and convey a strong impression of the magnolia's fleshiness.

The wrinkled-looking yellowish flower petals just right of center illustrate another way in which a sculptural quality can be suggested. Here, fibrillated glass, aided by striations, imparts a vivid impression of raised ripples that, in fact, do not exist.

In other areas, use is made of striations in a peculiar manner so that they appear extremely heavy at the center of the petal, gradually petering out toward its edges; the illusion of thickness thus attained is evident in the three long lavender flower petals (right of the wrinkled petals) in which the dark purple streaks in the center appear to be folds in the leaves. The background is bluish-gray interspersed with golden hues.

Dimensional effects were also achieved by lapping one petal over another. In some portions of the shade, petals overlap limbs and twigs, and, in so doing, protrude as high as ½" above the surface of the shade.

The shade is signed and carries the number 1509.

228

Magnolia on Blue-Purple   228

Here drapery glass is used in the fleshier petals; its high ridges can be seen on the upper right outline of the shade. Rippled glass is used for some of the smaller petals [228].

The color of the blossoms varies from white mottled with green, to mauve with purple striations, to yellow-brown with orange striations. Some of the flower centers are of rippled orange glass, others of lighter yellow color and of plain glass. The carefully grained branches are brown extending into green, and the leaf buds are green. The lower border row is rendered in rippled yellow-green.

In the upper portion of the globe, the background glass is light mauve, striated with blue. Farther down, it acquires darker purplish tones, striated with blue and spotted with gray; on the left side of the shade, as seen in the illustration (and on a portion of the unseen side), the background is predominantly blue, with pink and white striations.

The shade has the signature *Tiffany Studios N. Y.* (note the rare abbreviation) and the number 1509.

Magnolia on Red-Purple Ground   229

This shade best exemplifies the employment of deeply contoured drapery glass [229]. The blossoms are basically light green, with darker green and brown mottling, and a few whitish areas which are more transparent. As the flowers reach full bloom, they become brownish-white in color and are executed in thicker drapery glass (see large brownish petal at shade center). Some of the folds measure as much as ½" from peak to hollow. The flower centers are yellow with orange specks and are constructed from glass which is undulating or has low knobs.

229

The superlative floral interpretation is matched by the beauty of the background. From a light mauve, streaked with pink, around the younger blossoms and buds (most in evidence in the upper regions and at bottom left), the color deepens to a darker reddish-purple, streaked with gray, around the more mature flowers, and to blue-purple streaked with orange (in the back, unseen area of shade). All this is undulating glass, some segments of which have a finely filamented surface; it exudes a fascinating lighting effect in transmitted illumination.

The branches are masterfully delineated in dark, striated brown with touches of green. Since the leaves remain folded until the flowers have faded away, we only see them in bud form; brown with hints of yellow, they barely display the first tiny tips of green. The rippled horizontal row, which bands the bottom of the globe, is green with small amounts of yellow.

The shade is signed and carries the number 1509. It is also shown on the large floor base in figure [35].

8. IRREGULAR LOWER BORDERS

FOLLOWING our method of classifying the lamps of Tiffany in order of their importance, we now approach those shades in which the straight-edged round rims at the lower border have been replaced by the more realistic irregular contours observed in nature.

Though helpful as a physical reinforcement, the rigid lower border rows lend an alien and artificial air to the naturalistic patterns of the flower shades. When every care has been taken to portray blossoms, stems and leaves as living growth, complete with all their curves and convolutions, the straight, hard edges strike a spurious note.

In the shades to be shown in this chapter, the lower metal rim and the horizontal border row of glass have been discarded. Instead of this arbitrary "ruled" edge banding the bottom, we find an irregular border evolved from the leaves, flowers or fruits of the shade itself. Though this is a giant step toward freedom from mechanical confinement, the aperture row and the aperture itself still remain, along with the finial required to cover up the artificial opening.

The horizontal reinforcement wire assumes here an added significance since it must replace the function of the metal rim which binds the edge of shades with smooth lower borders, see figure [284]. It is connected by means of vertical reinforcements with both the aperture and the irregular border.

With the exception of the Trellises, all irregular lower borders are found only on globular shades.

Cupola Nasturtium 230

This colorful climbing herb has contributed examples to the hanging cones, the flowered globes and, in a novel shape, now penetrates the illustrous category of irregular lower borders. Among the flower designs, it shares this distinction of diversification only with the Dogwood and the Grapevine. The shade is 18" wide, 7" high, has a 3" aperture and is signed [230]. (An identical shade is known to bear the number 1463.)

The form of this rare shade is original and charming. Upon a gently curved globular shape, a secondary, more rounded cupola has been superimposed. Altogether, three curvatures can be distinguished: a convex one in the lower portion including the irregular border; a concave one at the transition from primary globe to cupola; and the final convexity at the cupola itself, which ends with an almost vertical aperture row.

The design, repeated three times, centers around a trellis which consists of three vertical and five horizontal slats. One of the latter is at the aperture; another is just above the irregular border and actually forms part of it at three small areas, about 2" wide. These interruptions of the border irregularity may have been intended as resting places for the support arms of a base.

Above, below and around the trellis struts flow buds, flowers, stems and foliage. The blossoms appear in yellow speckled with brown, brown with pink, pink with red and red with yellow. They are distinguished by exquisite textures whose surface faces the viewer: most of the petals are made from the rare and brilliant configurated glass, others are rippled or coarsely stippled. They impart the Nasturtium with an entrancing, dream-like effulgence.

The leaves (which again resemble the rounded lilypad leaves instead of the lobated nasturtium leaves) are in various tones of light and dark green with occasional additions of yellow and blue. The glass is also of choice quality, beset with cloudy area mottles and additional pinhead mottles which cause a constant change in their transparence. The carefully executed stems are of a pale yellow-green.

The background in the lower part of the shade is portrayed in a golden hue with light blue striations, changing toward the aperture to light blue with golden striations.

Blossoms as well as buds, leaves, stems and background participate in the irregular border; the indentations extend up to 1¼" beneath the lowest trellis strut, which prevents any upward extensions and thereby limits the extent of the all-over irregularities, already considerable for the small size of the shade.

The base can best be compared to a flower pot which measures 6½" at its widest diameter and is 6" high. Its upper and outer surface are decorated in low relief with replicas of plant materials, as if flowers and foliage spilled over the rim. The pot appears to stand on but is actually fastened to a round-ish tray whose outer edge has an upturned, molded lip. The upper surface of the tray, which is 7½" wide, is finely grooved and rilled. The pot carries five straight support arms, 8½" high at their ends. A three-light cluster is attached to an oil font which slips into the flower pot. The base is signed.

230

The Bat   231

This signed shade measures 17″ between opposing corners and 15½″ between the centers of opposite sides; its height is 6″, its aperture 2″ [231].

The lamp bears a certain kinship to the panel shades in that its lower half is composed of almost-flat sections. However, unlike the legitimate main line of the panel family, this

231

offspring has six, instead of eight, sides. Still, it is not this minor "birth" defect that bars the Bat from its geometric progenitors. It is, rather, an uncommon lower edge which allows this shade entry into the far more illustrious lamp family of irregular bottom borders.

Convex at the six rounded corners of the shade, the border is concave along the six "panel" sides in the up-and-down dimensions. The three down-hanging bat heads, which protrude beyond the lower rim, create an additional feature of border irregularity. More than ordinarily heavy, this metal rim is also distinguished by having been pre-cast instead of shaped. A cloud design is incised on its outer surface.

There are three repeats of the design which centers around this curious animal, the only mammal able to fly, and the only one depicted in a Tiffany shade. The bats' blood-colored glass bodies are outlined in heavy bronze and their solid bronze heads are exceptionally well sculptured; from the incongruously large ears to the carefully simulated hair, each detail received attention.

Spread wide between the long-stretched fingers of the front legs and the toes of the hind feet (both portrayed by lead lines), the bat's membranous wings reach from the lower border all the way to the aperture; between their upper tips we see the sky. In width, the wingspread of each creature covers an entire side and in addition one-half of each adjoining panel; only a small triangular section of the three alternating panels remains filled with geometric background rows. There is neither a border nor an aperture row.

Though all the wing glass is roughly stippled, the color differs in each repeat. The greenish-orange wings seen in the illustration are extensively and marvelously mottled in red.

One bat has purple wings; in another, the wings are grayish-green; both sets are mottled with deeper tones of their essential color.

From the textural continuity, it would appear that each wing was fabricated from a single piece of glass, cut into the required sections. These sections were then leaded together to conform to the horizontal and vertical curvatures of the shade; at the same time, the leading delineated the internal structure of the outspread wing.

The background glass has a strongly fibrillated texture, accentuated by random deep rills. In the triangles between the extended wings, it is a deep rich blue; at the apex of one such area, we see a pale evening star. Above the bats, the background is the misty green-blue of the sky; again we find a star in only one of the three repeats. This, however, is far brighter, presaging, perhaps, the dawn of a new day from which the nocturnal animals flee toward the safety of their dark abode.

Figure [232] shows a Bat shade from the Tiffany Album on a miniature mosaic base whose platform features three bronze bats in low relief; the number of the lamp is 353.

232

Butterflies 233

This strangely shaped shade is 20" in diameter, 9¼" high and has a 4" aperture [233]. From its widest circumference the shade curves sharply inward for as much as 5" in some places, so that it actually has a substantial underside. Its jagged inner border is formed by sixteen projections, the largest extending inward the aforesaid 5" from the outermost surface of the shade, and the shortest about 3". The open space thus left at the bottom of the shade measures from 10" to 14" across. On the lower right and left of the color plate, the shardlike ends of these projections are clearly visible.

The pattern of the shade, which is repeated three times, consists of a swarm of butterflies swirling through the air. Their widespread wings are orange and several shades of brown, mottled with red and green. Some are executed in an extraordinary glass that contains, in addition to the random streaks commonly seen, striations which form intricate patterns (see butterfly, center bottom); other wings are made of fractured glass, with tiny red and brown splinters introduced into basic orange or green.

The sky is constructed of a lovely light blue glass, delicately tinted with soft pinks, oranges and greens, and so heavily fibrillated that the texture is visible in transmitted

233

light (see center of illustration). The blue darkens toward the aperture and, in places, assumes a purple tone.

Despite the seeming fragility of the shade, there are no reinforcement wires; however, the few diagonal lead-lines, which we can see quite distinctly, probably serve the same purpose.

For a variety of reasons, this very unusual shade elicits the strongest admiration of many viewers.

The Tiffany Album shows the Butterfly shade on a mosaic base, whose design depicts leaves and flowers [234]; evidently it served as the oil font for the lamp. A metal ring near the top of the vase rests upon three ornamental legs. The shade in turn is supported by a series of curved metal rods which descend over the top of the font and rest on the metal ring; their upper ends are incorporated into the shade proper, along the diagonal lead-lines. The base is numbered 148.

An equally unusual lamp—number 146 in the Tiffany

Album—is distinguished by a spider-web shade [235]. Its irregular lower border appears to be as much a part of the bronze-and-mosaic base as of the shade itself. The pattern of the base portrays flower stalks and blossoms. The author has seen one of these lamps.

Another all-web shade—Tiffany Album number 151— tops a tall urn-shaped base, inset with mosaic and bearing a raised design of bronze wheat spears [236]. As in nature, the webs are appropriately placed atop leaves and flowers.

234

235

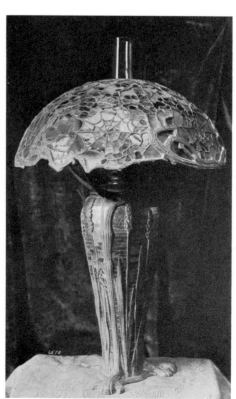

236

THE HANGING-HEAD DRAGONFLIES

This mournful title has no melancholic meaning; it merely indicates the physical position of the insects. Without a rim to hold them in, the heads and outspread wings project beyond their prior bounds to form the lower border. In all the other Dragonflies discussed, both cones and globes, the insects are inside of border rows and rigid rims.

These shades are 22" in diameter, 10½" high and have 5" apertures. There are nine repeats of the design, with one dragonfly, wings extended, in each. Although their wing-spread is the same as that of the insects in the 16" and 20" cones and they number nine instead of seven, the nine cover the circumference of 69" with a minimum of overlapping; there is far less, in fact, than occurs in the smaller cones. Where it does take place, the overlapping wing is raised well above the surface of the shade in order to create the desired three-dimensional effect. A fine network of bronze filigree covers the wings.

Of the three aperture rows always present, the middle one is usually the same color as the shade; the others either blend or offer a decided contrast. From four to six reinforcement wires run from the aperture rim halfway down the shade. The horizontal reinforcement wire, a standard for most shades with irregular lower borders, is not in evidence, its function evidently being assumed by the horizontal continuity of the dragonfly wings.

As the name of the shade indicates, the heads of the dragonflies hang below the rim; their large eyes, more prominent than ever because of this position, are made from half-round jewels. Their bodies, which extend upward to about the middle of the shade, mark the beginning and the end of each repeat. In addition to the four wings, each of the nine segments contains thirty-eight pieces of background glass; four of them are between the wings, the rest is arranged in four to five irregular horizontal rows between wings and aperture. These are irregular in size, some almost 4", others less than ¼", long. Dissimilar in shape as well, they are narrowly oblong in the upper portion of the shade and somewhat shorter and wider below. Among the background pieces, we find fourteen jewels of varying size in each repeat.

The texture of the glass accounts for much of the enthusiasm inspired by the Dragonflies. The soft sheen of their wings is largely due to the undulating glass so widely used in their construction. The luminosity of the sky in the upper third of the shade emanates from the fibrillated and stippled glass employed therein.

The dramatic impact of the Dragonfly is felt by virtually all viewers, yet it would be almost impossible to pick out a single element responsible for stirring such emotion. The design itself, the structural complexity, the careful execution, the intensity of color—all combine to make this shade the equal of the most exquisite flower lamps. The artistic genius of its creator, Mrs. Clara Driscoll, was recognized when the Dragonfly received a major award at the 1900 Paris Exhibition.

The effectiveness of these globes is undoubtedly enhanced by their having the largest area of background glass of any Tiffany shade, and also the greatest number of jewels. Since the background determines the "mood" of the shade, the changes in this area, made possible by the unlimited availability of polychromatic glass, resulted in unparalleled achievements.

We can think of no other Tiffany shade in which the water and sky are of such surpassing importance. Although the Studios entitled it "Dragonfly and Water Design," the fact that the insects inhabit the air makes the unmentioned sky almost as salient as the water. Because air and water impose far fewer restrictions than flora or fauna, the scope of this shade is limited only by the skill and imagination of the individual artist.

The author was once left alone in a remote house with a Dragonfly lamp. As time went on, it definitely induced a feeling of fear. The characteristics of the shade which instilled this sensation could not be dissected and definitely identified, but the effect it created was undeniable; thereafter, he referred to it as the "fear lamp." Later, in an attempt to evaluate the effect of the lamp on others, he exposed several acquaintances to its aura without any preliminary comment, and their reactions were almost identical. This experiment was subsequently repeated with another, essentially red, lamp, and the violence emanating from it was also felt by others; this may be ascribed to the psychological effect of color, enhanced by the mysterious Dragonfly design. Other Dragonflies have been described as depicting nightfall in the Florida Everglades, sunset on the Allegheny Trail, dawn in a flower garden, and so on, depending on the owner and his own orientation.

Green Dragonfly on Mauve   237

Purple is seen throughout the entire top portion of the shade. The only other color note is provided by the upper and lower aperture rows in rippled green [237]. Below them, oblong background pieces begin their transition from purple-blue to blue, and on to blue streaked with mauve and orange, pink and yellow. Proceeding downward to the wider pieces of background glass, the blue slides into pink-orange, striated with blue and purple. The four pieces between the wings are brown-orange, streaked with blue, purple and green. All the orange glass is stippled and finely fibrillated. The color scheme is so breathtakingly brilliant that no printing process is capable of reproducing its true quality; the missing ingredient is transmitted light.

The jewels are green and blue-green, except for a few of the round ones, which are orange-pink; on the inside surface of the shade, an extra layer of blue glass is set atop the five largest jewels of each repeat, presumably to improve the blending of colors. The bodies of the insects are of green-rippled glass; the eyes are blue jewels and the wings are blue with green and white splotches. Like almost all dragonfly wings, these are made of undulating glass. The shade is signed and numbered 1507–29, the high dash-number testifying to the many excellent Dragonflies already produced.

The base with its thirty-three iridescent balls is similar to the one described in figure [217], except that it can be extended from 28½″ to 34½″ by means of a sleeved stem; the adjustment screw can barely be seen on the very top of the stem, just below the wing, on the right side toward the back. Aside from the extension rod, both bases have the same features. Here, however, the bluish iridescence of the balls is even more arresting because of its complete compatibility with the blue tones of the shade. The base is impressed *Tiffany Studios New York 10922.* It is finished in light patina.

237

238

Dragonfly on Yellow-Brown
238, 239

The superbly mottled background glass of this shade possesses the quality of dichroism to a remarkable degree. In reflected light, the glass is dull green, and many brownish pea-sized dots may be seen in it. The three aperture rows are blue and the jewels red [238]. In transmitted light, the glass is a lively brown, and the formerly dark dots are bright yellow [239]. These spots are more numerous in the upper part of the shade where yellow mottling also appears over large areas of the glass, giving the shade an almost yellow cast. The aperture rows have turned into greenish-yellow. Because it contains fewer and smaller yellow dots and almost no area-mottling, the lower part of the shade looks dark brown. The jewels now appear bright yellow.

The wings of the insects are yellow-brown, with some blue and green; each body is composed of a single color, either green, blue, red or purple; red, blue and green jewels are inset for the eyes.

239

Dragonfly on Yellow-Blue 240

There are two rippled-green aperture rows with a blue row between; the blue is carried over into the upper third of the shade [240]. This magnificent marine-blue glass is enriched with streaks of lighter blue, pink and mauve, which vary in transparency; some of the oblate strips are glowingly alight while others are virtually opaque. Occasional yellow-orange striations in the blue glass become more pronounced at their lower end and eventually carry this color down to the wings, establishing a chromatic connection with the lower part of the shade. In that area, the slightly wider segments

240

are yellow with brown striations; the peculiar refractive quality of the glass is due to rough stippling, to extensive fibrillations and to masses of minute air bubbles trapped within it.

The wings of the dragonflies are a darker orange, mottled with yellow, and their filigree network, in comparison with others, is thin and open, allowing an exceptionally good view of the glass. The topmost row of large jewels is entirely green, and both green and yellow-brown jewels stud the midsection of the shade; the color is picked up again in the light green bodies of the insects. Their eyes are orange jewels. Two reinforcement wires reach the upper wings, two the heads.

The shade bears a 1½" tag, inscribed *Tiffany Studios*; a 1" tag, *New York* and a ¾" tag, *1507–32*.

241

Yellow-Winged Dragonfly   241

Here, the areas of radiance are diametrically opposed to those of the last-mentioned shade: the lightest portion is at the top, the darkest toward the bottom [241]. Rippled green aperture rings enclose a middle row rendered in yellow; that yellow, striated with green, continues into the first row of more or less oblong pieces. The second row of oblongs is green, striated with yellow. Below that, the rows return to yellow, streaked with brown; continuing downward, the striations become so dense that the last row above the wings appears to be almost solid brown. The heavily fibrillated texture of the oblate background glass lends this shade exceptional luster. The filaments are clearly visible in the illustration.

Most of the jewels, including the largest, are yellow, orange and brown, but a few green ones afford a mild contrast. This green, intensified in tone, appears again in the bodies of all the dragonflies, but the wings revert to yellow, with extensive but faint area-mottling of green. The eyes are yellow jewels. By means of this masterful juxtaposition of color, the top and bottom of the shade are tonally integrated.

To a previous owner, the background of this shade simulates a swamp, like the Everglades: with the yellow-brown above the insects representing the spongy mire; the odd, triangular striations, green and yellow reeds emerging from it; the glistening jewels, reflections from a patch of water in this natural habitat of the dragonfly.

The signature includes the coveted dash number and is also differentiated by the fact that the number-tag precedes the other two. The sequence is as follows: *1507-6, Tiffany Studios, New York.*

The shade rests on the renowned Root Base, which is essentially a simple construction and true to the Art Nouveau style. Six curved rootlets rise out of the earth and, by twos, converge into three larger roots which, retaining their separate identities, run upward, around the main stem of the base. An extension rod within the main stem can raise the lamp from 28" to 34", measured to the top of the finial. Other root bases have been shown in figures [41], [42] and [43].

Orange Dragonfly 242

The upper portion of the shade is a spectacular flaming orange—the color of a sunset over water—with the water itself in all probability represented by the green glass below [242].

A deeply saturated yet remarkably transparent orange glass makes up the center aperture row, which is bordered by two rows in green, and is also used for the topmost row of tapered oblongs. The glass is striated with yellow, which becomes increasingly more evident in the second row of elongated segments. In the lower, wider rows, we see the first striations of emerald green on yellow; descending, the glass becomes an almost solid green, with only intermittent streaks of yellow. The emerald green is bounded by the insects' wings, which pick up and reflect the sunset orange of the area around the aperture.

The largest jewels are bright yellow; the others are yellow, brown and white, with the white supplying sprightly highlights. The bodies are darkest orange, intermixed with green, and the jeweled eyes are blue.

This shade has been repaired. It carries the Tiffany Studios signature and the number 1507 on one 3" tag, and is fitted with three unequally spaced reinforcement wires.

242

Tri-Color Dragonfly 243

The sky of the Tri-Color Dragonfly [243] is, in spirit, entirely at variance with that of the preceding shade. A bright and inviting blue, it arches over a large expanse of light yellow, reminiscent of ripe wheat fields. The rare and highly prized blue glass is fairly solid in tone in the middle aperture row (the other two are rendered in green rippled glass), and in the topmost row of oblong pieces. Casting our eyes downward, we come upon the first few yellow and green striations. Little by little, the streaks of yellow spread until, in the lower rows, they have wholly taken over; here the glass is yellow, just gently brushed with blue and green.

Each set of wings is executed in a single color, and three colors alternate; blue, mottled with green, is followed by purple mottled with blue; this, in turn, abuts on red mottled with yellow. The bodies are light and dark blue, and the eyes, like the wings, alternate—red, then orange, followed by blue. The largest of the jewels are purple; the smaller, lower ones are blue, yellow, green and almost white.

This shade was repaired. Four reinforcement wires are present. On the signature tag, the number *1507* precedes *Tiffany Studios, New York.*

243

Dragonfly on Deep Blue   244

The upper and lower aperture rows of this Dragon-fly are a diluted blue; the band between them is orange, shaded with blue, which color continues and intensifies in the two rows of irregular oblongs [244]. Here, the fibrillated glass is an orange of medium saturation and more than ordinary brilliance, extensively mottled with much mauve-blue and a smattering of gray. The mottling is of two kinds: area-coverage, which extends the blue over a fourth to a third of the glass segment involved; the other is spot-mottling with scattered dots ranging from a pinpoint to pea-size. In addition to the blue mottles, some orange spots and a sprinkling of green are also present in these remarkable pieces.

In the next row, blue becomes the basic color, and orange serves as the mottling agent. Finally, farther down, the glass deepens into dark blue, with mere traces of gray mottling. This color even intrudes upon the intrinsic orange of the insects' wings. The texture of these dark blue segments is both undulating and knobby. Blue jewel eyes accentuate the orange and blue bodies. All the jewels are blue, but somewhat lighter in tone than the livid background.

The shade has two signature tags; a 2½" seal is stamped *Tiffany Studios New York* and a ¾" tag is inscribed *1507*. Instead of the usual four, we find six randomly spaced reinforcement wires; three run from the aperture ring to the upper wings, three, all the way down to the hanging heads.

244

Dragonfly on Red-Green   245

This shade is somewhat similar to the Orange Dragon-fly of figure [242] except that the color scheme is reversed, the green now appearing at the top of the shade [245]. The outer two aperture rows are of green-orange rippled glass; the dark green of the middle row is drawn into the upper portion of the shade, and is particularly intense in the first series of oblong segments. Traveling downward, the green is increasingly mottled with yellow. In succeeding rows, yellow glass is mottled with red, which produces an orange hue; red is then mottled with yellow, and, finally, red is dotted with deep wine.

The bodies of the insects are orange, tinged with purple; the eyes are orange, and the wings yellow with orange undertones. The jewels are yellow and orange, emphasizing the strong contention that already exists between the green and the red.

This shade has been repaired. It is signed and numbered 1507.

245

Dragonfly on Blood-Red 246

This sanguine color [246] which is rarely seen in Tiffany shades comes close in tonal quality to that used in the cone-shaped Dragonfly of figure [148], and is made from a similar configurated glass. The color of blood, it is employed in such a way that it appears to be fluid and dripping. While a sky of this color is improbable, any other interpretation would be too ominous.

In the middle aperture row, between two green rows, the red is rather solid. As it spreads down the shade, it diminishes in intensity but somehow becomes more sinister. Throughout the two upper background rows, the oblongs are striated with gray, yellow and touches of blue; farther down, the gray and yellow—and especially the blue—become the basic colors of the glass, with the red confined to the striations which continue into the bottom background row, between the wings.

The bodies of the insects are blue; the eyes are green jewels; the wings are green, mottled with small amounts of orange and blue. The large jewels, uppermost on the shade, are the same venous red as the background glass, but all the others are blue and green, quietly complementing the glass in the lower stretches of the shade.

The first of the two signature tags is 2¾″ long and reads *Tiffany Studios New York*; the second is 1″ long and bears the dash-number 1507–16.

The Dragonfly rests on one of the Studios' choice bases. Its round platform is 10½″ in diameter, and is similar in design to those shown in figures [217] and [237]. Like them, its periphery is edged with thirty-three glass balls, but these balls, though iridescent, are black rather than the gray-white employed in the other bases.

Six curved legs, with raised center ribs, support the stem; on the lower end of each leg, the rib spreads into a round, flat foot. An extension sleeve, which allows the lamp to be elevated from 28″ to 34″, fits inside the stem.

The base is finished in dark bronze with a hint of patina, and is impressed with the Tiffany Studios' signature and the numerals 10901. The same base is shown in the Tiffany Studios Album, numbered 392.

Another base featuring iridescent balls is illustrated in the Album [247]. Here the stem is supported by four legs, designed in such a way as to suggest roots, each of which separates into four smaller rootlets, all sixteen of which rest upon iridescent balls. The base, numbered 390, carries a geometric shade, with a horizontal row of iridescent balls imbedded about a third of the way up from its bottom edge. These harmonize with the balls in the base. To the author's knowledge, there is at least one such base still in existence.

246

247

Blue Dragonfly on Yellow   248

In the illustration, the shade appears blander than it really is, because the innumerable and variegated light refractions blazing through the white areas are impossible to reproduce on paper [248]. This also reduces the effectiveness of the mottling, which is outstanding in this shade, ranging from almost imperceptible shadows to heavy shrouds.

In the upper section, it consists of gray and yellow mottling on white; in the middle area, brown on yellow; and in the insects' immediate vicinity, yellow on orange-brown. This is not run-of-the-mill mottling, but a carefully preconceived, precise placement of selected specks, all relating to each other in size and shape, transparency and tone. Together, they create an ominous and somewhat eerie aura as of storm clouds gathering, or some other natural disaster in the offing.

A slightly undulating, stippled glass is used in the upper areas.

All three of the aperture rows are of the same color, which is not usually the case; these are gray-blue with yellow. The jewels are several shades of yellow. The bodies of

248

the dragonflies are brown, tinged with green, and their eyes are orange jewels. The only strong contrast is provided by the wings, which are blue, with touches of purple, red and green. The shade is signed and numbered 1507.

249

Blue Dragonfly on Orange-Brown   249

The color scheme is very simple, yet surprisingly effective [249]. Blue upper and lower aperture rows edge a middle row of pale orange. The orange color, which is quite light in the upper area of the shade, increases in intensity as it descends. In the vicinity of the insects, it has become a tawny orange-brown. All the background glass is both striated and mottled with deeper tones of the same color. The finish of the leading is gold.

Dark orange eyes gleam out of blue bodies. The wings of the insects are also blue, mottled with gray and green. The jewels, ranging from yellow to orange to brown, are almost lost in the background glass.

Three reinforcement wires run from the aperture ring to the lower rim of the shade, which is signed and numbered 1507.

The style of the elaborate base is pure Empire. Four ornate legs rise from a four-cornered platform, merge to make the slightly bulging body of the stem, then narrow and flare out again to form four scrolls; above the scrolls, the stem ends in a flattened orb of openwork. The base is 32" high, and is signed and numbered 550. Both it and the unusual finial are finished in gold doré.

250

In figure [250], the Tiffany Album demonstrates a different type of Hanging Head Dragonfly. Perhaps it should be called "Head Down" to differentiate it from "Hanging Head," since these heads do not protrude to form a part of the irregular rim; neither, in this instance, do the wings. Below the insects, we see two additional rows of background glass, the lower of which constitutes the true border of the shade. A continuous line of horizontal leading connects the nethermost portions of all the wing tips, and the first additional row of fairly uniform background pieces fills in the space between this wire and what would have been a "Hanging Head" border. The second and last row consists of irregular curved segments, which give the impression of waves, thrown up by a heavy wind.

The number of the shade is 1507. The 11"-diameter base consists of eight perforated bronze sections which extend upward into a tapering stem; four of the extensions are decorated with bronze "pearls" arranged in a leaf-like pattern. It is numbered 397.

Dragonfly Ornaments   251

Separate Dragonfly Ornaments, 10" wide and 7" high, were produced in several color schemes; provided with chains, they were suspended from shades to serve as additional decorations [251].

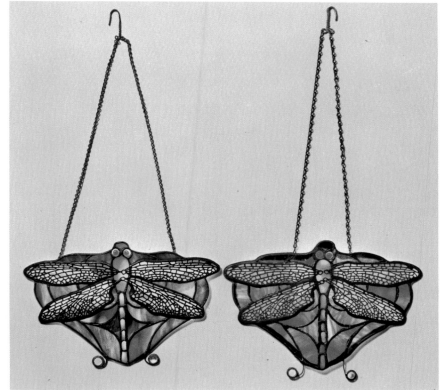

251

TRELLISES

Because each structure appears to be supported from below—like an espalier—the trellises in the irregular border group are more realistic than those belonging to the cones or globes where they are mainly figurative. Octagonal, with eight flat sides and a straight 4″ apron, the architectural aspect of the trellis is heightened by the "uprights" which extend downward, toward the ground. Five horizontal lattices (one around the aperture, two encircling the main surface of the shade, one starting and one ending the apron) connect the eight verticals.

Each shade measures 25″ from side to opposing side, 26″ between opposing corners, has a 4″ aperture, and is 10½″ in height. A reinforcement wire runs from the aperture, along each lattice slat, to the lower border.

252

Autumn Leaves Trellis 252

The shade features foliage in a riot of autumn colors; we are treated to the entire seasonal spectrum of yellows, oranges and red in addition to some greens, blues and purples [252].

The leaves, varying in size, but uniform in shape, are clustered in groups of five, and almost cover the shade surface. The branches are a soft green and twist around the lattice like a climbing vine. A few bunches of small blue-green berries may be seen in the apron.

Since no part of the plant extends beyond the straight lower border, the projection of its vertical lattices is the only reason for including this trellis among the irregular borders. The lattice work is blue-green and is only slightly mottled. The shade is signed and numbered 609–21.

Clematis Trellis 253

The Trellis in figure [253] is almost completely covered with the multitoned blue flowers of this climbing plant. The Prussian blue petals are mottled with lighter shades of blue or gray, or speckled with darker blues and touches of purple; despite its essentially monochromatic color scheme, these variations provide a surprising diversity of tone. Small green leaves sprout from thin, winding stems.

The background is fabricated from two different types of glass, one speckled, the other striated. The light gray segments are spattered with blue, green and yellow; the darker gray pieces (see center section, above apron) are streaked with darker blue, green and orange. The lattice, most of which is exposed, is blue, mottled with gray and green. In this shade, both blossoms and leaves extend below the last horizontal lath of the apron, thus establishing a true irregular border. The shade is signed and numbered 612–3.

Grape Trellis 254

The last example in this group has no blossoms and comparatively few leaves; however, these deficiencies are more than balanced by the artistry of the design, the exquisite coloration and the truly remarkable background [254].

The foliage is portrayed in various stages of development. The smallest leaves are either a self-mottled dark green or a white mottled lighter green. As they increase in size, their color changes to yellow-green, and finally, in foliage past its prime, palls into grayish green, speckled with orange. The

254

yellowish stems meander at random around the shade, sometimes over the lattices, as often under them. Most of the grapes are a deep plum purple, highlighted with brighter shades of the same color; some are red, and, as indicated by the subtle green and yellow striations, not quite ripe.

The potent visual impact of this comparatively simple shade is in large measure a result of the lavish use of many types of textured glass. The purple background glass is knobby; the reddish segments are heavily stippled; the yellow-green leaves are both fibrillated and undulating; the green leaves, rippled; the purple grapes are partly stippled, partly rippled and those that are reddish-green are strongly grained.

All the grape clusters, and a few leaves as well, fall past the lower lattice of the apron, leaving no doubt that the Grape Trellis is properly classified as an irregular border design. In addition to bearing the Tiffany Studios signature, the shade is distinguished by dash number 619–1.

HYDRANGEAS

With very few exceptions, the Tiffany shades we have so far seen were all shaped in the old traditional styles. As in the era of gas jets and oil lamps, they were designed to "shade" (in the most literal sense) the concentrated source of light.

While the Lily Orb and the Flower Basket, see figures [120], [121], among others, are interesting deviations, they lead to no fresh forms. The Trellis, on the other hand, is a definite step in a new direction, although it is plain to see that the "shade" concept still rules supreme.

The Hydrangea, however, represents a major breakthrough; for the first time, the contour of a plant determines the actual shape of the shade. From a light, camouflaged by flowers, we have arrived at flowers brought to life by a light.

The Hydrangea shade is 25" wide, 15" high and has a 5" aperture. Parabolic in shape, it consists of an almost spherical upper portion which gradually loses its rotundity toward the lower border. The curvature of the shade coincides with the contour of the blossoming bush; even the softly scalloped edges of the irregular lower border are attuned to the easy sweep of the shade outline. The design is repeated three times.

As compared with the previously shown hanging Hydrangea shade, it becomes evident that this gently flowing flower is superior to the confining surface of a cone. Furthermore, it can be readily viewed at low angles without the danger of distortion.

The glass in Hydrangea shades is unusually transparent and requires that low-wattage bulbs be used for illumination.

From four to six vertical reinforcement wires connect with a similar horizontal support a few inches above the lower border. Even with this precaution, the Hydrangea is rather fragile and bendable. This is due to its considerable width and length which, utilized to their fullest extent in an expansive shape, provide it with the largest glass surface of any Tiffany shade. Under these circumstances it is amazing that so many Hydrangeas have endured. These shades may be supported on the small floor base or hung from the ceiling.

Light Blue Hydrangea 255

Among the three examples of this group, the individual components of each flower cluster are here least noticeable [*255*]; these subdivisions, indicated by roundish, milky-white or slightly yellowish speckles on a more transparent white glass, are observed in only a few of the large globular blooms (see the last one of the rounded blossoms near the left border, a little below the center).

At the bottom of the shade, the speckles are yellow and green and cover sizable areas. Smaller dot-speckles are sparsely employed. In addition to the mottling, the glass used in the flowers is exceptionally interesting from the textural viewpoint: in most instances, its inner surface is knobby or rippled; in others, white fractured glass with green flakes has been used most effectively. The radiant image created by these diversified glass modifications is truly fascinating.

Almost all the foliage is in the upper portion of the shade. Its color leads one to assume that the plant is just past its peak; though most of the blooms are still pristine, the green of the leaves is heavily streaked with yellow and brown—evidence of age. Sometimes rippled glass is employed on their outer surface, and in other instances, turned inward. The rather heavy branches of the plant are light and dark brown, with considerable striation, and all the twigs and offshoots are extremely well delineated.

The background glass in the lower sections is a translucent light blue, with gray striations and a touch of purple mottling; close to the aperture, it becomes darker in tone. The shade is signed.

255

Dark Blue Hydrangea   256

Most of the blossoms of this Hydrangea [256] lack the uniformity of those shown in the previous shade; the large amount of spot mottling clearly delineates the masses of tiny, individual florets which make up each whole hydrangea head. The translucent white, bluish-white and yellow-white glass incorporates semi-opaque dots many of which contain still lighter spots at their centers; these spots-within-dots are oddly intriguing. In other blossoms, green spot-mottling is employed. Noteworthy also is the yellow, blue-gray and green area mottling.

In addition to the mottling, extensive use has been made of basically white fractured glass in the flower heads; green, pink and brown splinters and flakes are embedded in the surface of the glass that faces inward, and are seen by the viewer as shadowy soft-toned shapes. No rippled glass is employed in this shade. Apart from the fractured glass, the only texture to be seen is on the grained inner surface of the green-white pieces, with much of the design's effectiveness being assigned to the extensive mottling. In the upper section of the shade, the foliage is green; in the lower, yellow-green.

This shade differs in several respects from the last one shown. Perhaps the most obvious is the interchange of design elements whereby several leaves in the former have become background glass in the latter. Then, too, the branches in this are much thinner and more angular than in the Light Blue Hydrangea. A major color difference also exists in the background which, in the shade under discussion, is not only a darker blue near the aperture, but maintains almost the same intensity all the way down. The glistening quality of its sister shade, brought about by its multi-textured glass, is entirely absent.

The Tiffany Studios signature tag is affixed.

256

Purple Hydrangea 257

As its name indicates, the color scheme of this shade [257] is quite different from that of the two preceding ones. For one thing, we find no white flowers at all; instead, the hydrangea heads are light yellow, pale green and bluish-gray, mottled as before to denote the existence of the individual florets. In addition, a good deal of area mottling may be seen, as well as sporadic striations.

The prevalence of green rather than white in the heads may connote the maturity of the plant. At the left, the foliage is green, brushed with yellow, with more heavily saturated green leaves at the right.

The extra-heavy branches are a yellowish-brown, shading into brownish-green as they attenuate to stem size. In exciting contrast to the quiet yellow flowers, the background glass is almost clamorous with color; from shimmering blue and rosy violet in the border area, it deepens into darkest purple and densest blue around the aperture. The blue glass is streaked with white and purple; the purple, striated with blue and pink. The shade is signed.

257

The Tiffany Album illustrates a Miniature Hydrangea [258] which appears to be composed of many whitish flowers, combined with dark foliage and a striated background. Rippled and mottled glass has also been used, the mottling in some of the larger flower segments clearly indicates the components of the cluster.

No shade measurements are supplied, but from the size of the base (which has a 9" platform and is 26" high), it can be deduced that the shade is about 16" in width and 11" in height. It is numbered 1571. Some Miniature Hydrangeas are still in existence.

258

259

Dogwood in Tree Shape   259

A Tiffany Studios favorite, the Dogwood design, has been seen in transition to flowers, cones and globes, but this is the first time that we encounter it with a natural lower border and in the shape of a tree [259]. Actually, this Dogwood has the same parabolic profile as the Hydrangea, and the same dimensions: width 25", height 15", aperture 5". Even for a small tree, its crown appears to be very narrow and deep; the shape seems better suited to a shrub.

A stunning array of flowers sweeps over the entire surface of this shade; from aperture to irregular border, each area is equally embellished. Most of the blossoms are in full bloom, their petals (bracts) as widely spread as possible. Although adjoining flowers often overlap, no dimensional effects have been attempted. Some blossoms are a translucent white, mottled with opaque specks of the same "color." Others, equally limpid and similarly mottled, are yellow or greenish in tone. All the flower centers are yellow-green.

The ovoid leaves are a light, glowing green, speckled with darker green, and are fabricated of granular glass, with the texture turned inward. Interspersed between flowers, the small leaves help form the irregular bottom border. The branches, heavily laden with flowers and leaves, are mainly a self-mottled brown, with traces of green and mauve.

A highly transparent, scintillating blue glass, striated and mottled with darker blues, greens and a touch of mauve, makes the background worthy of special study. Unlike the thick segments employed in the petals, this glass is exceptionally thin. Because of the great discrepancy in gauge, the juxtaposition of blossoms and background creates an odd surface condition. While the outside of the shade is smooth, the inner surface resembles a relief map; each heavy petal is a visible protrusion.

The color scheme of the shade is pastel-soft, but far from innocuous. Obviously the most exquisite care was shown in the selection of glass. Its delicate beauty was attained at a certain sacrifice; since the fragile glass is extremely transparent, even low-wattage bulbs cause an acute glare. It is therefore advisable to cover them with small individual shades of translucent fabric in order to diffuse the light before it reaches the glass. The shade is also surprisingly attractive in reflected light.

The shade is supported by one horizontal and six vertical reinforced wires. It is signed.

LABURNUMS

Informally known as Goldenchain, the Laburnum is generally conceded to be among the most beautiful of flowering trees. With its drooping golden flower clusters and well-defined trifoliate leaves, it is easy to see why Tiffany was so attracted to it. In the irregular borders, the Studios immortalized the Laburnum in three sizes: 22", 24" and 28".

Unique to this design is the way in which its flower clusters bulge beyond the basic spherical shape of the shade. Between the bulges, the shade curves inward, forming shallow depressions. There are three repeats of the design, each including two bulges and two depressions.

The deviation from the strictly circular cross-section toward the irregular, undulant contour of a tree adds a particularly realistic touch to the Laburnum shade. In only this one instance did the Tiffany Studios alter the smooth circularity of their globes in order to portray the natural shape of a living entity. The technical difficulties inherent in these repeated transitions from convex to concave curvatures in the horizontal plane, while at the same time maintaining an additional curvature in the vertical plane, were certainly considerable.

This delightfully different contour remains the sole property of the Laburnum, and serves to place it on an equal plane with the best shades Tiffany ever made.

A readily discernible trend toward smaller flower elements, as his shades became progressively more subtle and refined, almost reaches its summit in the Laburnum. The multitude of extremely small floral petals to be leaded called for the most meticulous craftsmanship and the expenditure of infinite time and patience.

Because of these factors, interchangeability of design elements assumes major importance. In the Laburnum, flower petals, some leaves, and virtually all background glass, may be substituted one for another, without destroying the established pattern. When large flowers, such as tulips or poppies, which are made up of a known number of comparatively large components, are depicted, such interchanges are, on the face of it, unfeasible. First, of course, a flower with, let us say, five petals cannot arbitrarily be cut to four or increased to six petals, even if the adjoining glass sections were similar enough in shape to be substituted. Second, such great differences exist in the shape and the location of the various design elements that interchanges are impossible in any appreciable number.

We have already encountered interchangeability in the Hydrangea. Because of the large quantity and great irregularity of the flower, foliage and background segments of that shade, such replacements can only be detected when the two specimens are carefully compared. In the Laburnum, the smaller and less uniform constitutents encouraged even more substitutions. This afforded the designer or artisan unlimited opportunities for innovation. Without altering the intrinsic character of the original design, any number of variations might be introduced in either or both color and pattern. The same held true for other small-segmented designs that will be shown.

The irregularity of the lower border is more pronounced in the Laburnum than in the Dragonfly, Trellis or Hydrangea; in fact, the difference of as much as several inches which exists between its highest and lowest points is not exceeded in any other irregular border shade.

Like the Hydrangea, the Laburnum shade is equipped with a complex reinforcement system. An examination of its inner surface will reveal from four to six vertical wires; these cross a horizontal reinforcement wire, which can be found a few inches above the border, and continue on to the border itself.

Twenty-Two-Inch Laburnums

These shades are 22" in diameter, 11½" high and have 5" apertures. Between the three longest clusters which mark the three repeats at the irregular lower border, we can count seven smaller projections, created by clusters of dissimilar length and breadth. The maximum difference between the lowest and the highest points of the border is about 2".

Branches and a veritable blanket of foliage comprise the upper portion of this Laburnum pattern. Each of the six bulges is composed of two cascading flower clusters, whose tiny blossoms make up most of the lower two-thirds of the shades. In the concave areas, heavily leafed limbs droop downward between the flower clusters. However, they stop short of the lower border, unlike those seen in the larger Laburnums. The largest petals are about 1" long, the longest leaves 2½".

260

Pale Gold Laburnum   260

The shade is distinguished by petals mottled in such a manner that each has clearly defined darker and lighter areas; as in nature itself, no uniformity of color exists [260].

Between the bulges, the brown tinge of some blossoms betrays their age. Here, too, the leaves change hue as if about to fall; bluish-green with gray mottles, they lack the lively verdant look of fresh foliage. The young leaves, toward the top of the shade, are an almost unvarying dark green; farther down, as they begin to fade, yellow mottling becomes evident. The heavy branches bearing them are rendered in dark brown glass, with few striations; some of the limbs stretch to the bottom border.

The background is formed of exquisite fractured glass, colorless but for the blue, green and brown flakes imbedded in it. The shade is finished in gold and is signed.

The Pale Gold Laburnum is shown on the Lily Stem Base, which is finished in dark gold doré; in figure [159] it was shown in patina. Since this photograph was taken at a lower angle, more of the stand can be seen. The twisting stems harmonize especially well with the flowing clusters indigenous to the Laburnum design.

Laburnum on Brilliant Blue   261

Reddish speckles are present in some of the petals of this plant [261]. The ruddy tinge can be seen clearly at the lower left of the illustration. Indicative, perhaps, of an early growth stage, many clusters are a grayish-green, untouched by red. The branches are also a subdued gray-green, and in several places descend within a petal's breadth of the bottom border. Pale green leaves, mottled with gray, are very prominent in the upper portion of the shade. Elsewhere the foliage is green with yellow mottles and darker green striations.

The background glass is the most outstanding feature of this shade. Light blue and very transparent, it glistens like cascading water. The glass is finely fibrillated, with hair-thin longitudinal grooves impressed on its inner surface. Adding even more interest to the texture, a multitude of the tiniest air bubbles are also embedded within these segments. Unfortunately, the great effectiveness of the two combined textures is not wholly reproducible.

The shade is signed and dash-numbered 1539–3.

261

Rose-Tinged Laburnum   262

The last 22" shade [262] contains quite a bit of pink in the essentially yellow petals. Again, we find that some of the florets are still green, with yellow mottling. The rosy hue embellishes only the most mature blossoms, but is sufficiently strong to lend a special essence to the entire shade.

The leaves may be divided into three color categories: dark green mottled with light green; light green mottled with yellow and blue-gray mottled with white. Much of this foliage is made from granular glass, with a more or less heavy texture on its inner surface. The leaves cling to dark brown branches, well mottled with a lighter brown.

The blue background glass is streaked with green and yellow. Comparatively pale in the lower portion of the shade, it becomes darkly opulent in the aperture area. Many segments which belong to the background in other Laburnums here help to fill out the flower clusters. This shade represents a prime example of interchangeability.

The Rose-Tinged Laburnum is signed and numbered 1539. It is finished in gold.

262

Twenty-Four-Inch Laburnums

Twenty-four inches in width, 13½" high and possessed of 6" apertures, these shades may be supported by a large floor base or hung from the ceiling. Again their pattern is repeated three times, and each repeat contains two bulges and two depressions; eight border projections can be counted, as compared with the seven seen in the 22" shades. Deeper as well as more numerous, these projections vary as much as 3" in length, rather than the 2" maximum measured in the smaller shade.

The 24" Laburnum also differs in design. The branches are heavier than the increased size of the shade alone would warrant, and they fork off at distinctly dissimilar angles; nowhere, for example, do they come as close to the bottom border as in the smaller size. On the other hand, the foliage does hang all the way down, which is not the case in the 22" category. Displayed with such prominence, the distinctive trifoliated leaves show to much better advantage. The largest leaf is 3¼" long, the largest petal measures 1½".

263

Burnt-Gold Laburnum 263

Here the flower clusters in full bloom are golden brown, mottled with yellow while the less mature blossoms are yellow mottled with green [263]. All petals are constructed of either fine-grained or stippled glass, both textured on their inner surfaces. With a few exceptions, the cluster ends which form the irregular border are fairly light in color.

The brown branches, tinted with mauve, bear medium green leaves streaked with light green and yellow. Those overlaying the clusters are dappled in yellow, as if the blossoms themselves showed through; the mottles are the size as well as the shape of the underlying florets. The inner surface texture of this foliage glass is roughly undulating.

The blue background, streaked with green, deepens in tone toward the top of the shade.

The Burnt Gold Laburnum is signed and numbered 1537.

Large-Mottle Laburnum   264

264

Color change achieved through the use of speckled and spotted glass is characteristic of this whole category, but it is so pronounced in this shade as to merit inclusion in the very name of it [264].

In the various florets, the mottles are white on yellow, green on orange and orange on brown. The specks are in the center of the petal or on one side. Occasionally, they may be found on both sides, leaving only the middle its original yellow hue.

Similar mottling dominates a large number of the leaves, especially those which overlay the flower clusters. When this occurs, we again encounter the epitome of spot-mottling, in which the yellow of the blossom is made to show through in the actual shape of the unseen petal. (See center leaves in illustration.) These faded leaves are obviously as thin as tissue, while the fresh green foliage is almost completely opaque.

The slender branches, greenish-brown with dark brown

striations, are delineated with such care that every knurl and growth ring is easily discerned.

The background glass ranges from light blue near the border to dark blue at the aperture. It is streaked with green and several shades of blue.

The Large-Mottle Laburnum is signed and numbered 1537.

The shade rests on the Tree Base, reputedly designed by Louis C. Tiffany himself. A tangle of roots rises from its 14½" round platform; in true Art Nouveau style, they creep upward along its trunk, and, in so doing, metamorphose into bark.

As a rule, the Tree Base has a special rod-and-sleeve fitting at the top to receive the shade. In some instances, however, as in this example, the Tree Base had originally been equipped to carry a 6" aperture ring instead.

The base is signed and numbered 553.

Blue-Tinged Laburnum   265

No one can look at this Laburnum [265] without commenting on its glorious background glass. Fibrillated, it transmits a muted yet strangely resplendent light. Portions of this glass are an extremely transparent light blue; other segments, tinged with mauve, are more opaque. Toward the top of the shade, this darker hue becomes dominant. Apparently in tribute to the extraordinary tonal and textural qualities of this glass, the craftsman chose to interchange many flower petals for background pieces, thereby intensifying the blue brilliance.

265

Further to enrich this superb shade, he employed other exceptional textured glasses in its production. Of all the foliage, only the light green leaves with yellow striations are made from smooth-surfaced segments; the others, in which darker greens and browns prevail, are of configurated glass, which is both ridged and nodular. Glass of a similar texture, used for the yellow-green blossoms, imparts a polished sheen, as of faintly glimmering gold. Other petals are constructed of yellow stippled glass, intricately mottled with orange. Branches and stems are greenish-brown with some striations showing.

Three separate signature tags are attached to various sections of the leading along the stems, since no one line is sufficiently long and straight to accommodate them all. The 2" marker reads *Tiffany Studios; New York* is on one 1" marker; the other 1" tag contains the well-deserved dash number 1537−2.

The Twenty~Eight~Inch Laburnums

While 4″ wider than the last Laburnums, the 28″ shades are the same 13½″ in height; this change in proportion results in a more extensive spread, and therefore a more true-to-tree appearance. Next to the Spreading Cherry Tree, it has the most lifelike tree form of any Tiffany shade. At 6″, the aperture remains the same.

As in all Laburnums, the design is repeated three times, but, in order to cover the larger circumference of the 28″ shade, each motif is of a larger size. This extra coverage is not accomplished by increasing the size of its glass segments, as one would suppose; the longest floret is still 1½″, the longest leaf 3¼″. Instead, the *number* of petal and background pieces has been increased. Only the number of the leaves remains unchanged.

The large Laburnum, majestic in spread, splendid in design and magnificent in coloration, is certainly among the finest of the Tiffany Studios shades. Next to the Hydrangea, it represents the most extensive glass surface of any shade.

Green-Tinged Laburnum
266

266

In this shade [266], the exceptionally heavy clusters are composed of clearly defined florets, almost all of which have an underlying hint of green, in addition to other tonal modulations. The mainly yellow petals are mottled with citron and orange, and much orange may also be seen in the greenish clusters. Scattered petals, in all parts of the shade, are made from fine-grained glass, with the texture turned inward.

The greater part of the foliage is dark green, with blue-green prevalent in the upper portion of the shade. The characteristic spot-mottling of leaves, outlining the blossoms over which they lay, is again in evidence. Some of the lowest leaves have a brownish soon-to-be-shed look.

The branches and offshoots are faithfully portrayed in brown, with green-gray mottling and stray tints of red. As the twigs thin toward the bottom, the green disappears.

Three distinctly different groups of glass have been used in the background. The most extensively employed is a gray-blue glass, speckled with dark purple; it starts appearing in the center of the shade and the mottles become larger and deeper in tone toward the aperture. In addition, milky blue segments, seen close to the bottom border, alternate with very transparent pale blue pieces, interestingly pin-mottled. The designer attained superb subtleties of color.

Within this Laburnum, three vertical reinforcement wires connect with a horizontal reinforcement wire. Rather than girding the shade in one fell swoop, it circumnavigates it in sweeping curves, sometimes ¾″ from the border, then as much as 5½″ above it. Despite this additional support, and undoubtedly owing to its odd proportions, the Green-Tinged Laburnum is very fragile—almost bendable. It is signed with three tags, one stamped with its number 381–1.

267

Laburnum on Mauve   *267*

The last of the series is a shade which is also the most captivating in terms of color [*267*]. An almost ethereal quality has been achieved.

The variations apparent in the six flower clusters are testimony to the fastidious taste of the artisan involved. The tonal nuances prove that each piece of glass was picked for its precise purpose.

One cluster is predominantly green, mottled with a small amount of yellow; another has slightly less green and correspondingly more yellow; orange petals are tinged with green; yellow florets are flushed with orange; orange blooms are mottled with brown. Much of the glass is fibrillated, but its filaments are coarser and less numerous than those generally seen in this texture type. Some petal segments are filled with minute air bubbles, each of which acts as a little light diffuser.

In the uppermost portion of the shade, the foliage runs through a good part of the green range; yellow-green, orange-green, green-orange, green-brown and undiluted greens of every density. Where leaves rest on blossoms, show-through mottling can be seen, but the outlines are not as sharp as in other shades. Through the dark green leaves, petals are a faint orange; the blossoms behind the pale bluish-green foliage are a yellow-gray. Most of the foliage is rendered in glass textured on its inner surface; some is granulated, some undulating.

The branches of the plant are brown, thoroughly striated with yellow and darker brown; in the aperture area, reddish striations are also present. Quite thick around at the aperture, the branches continue to be more than ordinarily heavy all the way to their ends and are exceptionally well portrayed.

It is in the background glass, however, that the true artistic quality of this Laburnum can best be seen. In the main body of the shade, the glass is purple, streaked with several shades of blue. Along the lower periphery, we find a highly transparent, more richly purple glass; since their inner surfaces are undulating in texture, these segments are strongly refractive. At the top, the glass is a resplendent reddish-purple, and rippled in texture.

Once again the craftsman exercised his option to increase the background area by incorporating segments which, in other shades, are flower petals.

Six vertical reinforcement wires run from the aperture rim to the same kind of dipping, curving horizontal reinforcement wire seen in the Green-Tinged Laburnum; crossing this, the verticals continue to the lower border. The shade is signed.

Comparable to the best ever created by the Studios, the shade somehow combines great delicacy with strong drama. Although it seems inconceivable that this magnificent shade was not awarded a dash number, no number – not even a production code – can be found.

Flowering Lotus   268

268

269

In the Lotus we encounter a completely new shape [268]; long and narrow, it is the ideal form for the depiction of flowers which droop down instead of standing erect, atop straight stems. Variations of this shape will be found in the pages ahead.

The Lotus is 18" in diameter and from 13" to 14" high, depending on the border point from which measurements are made. It has one horizontal and six vertical reinforcement wires. The height of the lamp is 26½".

Yellowish-green in color and clearly segmented, the thin, supple stems of the Lotus emerge from the top center of the shade and hang halfway down before bursting into bloom. Between these slender stems, the superbly striated blue and purple background glass suggests evening mist falling softly from the sky; the glass is of a fibrillated texture, highly luminescent. By any criterion, this stem-filled, gently curved section is the most splendid part of the shade; the flowers serve only to frame it.

At the crown, the stems converge on a tiny aperture, whose rim rests on a 2" ring; ordinarily the small finial is invisible, submerged as it is below the incurved top section of the shade. This very small, hidden aperture may serve as a link to the shades which have no aperture at all, to be dealt with in the following chapter.

The lowest of the three flower layers forms the irregular bottom border. The height variations of this edge are limited to about an inch. Because of the outward curve of the border, the blossoms appear to float on some unseen water surface.

The flowers are mainly milky white, tinged with orange and blue; some of the petals are bright yellow, mottled with opaque orange. Most of the petal glass is knobby textured; the remainder is stippled. In the middle row, the unfolding bracts are greenish-yellow; in the top tier of buds, which are just barely open, the bracts are greenish-brown. The sparse leaves, which should not be confused with the bracts around the blossoms, are a bright green.

Each of the four pattern repeats contains three blossoms at the bottom border, two blooms and one closed bud in the row above, and four unfolding buds in the uppermost row.

The Tiffany Album shows a Lotus shade with the entire background made from rippled glass. A miniature version of the Lotus was also produced [269]. It is seen on the smaller Lily Pad Base, whose platform is 4" high and an average of 9½" in width. With these measurements as a yardstick, it would seem that the miniature shade was the same 18" in height as the standard Lotus, but very much narrower—apparently about 10½". Consequently, fewer flowers could be accommodated. The contour of the shade differs, as well as the design; instead of a gentle curvature from crown on down, the horizontal top section arcs sharply into long vertical sides. The base bears identification number 345.

The integrated base reaffirms the Lotus *leitmotif* in a massive platform consisting of carved water-lily leaves; since the lotus belongs to the same botanical family, the leaves are, in this instance, properly employed.

Five inches high, the platform varies from 11" to 13½" in diameter, because of the unevenness of its leaf-outline edge. It thereby exceeds the measurements of the Lily Lamp Base in both dimensions. Seven lotus stalks in close conjunction make up the heavy main stem.

This shade originally was provided with a rather peculiar lighting arrangement in the form of two rows of bulbs—one of the candelabra type—at two different levels. The light quality created by the size and placement of these eight small (7½ watt) bulbs can only be compared with the glimmer of glowworms reflected in water. To accentuate this effect, eight more tiny lights, in two additional rows, were subsequently installed as an adaptation. These "glow" lights can be seen in the illustration.

9. IRREGULAR UPPER AND LOWER BORDERS

PPROACHING Irregular Upper and Lower Borders, we have taken the last, most exhilarating, step in pursuance of the consummate Tiffany Studios shade. The Laburnum showed us the best of the "natural" lower borders. Now we come to the final, incomparable, category: in these creations, both upper and lower borders abandon the artificial straight edge and adopt the outlines dictated by Nature.

In this group, the aperture has been replaced by an openwork metal crown which simulates bows and branches of a tree or shrub; at the juncture of the bronze crown and the glass-covered portion of the shade, an irregular upper border comes into being.

The bronze crown assumes the support function of the aperture by means of a metal tubing or sleeve which is attached to the center of its under surface; this slides over a rod at the top of the base, see figure [26a]. Sometimes, in a reversed manner, the rod is attached to the shade and the sleeve is on top of the base. Rod and sleeve are either smooth or threaded. In the standard size, the rods are about 1¾" in diameter; in the miniature size about ½". Because of the elimination of the aperture, it is not possible to place these shades upon ring-equipped bases and interchange them at will. Instead, they are definitely integrated with the specially designed Tree Bases which are interchangeable, provided that the arrangement of rod and sleeve corresponds.

The bronze crown also substitutes for the finial, both aesthetically, by concealing cluster and support mechanism, and in a utilitarian way, by allowing the heat of the bulb to escape through its opening.

BEGONIAS

Although the two semi-tropical plants bear little resemblance to each other, this shade design is frequently referred to as Bougainvillea. Actually, the Christmas-flowering begonia – developed by a governor of Santo Domingo named Begon – has a highly individualistic blossom, consisting of two pairs of petals on different planes. The upper two petals lay crosswise on the lower two, covering part of the latter pair. The leaves are large, asymmetric, serrated and strongly veined. All these characteristics are so clearly portrayed in this shade that there can be no question as to its botanical classification.

Almost, but not quite, spherical, the Begonia is 7½" high and achieves its maximum 13" width at its lower border. The design, which is repeated three times, is made up of masses of flowers, interspersed with extra large leaves.

Begonia on Gray   270

The flowers, all with soft gold or green centers, range from pale pink, striated with white, to dark pink, streaked with red [270]; a few deep-red blossoms serve as accents. Many of the flower petals are fabricated of finely textured glass segments, some with surface grain, others stippled or minutely fibrillated.

Being far from uniform, the tonal density tends to increase from top down, so that the flowers which form the irregular border are the deepest red. Limited as it is to the length or breadth of a single petal, the border is only slightly uneven.

With great fidelity to nature, Tiffany artisans assembled the flowers as they appear in life. Some were constructed on three planes: the flower centers are lowest; raised slightly above them, we see one pair of petals; and higher still, the second pair of transverse petals. These gradations were achieved through the employment of thicker glass, or the physical elevation of regular glass by leading it somewhat higher than surrounding segments. As a result, the normally smooth outer surface is, in the Begonia, rough and craggy.

The three leaves in each repeat are light green, streaked with pinkish-brown and yellow, and reach from the upper portion of the shade to the lower border. A few small green sections can also be seen near the crown section; in all probability these represent a background leaf almost buried under blossoms. The leaves are made from textured glass, knobbed on its inner surface. While branches *per se* are not shown, their presence in some places is hinted at by heavy lead lines.

The entire background is executed in fractured glass. In the lower third of the shade, the segments are a very transparent gray, virtually colorless if not for the embedded flakes of pink and rose. In the upper area, the basic background color is pale green, also inset with pink and rose.

The crown of the shade, which encompasses the area of the old aperture, consists primarily of nine cast-bronze branches. Splaying outward from the top center of the shade, as if actually emerging from the big main stalk of the plant, these extend to the heavily leaded, highly irregular upper border of the glass portion. Between the nine branches, an intricate network of bronze twigs fills what was once the open space of the aperture—in this instance, some 6" to 7" in diameter. In conformity with the flowered section of the shade, the pattern in metal is also repeated three times.

No reinforcement wires have been employed. The shade is signed with a ¾" tag affixed to the inside of its lower border.

The Begonia is shown on the Miniature Tree Base, utilized for all the smaller lamps in this category. From the periphery of

270

its 6¾" circular platform, small low-relief rootlets converge on the stand in tangled skeins. There they combine and creep up the stem, covering it with a gnarled bark made of their layered mass. The base carries a three-socket cluster. It is finished in light copper, signed and numbered 554.

Begonia on Blue   271

More vibrant colors and more striking contrasts are immediately evident in this shade [271]. Once again, the flowers are pink and red, but the red is brighter and more ebullient. All the petal glass is strongly self-striated. The dimensional effect described in the last Begonia is noticeable in some petals and centers, and both leaves and background glass are slightly elevated in many areas, but the technique has been applied less systematically than in the previous example.

The foliage is made from deep green fibrillated glass, while the bluish-green, blue-streaked leaves are of knobby glass, with the texture turned inward. In the lower part of the shade, the blue and green-blue background pieces are also knobbed on the inside; because of the exceptional transparency of the glass, the texture shows through and adds a remarkable faceted quality to the normal refraction. Toward the top of the shade, the finely grained background glass is a highly transparent pale green, with pink and orange streaks. Both of these tints and texture types co-exist in the center of the Begonia; though some of the green-orange descends into the lower area, the blue never strays above the midsection of the shade.

A fascinating shade, superb in transmitted light and extremely attractive even when unlit, this Begonia was awarded

a dash number. The three signature tags, two close together, the third, 2" away, are attached to the upper irregular border; they are inscribed *Tiffany Studios, New York* and *350–9*.

The Miniature Tree Base is finished in patina, signed and numbered 350.

271

Next we will show some LEAF-PATTERN LAMPS from the Tiffany
Album. The design accounted for a small but interesting portion of the
Studios' output.

272

The shade illustrated in figure [272] is completely composed of large,
overlapping leaves, whose contours create irregular borders at both top and
bottom. By the employment of sculptured glass, it was possible to define the
veins and ribs of each leaf in an extremely lifelike manner.

The platform of the base resembles that of the Miniature Tree Base,
showing an Art Nouveau type of plant motif; its stem supports a three-light
cluster equipped with three Lily shades, portions of which may be seen at the
aperture. The lamp is numbered 354.

273

A similar type of lamp is shown in figure [273]. In this, the sturdy main
stem separates at the top into numerous drooping bronze branches which
support the shade. The latter is almost entirely made up of overlapping
leaves, though some flowers can be discerned. Illumination is furnished by an
array of light bulbs which depend from lily stems.

An abstract root design decorates the platform of the base; from its
outer scalloped edge, the radicals converge upon the center and ascend the
stem. The lamp is numbered 352.

CHERRY TREES

This design is often called Apple Blossom, but the size of the fruit, the pink color of the flowers, their arrangement in clusters and the smooth-edged pointed leaves indicate that the cherry tree inspired this shade.

The Cherry Tree was produced by the Studios in two sharply different shapes. The one made to resemble a widespread tree marks a revolutionary departure from all previous lamp profiles. The other shade, far deeper and much smaller in circumference, seems to share kinship—at least in shape—with the weeping willow. Many other forms of plant life have also been cast in that contour by the Studios.

In these designs, we once again find that leaves, fruit and flowers, heedless of season, co-exist in the same shade. The simultaneous appearance of all these elements is, no doubt, an expression of artistic independence.

Spreading Cherry Trees

This is without question the most realistic tree shape that Tiffany ever produced. With his Tree Base, it constitutes a perfectly integrated entity. The closest comparable shade is the largest (28") of the Laburnum series which, however, lacks the crown of bronze branches, an essential tree characteristic.

The Spreading Cherry is 25" in diameter, and a comparatively shallow 12" in height; some of this already scant height is appropriated by the network of branches in the tree crown, leaving only about 8½" for the leaf-and-flower portion of the shade.

Measuring from the small (2") flat area at the top of the shade, the bronze crown extends downward at an approximately 30 degree angle for a minimum of 5½", a maximum of 7½" to meet and merge with the heavy bronze edge of the irregular upper border. Some of its branches intrude an inch or two into the glass portion of the shade where they are continued by glass branches. There are four repeats in the branch pattern of the crown.

The aforementioned (2") flat section at the top center of the shade is slightly recessed and is therefore invisible at, or above, eye-level; if viewed from above, however, it is somewhat unsightly. An attachment on its underside secures the shade to the stem of the base.

The glass area of the shade consists of a gently inclined top section, adjoining the (steeper) crown, and a nearly vertical side section or apron. With only a slight downward slant of about 15 degrees, the upper area of the glass shade extends sideways from 5" to 7", depending on where one measures; this "spread" is due to the fact that the upper bronze-glass border is so extremely irregular. By means of a rather abrupt curvature this slightly inclined surface turns into the almost vertical apron; the depth of the latter varies from 6" to 7" due to the irregularity of its lower border which fluctuates within an inch. The apron has a hardly detectable outward slant.

Like the crown, the glass portion of the shade consists of four repeats, each containing blossoms, cherries, leaves, branches and background. Four large branches, laden with heavy foliage, sag down from the crown to the bottom border, and, in so doing, neatly divide the shade into its four repeats. Since the branches descend so low, leaves play a part in the formation of the border. However, most of this edge is made up of flower petals and fruit. In the apron, the blossoms appear singly and in clusters, and the same holds true for the cherries.

Interchangeability is evident in all these shades. A leaf in one becomes a cherry in another, a petal in a third, and, in the fourth, perhaps a piece of background glass. This interchange factor, combined with possible color variations in each of the four components, explains the fact that each shade in this design is different in mood from every other.

Most of the shades have four vertical reinforcement wires which run from the crown to a horizontal wire near the lower border.

The Spreading Cherry shades are designed to fit the Tree Base shown in figure [275]. In this combination, the Tree Base is 27½″ high and has a six-light cluster whose sockets and bulbs encircle the stem and are more or less parallel to the apron.

As a rule, the base has a special switch with four settings to control the six bulbs. The first turn illuminates three of the bulbs; the second position switches on the other three; at the third setting, the first three go off; the fourth turn darkens the entire lamp.

274

Green-Leaf Cherry Tree   274

The name is attributable to the fresh verdance of the shade's foliage [274]. The tonality ranges from dense, deep greens at the crown to lighter greens below; the green is self-striated or intermixed with orange and yellow. Much of the leaf glass is stippled or fibrillated, thus producing a delicate radiance. Many of the foliage pieces here are fruit or flower petals in other shades.

The lush green look is augmented by background segments of essentially the same hues; these, however, are mottled with white and yellow, and somewhat less trans-

lucent. The green branches, spotted with dark orange, are not readily discernible. Even the bronze crown is in bright green patina.

The predominantly white blossoms are lightest at the irregular lower border. Higher up, they are interspersed with pink flowers which proliferate as they approach the crown. The darker pink, red-speckled cherries are made of a vivdly transparent glass which is either knobby or rippled in texture. The flower centers are a transparent yellow.

No reinforcement wires are to be found.

275

Red-Cherry Tree 275

This shade is easily recognized by the clear cardinal color of its fruit [275]. The vibrancy of this exceptional red glass is intensified by the knobby texture of its inner surface.

The cherries are not only brighter than those seen in other shades, but are also more numerous. Interchangeability accounts for the increase as fruit has here been substituted for other plant elements. Now we find three cherries where elsewhere there are only two; two where – in another version of this design – there is only one; and even a few single fruits where we have previously seen a small piece of background glass, a tiny leaf or part of a flower petal.

In the main, the blossoms are light pink, with some white flowers interspersed among them. The foliage is rendered in two distinctly different greens. The extremely trans-parent glass employed in the leaves seen in the upper portion of the shade is striated with deep orange; descending, the green is denser, with pale green mottling. The branches are mauve, striated with green and brown.

Two types of mottling add special interest to the pale emerald-green background. One is a light green with overall pinhead spotting; the other consists of multitudinous opaque specks in faint mauve, pea-sized or larger and irregular in shape. Some bluish background pieces at the lower border lead one to believe that blue flowers may grow in the garden beyond those low-hanging branches. The shade is signed.

The shade is shown on a Tree Base in patina finish; it is signed and numbered 6902.

276

Cherry Tree on Fractured Glass   276

Here, pink and white blossoms appear in just about equal numbers [276]. The white are most abundant at the lower border, while the more colorful flowers are found higher on the shade. It is there, too, that the foliage is most deeply green; farther down, yellow encroaches on the leaves, and, at the lower border, some are mottled with the yellow-orange and brown of autumn, which portends their end. Most of the foliage is fabricated from undulating glass, textured on its inner surface. The heavier branches are brown, streaked with orange; the thinner limbs are green with orange.

The pearly background is made of a strikingly beautiful fractured glass, containing some milky spots. The green, orange and rose flakes and splinters imbedded in it evoke an impression of far-off flowers and trees. Because some of the shards are not completely integrated, the inside surface of many segments is uncommonly craggy. The shade is signed.

277

Cherry Tree with Bronze Branches 277

What strikes one first in this shade [277] is the substitution of metal for colored glass in the execution of its branches and stems. Growing out of the bronze crown, the heavy metallic branches twist and twine through the siliceous section of the shade, entirely obscured at times by blossoms and leaves, but emerging at intervals into the open; some of the thinner stems reach all the way to the bottom border. The main branches are somewhat thicker than those executed in glass; sculpturally treated, they project ¼" or more above the surface and lend a very realistic touch to the tree-concept of this shade.

The blossoms are all white, or white with pink tinging just the periphery of the petals. Most of the petals, especially those flushed with pink, are fabricated of undulating glass with the textured side toward the viewer. The flower centers are yellow, and the foliage is a transparent pale green, mottled with yellow, darker green and gray opaque splotches. The unusual brilliance of the cherries originates in the partly stippled, partly fibrillated texture of the glass employed. Some unripe cherries are rendered in pale rose, striated with green.

The background of this Cherry is also constructed of fractured glass. In the apron area, the basic alabaster glass contains large numbers of completely transparent dots, the size of pinheads; small green, orange and rose splinters are superimposed in these segments. In the crown area, the greenish base glass is lavishly strewn with large splinters of green, pink and purple which overlap each other in all directions. This innovative technique adds a wholly new dimension to the upper section of the shade.

To match the solidity of the bronze branches, the leading of the blossoms is unusually heavy; because of this, many petals and flower centers are thrust above the surrounding surface. Most flowers hang from thickly leaded stems, as do quantities of fruit and foliage. Background segments add their own irregularities to an already fitful surface. Thus the three-dimensional approach, inherent in the bronze branches, pervades the entire shade; there is the Tiffany Studios signature.

Pendant Cherry Trees

These shades were made in a standard and a miniature size, and, though similar in some respects to the Widespread Cherry, they are distinctly different in their essential shape.

Comparing the standard sizes, we find the 25" width of the Spreading Cherry reduced to 18" in the Pendant. On the other hand, the vertical sides increase from 7" in the former to 10½" in the latter. In the miniature size, these dimensions are proportionally smaller. In addition, the high bronze crown of the Spreading Cherry becomes a less inclined, almost flat surface in the Pendant.

Miniature Pendant Cherry Tree 278

In its crown portion, this 10"-wide and 9"-high shade bears a certain resemblance to the Begonia [278]. As in that design, a skein of branches begins to spread from the top center of the shade and continues until the bronze web reaches the glass; at the start of the glass section, the branches merge into a heavy and irregular bronze border. Considerably reduced in size, the thick limbs invade the leaded area of the shade for a short distance.

The bronze web, which consists of a single flowing pattern with no repeats, covers approximately two-thirds of the crown portion of the Miniature Cherry, with the remainder given over to leaded glass. The glass part of the crown has only a slight downward slope. A sharp curve at its periphery, again as in the Begonia, marks the beginning of an almost perpendicular apron, whose sides descend from a minimum of 6" to a maximum of 7½". This is accounted for by the fact that the highest and lowest points on the irregular border are 1½" apart—a considerable variation for such a small shade.

The frosty pink and white glass employed in the plentiful flowers is spotted with more transparent mottles. A few petals overlap and, where this occurs, the surface is unevenly raised; the cherries are also raised. Against the opacity of the petals, the transparent yellow or orange flower centers shine with extra sparkle. The rose-red cherries, constructed of knobby glass, with the textured surface turned inward, are even more dazzling. Some of the emerald-green and extremely transparent leaves reach so far down that they form part of the bottom border along with the blossoms. The design is repeated three times.

The branches, originating at the bronze crown, are surprisingly light in color; a wan greenish-brown, they seem unworthy offspring of the dark bronze parent branches. While the very light yellow-green background glass is not assertive either, slightly darker green and orange mottling, plus pinhead stippling, give it strength and character. The shade is not reinforced. It is signed with three small tags at the upper irregular border and bears the number 384–5.

The Miniature Tree Base on which it stands, (described in connection with figure [270]), is finished in gold bronze, a few shades lighter than the patina of the shade.

278

The profile of the STANDARD PENDANT CHERRY is precisely that of the Miniature, though proportionately larger in all its parts. These shades are 18" in width and, because of a 2½" variable between projections and indentations at the lower border, range from 8" to 10½" in depth. The over-all dimensions of the shade, whose form is extensively employed for other plant designs, always remains the same, but the degree of irregularity at the bottom border is subject to change.

As we have learned to expect in a "tree" shade, the crown consists of intertwined bronze branches, arising out of and radiating from the very top of the "trunk" for a distance of some 6½" to 7½". There are two thick sprawling limbs in each of the five repeats of the bronze crown. Their ends merge into the irregular bronze border of the crown's glass portion. The latter extends another 2½" to 3½" toward the well-rounded corner leading into the apron; however, individual bronze limbs break through the irregular upper border and continue into the apron, where they finally end and the glass branches begin.

Although the diameter of this shade, measured straight across, is 18", measured along the slightly curved upper surface of the crown, results, of course, in a larger figure – in this case, 20".

After negotiating the curved corner, the leaded-glass crown becomes a vertical apron from 9" to 11" in depth, again depending on where one chooses to place one's rule on the irregular bottom border.

The Pendant Cherry, like all the Pendant Flower shades, is integrated with the Tree Base, but the height of the latter is slightly less than in the Spreading Cherry, between 14½" and 16½" (there is this much variance); also, the light cluster is different in that it consists of four sockets placed perpendicular to the stem, see figure [26a]. A switch on the platform controls the four lights in units of two.

279

Cherry Tree on Green   279

Both the color and texture of the background glass are exceptionally interesting [279]. Fair-sized opaque mottles and pale gray pinhead spots add internal enrichment to the transparent ice-green glass. An undulating texture enlivens the inward-facing surface. The combination of all these elements causes the appearance of the shade to change with every shift of the onlooker's eye.

An even rougher-textured glass makes up the whitish-pink cherry blossoms, which are the same shape but slightly smaller than the blossoms seen in the Spreading Cherry Trees. Again the textured surface—a combination of knobs and ripples—is on the inside. The glass is more opaque than that of the background, and the unevenness of the inside surface produces spotty highlights in the petals. The cherries, most in clusters of two and three, are constructed of the same type of glass, in darker pinks and glossy reds.

The irregular lower border has extremely deep indentations and correspondingly long projections. Some of these are made up of a single blossom; others contain both blossoms and leaves; a few include cherries as well. There are no blossoms or cherries in the crown section of the shade.

An impressive pattern of green-orange branches—continuations of their bronze counterparts in the crown—ranges over the entire shade and stops but a leaf-breadth away from the lower border. Cleanly drawn and clearly segmented, they are forced into even sharper focus by the scarcity of flowers. Even the tiny stems of individual blossoms and cherries are clearly delineated, by lead lines.

Only a comparatively small number of bright green leaves are to be seen, most of them in the blossomless crown section. This paucity of foliage is botanically more accurate than its abundance in the Spreading Cherry Tree, since, in nature, leaves appear only after the flowers have fallen.

Inside the shade, five vertical reinforcement wires extend from the bronze crown to a horizontal wire above the lower border. Signed with three tags and numbered 347–1, the Cherry Tree on Green ground stands on patina-finished Tree Base, which is impressed with the signature and the number 9919.

Cherry Tree on Fractured Glass 280

In this shade the background glass is strikingly beautiful [280]. Basically milky-white, each segment is modified by an array of tiny transparent shapes, irregular in outline. Large and small flakes of green, pink and rose have been superimposed on this shimmering foundation to form a spectacular type of fractured glass in which the shards not only interpose on the basic layer but overlap each other. The roughness of the inner surface, arising from the fact that the edges of the flakes are slightly exposed, adds another refractive dimension. The end result is an astonishing display of subtle multicoloration and scintillation such as few shades can offer.

The blossoms are both white and pink. Most of the cherries are only slightly redder than the rosiest of the petals, and are spotted with darker red; undulating glass, with the texture on its outside surface, forms all the fruit. The branches are orange-green, liberally striated with darker green, and the leaves are fashioned of a glittering transparent glass, streaked with yellow and orange. Utilizing the principle of interchange, some pieces, which on sister shades are shown as leaves, here appear as part of the background.

Two factors account for the extreme unevenness of this shade's outer surface: because the background glass is much thinner than that used in the blossoms and fruit, much of the irregularity is inherent in the construction; some is due to the conscious overlapping of petals, leaves and cherries to create a dimensional effect.

280

THE PENDANT VINES, climbing vines in pendant shades similar to the Pendant Cherry, play an important role in this final and exclusive chapter. Here belong the Trumpet Vine, the Grape Vine and the Wisteria. The pendant shape is actually more appropriate for the climbing vines than it is for fruit trees, since vines naturally tend to droop downward after spreading a short distance. The shade is made in two slightly different forms: with a rounded apron corner where the angle between crown and apron is soft and rotund; and with an angular apron corner where it is sharper and more abrupt. Five repeats are always found in both its bronze crown and glass body.

281

Trumpet Vine   281

The shade, which exemplifies the style with a rounded apron corner, is 18" wide and ranges from 9½" to 10½" in height [281]. Bronze branches, which are heavier though less numerous than in the Pendant Cherry, stand out starkly; some reach to within a few inches of the lower border. Lesser limbs, rendered in brown and green glass, fork from the metallic branches and lead, in turn, to twigs and leaves.

The shade is dominated by clusters of the large trumpet-shaped blooms from which it derives its name. Light orange, mottled with dark orange and red, these are depicted full-face and from every conceivable angle. The glass in the petals is textured on the inside, coarsely grained and, in places, almost knobby in texture. At the center of the young clusters we see green buds.

The leaves range from light green, streaked with yellow, to a dense dark green, and supply the strongest possible contrast to the orange flowers. At intervals, the foliage participates in the formation of the irregular lower border.

The background is constructed from an almost colorless fractured glass, containing greenish and orange flakes and splinters; the inner surface of these segments is finely fibrillated.

The juxtaposition of chromatically opposed colors makes the Trumpet Vine a showy, almost gaudy, shade. It is signed with a 1⅜" tag, inscribed *Tiffany Studios*; a ¾" tag marked *New York* and a ¾" tag bearing the figures *340–5*.

The integrated Tree Base on which the Trumpet rests is finished in a matching light patina, signed and marked with the number 342.

GRAPE VINES

This highly ornamental plant which carries its portentous berries in graceful clusters, served as an inspirational model for many Tiffany Studios creations, such as we have encountered among the hanging cones, globes (Fruit shade), and irregular lower borders (Trellis). Here is assumes its most distinguished representation.

Green Grape Vine   282

The gradual intensification of color indicates several stages in the ripening process of the fruit [282]: from milky-white with green striations and mottling, we go to green with gray opaque mottling, green with blue speckles, green with orange speckles, medium dark green and a mellow blue. Some grape clusters contain rippled glass, textured on the outer surface; knobby glass, with the texture turned inward, is found in others.

As in the case of the grapes, foliage color seems based on seasonal change. Young leaves are pale green; aging leaves are darker; approaching the end of the cycle, they are increasingly streaked with yellow and brown, until, at last, they are predominantly brown, with just memories of green remaining. Undulating and knobby glass is employed for much of the foliage.

An extraordinary leaf treatment may be seen in the lower third of the shade, to the left of center. While the base and central area of the leaf are a rather dark green in a well circumscribed outline, its tip and outside edges are not only lighter, but quite a different yellow-brown color. Color combinations of similar artistry are found in other leaves.

The bronze branches in this shade are shorter, thinner and, in general, much less important to the pattern than those in the Trumpet Vine; their glass offshoots are yellow, speckled with brown.

To enliven the soft tones and subtle blends of its other elements, the background was made a fantasy of fractured glass: orange, carmine, apricot and sienna flakes create a kaleidoscopic spectacle. The flake applications, like the pigment dots of a pointillist painting, cause constant shimmering color changes.

The shade has a rounded apron corner; it is signed and numbered 348-3.

282

Purple Grape Vine 283

In its lush ripeness, this Vine is the direct antithesis of its almost virginal sister shade [283]. Instead of cool, dewy colors, these grapes are executed in the deeply saturated hues of harvest-time: dark blue, dappled with transparent gray; pink and wine-red, striated with blue; royal purple, mottled with blue and red. Mottling has been employed as deftly as color. In one bunch, for example, all grapes are speckled on the same side—obviously the surface exposed to the sun. In another, the darker areas are at front center of the fruit; elsewhere, they may be seen around the circumference of some grapes, or disseminated in seemingly random style. When this shade is viewed as a whole, however, it is obvious that every speckle was placed with the utmost precision.

Because the same exquisite care was exercised in evolving the leaves, the foliage vies with the grapes for the viewer's attention. Decayed-looking yellowish-green leaves, dotted with gray, are highlighted by their nearness to healthy growth in hearty greens. Young leaves, streaked with the dark-green of life, lay next to drab faded foliage, marked with the orange-brown striations of impending death; wrinkled leaves, ready to fall, make the unfolding of the fresh new greenery even more miraculous. Some leaves are fashioned from undulating, others from knobby, glass which endows them with an alluring luminescence.

Grapes and foliage have been tied together with a beautifully color-balanced blue background, speckled with orange, red and brown. The final tribute to the craftsmanship embodied in this shade is the fact that it carries its varied and often vehement colors with quiet dignity.

The shade has one horizontal and four vertical reinforcement wires and contains three tags: a 1¼" plaque inscribed *Tiffany Studios*, a 1" tag marked *New York* and a ¾" tag bearing the number 348–6. The base is impressed with the same number 348.

283

WISTERIAS

The Wisteria, native to North America and an incomparably picturesque ornamental, is probably the best-known and most cherished of all Tiffany shade designs.

A vine, like the Trumpet and the Grape, the Wisteria is again depicted in the Pendant Tree profile. Besides the more prevalent standard, a miniature size was also produced in this pattern. In conception, as well as workmanship, these shades represent the apogee of all Tiffany's creative accomplishments.

Infinitely delicate in design, the standard Wisteria is made up of more than a thousand small pieces of painstakingly selected glass in highly complicated, meticulously cut, curved shapes. Five vertical reinforcement wires give additional support to this fragile shade; they run from the bronze crown along a torturous path of curving lead lines to a horizontal wire near the lower edge from which offshoots extend to the irregular border [284].

In the Standard Wisteria again, we clearly distinguish two slightly different shapes: one with a gently rounded corner between crown and sides, the other where the corner is abrupt.

A number of medium-heavy bronze branches run from the metal crown about halfway down the sides of the shade; they continue into thinner stems executed in sculptured leading, which carry the leaves and flower clusters.

Since the lower blossoms open and mature earlier than those higher on the cluster, and since adjoining clusters may also mature at different times, subtle as well as pronounced color variations can exist both within and between clusters. This diversity, along with the possibilities presented by leaves and background, offer infinite scope to the craftsman and colorist.

The small size of the leaded glass segments also facilitates the interchange of petal, leaf and background pieces. In some instances, even the bronze branches have been made thinner or cut short and replaced by additional leaves or flower petals. This explains the extent of the dissimilarity between Wisteria shades of the same size and shape.

In this design, which is repeated five times, the foliage is concentrated in the crown portion, and few leaves extend past the midpoint of the sides; none reach the lower irregular border, which is formed entirely of blossoms. The indentations at this edge may be as much as 2⅞″ deep.

The Wisteria fits the Tree Base, with which it integrates exceptionally well. The supporting rod, which extends from the top of the base, and the matching sleeve, attached to the inside center of the bronze crown, are usually impressed with the same number. This also holds true when the arrangement is reversed and the rod is attached to the crown while the sleeve juts from the stem of the base. These markings must not be confused with the regular design numbers of shade and base. The height variations in the base, from 14½″ to 16½″, has already been mentioned.

The Miniature Wisteria resembles the more common standard size both in shape and general characteristics, with only a few exceptions. In the smaller shade, the bronze branches run farther down the sides, with the remainder of their length executed in sculptured leading.

Although the irregularity of the lower border is virtually the same, because of the smallness of the shade the unevenness seems disproportionately great in the Miniature. Despite the reduced dimensions of this shade, the blossoms are, surprisingly, the same size as those seen in the Standard. The Miniature Wisteria is integrated with the Miniature Tree Base.

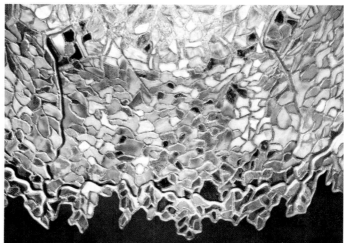

284

285

Light Blue Miniature Wisteria   285

The almost-white petals, uppermost in the clusters, are followed in descending order by blossoms in light blue, light blue streaked with medium blue, medium blue and, at the border, dark blue [285].

Alternating clusters, evidently more mature and so somewhat darker, start with blossoms of a richer blue. Interspersed between them are petals spotted with purple and some which are mauve-white, with hints of rose. At the border, the blossoms are a dense stygian blue and form an edge so irregular that its highest and lowest points are 2¾" apart.

Green in the crown, the leaves become progressively more yellow in the apron area. The branches are all metal: the heavy ones executed in bronze, their offshoots in lead. In the lower section of the shade, the small amount of background is a highly perceptible golden yellow; toward the top, the color fades until the background segments are almost indistinguishable from other design elements.

Dark Blue Miniature Wisteria   286

This shade is more somber in hue throughout [286]. Some of its floral cascades are wholly blue, but varied in tone, with tints appearing at random rather than in a sequential arrangement, as in the last shade. Instead of a gradual tonal transition from top to bottom of the same cluster, the lighter greenish-blue blossoms are scatter-mixed with those of a darker reddish-blue.

The Dark Blue differs from its companion shade in still another respect; darker and lighter clusters do not alternate. In all three repeats, two of the paler clusters (at center of illustration) adjoin each other, each flanked by a darker agglomeration.

The leaves are either green, striated with yellow, or yellow, striated with green. Faintly yellow fractured glass, enriched with red and green splinters, makes up the background.

286

Standard Wisterias

From a purely chromatic viewpoint, two different types of coloration may be observed in specimens of this shade. One features clusters which are sharply delineated and almost uniform in color by themselves, yet in strong contrast with adjoining clusters; some, for instance, may be predominantly white, the alternating ones predominantly blue. Although highly effective visually, such vivid contrast is seldom seen in nature on clusters of the same plant. The other type of coloration is characterized by the fact that most of the chromatic variations occur within each cluster rather than between adjoining clusters. Here some older blossoms may already be blue while the newly opened ones are still pale. This is more in keeping with the horticultural habits of the Wisteria plant, since the individual blossoms within each cluster mature at different times.

The first category to be shown will be the WISTERIAS WITH SHARPLY DEFINED CLUSTERS.

287

Blue-Gray Wisteria   287

The flower clusters are clearly outlined and well separated from each other [287]. At least three different tonal modifications, light, medium and dark blue, each modified by self-mottling, appear in the predominantly bluish clusters. The flower masses in the remaining clusters are white with blue or bluish-white mottles. The coloration at the irregular border conforms to that of the clusters which create the projections. Knobby glass, textured on the inside, gives the petals a strange luster.

Except in the crown, where a few all-green leaves may be found, the foliage is mainly yellow, striated with green. The background glass is purplish-blue and gray, speckled with green. No attempt has been made to draw a strong color distinction between blossoms and background and the main difference is, besides the purple tint, the latter's greater transparency and stippled texture.

By the selection of this subdued color scheme and its execution in precisely the right texture types, the Studios succeeded in producing a shade of wondrous serenity and outstanding elegance. The Blue-Gray Wisteria is signed and bears the number 1073; it is rendered with the rounded apron corner. The base is impressed with the same number.

Multiple-Stage Wisteria   288, 289

Several stages in the life cycle of the flowering vine are encompassed in this single shade. On one side of it, shown in figure [288], we notice that some of the clusters are still white while others, which apparently started to bloom earlier, are already blue. As we follow the progress of the season (from right to left in the illustration), the warmer sun starts

nitively than any encountered in life. To add further emphasis to the contours of the clusters, the artist freely employed the principle of interchangeability. By substituting blossoms for background glass, the clusters were made wider than in other shades. Near the crown, shortened branches carry blossoms in lieu of leaves, thereby lengthening the clusters

288

289

to tint the white petals a pale blue, the bluish petals a much darker blue.

As the season advances into early summer, as depicted on the other side of the shade [289], the formerly white clusters have changed to a median blue while the originally blue clusters have assumed a still deeper hue and a purple tinge. The leaves that were a fresh and glossy green on the spring side of the shade are now a faded echo of their former color; yellow and brown striations clearly indicate their slow decay.

In this shade, which is of the angular apron type, the flower clusters are separated from each other far more defi-

at their upper ends.

Though little background is left, that little is amazingly effective. Fabricated of a milky-white transparent glass, shot through with rippling blue streaks, the sparkling segments seem to glisten with reflected sky glow.

This completes the examples of shades with sharply defined clusters and leads us to the discussion of the second category, the WISTERIAS WITH COLOR-INTEGRATED CLUSTERS, where the sharp demarcation between them is no longer in existence.

Wisteria with Fractured Glass 290

Here, the artificial color variations between clusters are absent, and all the blooms merge in a magnificent floral mass [290]. As in nature, tonal gradations occur between individual blossoms rather than between bunches.

Throughout the shade, the lightest blossoms are directly below the crown, with darker petals appearing in vaguely

290

eye, peering between the clusters, would perceive other similarly colored clusters in the background.

In the area of the bottom border, where wider spaces offer more extensive vistas, a superlative fractured glass simulates the splendor of the barely seen but glowing garden, reflected in the background glass. Single and double layers of green, pink and orange flakes were pressed into a colorless, completely transparent base sheet; through overlapping, an infinite variety of color combinations could be achieved. Enough of this imbedded glass projects from the inner surface of the fractured segments to produce a sharp-toothed texture.

Looking closely, an oddity may be perceived in the placement of green glass splinters; while some are inset in the usual more or less straight lines, others inscribe circular outlines in the base glass.

The shade has a rounded apron corner; it is not signed, but the number 7806 is impressed upon the sleeve attached to the underside of the crown, which fits over the rod emerging from the top of the base; the base has the same number inscribed on the underside of its platform, indicating that the two components were made to go together.

vertical sequence and at random. Both the mauve-tinged milky-white glass, striated with light blue, and the darker grayish-blue glass, with blue-purple area-mottling, are knobby-textured on their inside surfaces. Most of the foliage is a dense olivine green, with some leaves heavily striated with yellow, orange and ocher.

In the upper portion of the shade, the blossoms almost obliterate the background. Since both are formed from the same knobby-textured, basically bluish-white glass, striated and mottled with darker blue, only the slightly more angular shape of the background segments enables us to identify them. This color congruity may be due to the fact that the

291

Purple-Edge Wisteria   291

Here, the more angular of the two shapes used for this vine design has been employed [291]. (Note the more acute curve between crown and sides.)

In this shade, the clusters again are integrated and one cannot readily be distinguished from the next; the lines of demarcation have almost completely disappeared. However, the color differences within each cluster are more pronounced than those observed in the last Wisteria.

Once again, the freshest, lightest flowers are found principally in the upper portion of the shade: milky-white, with or without mottling of a mild blue, they are rendered in stippled glass, textured on its inside surface. Farther down, the petals are a pale cerulean hue, lightly spotted with dark blue. Closer to the border, the predominant blossom color is Prussian blue, with exceptionally heavy purple mottling in many petals. Some of these mainly purple flowers form a part of the irregular lower border.

Adjoining the clusters, and occasionally penetrating them, the background glass is of two different types, both more transparent than that of the blossoms. Near the bottom border, the segments are light blue, striated with purple, orange and green. Higher on the shade, the background is made up of a bleached blue glass, generously dotted with tiny gray pinpoints; larger specks of opaque blue are also present.

The coloration of the foliage is quite uniform and consists of green modified with varying amounts of yellow in the form of mottles or striations.

The tranquil aura of this Wisteria was assured by the employment of practically the entire blue spectrum. However, it is the unexpected accents of acid yellow-green that elevate this shade from placid beauty to positive brilliance, augmented by the purple highlights at the lower border and the shiny, highly textured, bluish-white glass.

The shade is signed.

292

Multicolored Wisteria   292

This shade has the angular apron corner. It consists of completely integrated clusters [292]. They display the wide range of the bluish scale from white, streaked with blue, to pale blue and gray-blue, to cerulean tones, to dark blue and midnight blue, to lavender and purplish-blue. Interposed with this symphony in blue is the foliage in an almost equal diversity of tones of light and dark green, and green mottled with various shades of yellow. The older leaves introduce stronger patterns of orange and reddish brown which, in juxtaposition to the blue flowers, establish a firm contrast.

The chromatic scheme is further enhanced by one of the most dramatic backgrounds seen in any Tiffany shade: highly transparent, partly of granular and partly of fibrillated texture, it features a brilliant azure blue with turbulent swirls of yellow, orange and red. Other sections are made of a shimmering green glass with area-mottling of blue and orange and with striations and pinpoint mottling of the same colors.

In a reversal of the usual procedure of interchange, blossom petals and leaves have here been converted into background, conferring upon the latter an exceedingly predominant role in the over-all appearance of the shade. This impact is further strengthened by the impressive quality of the background glass and its marked transparency.

However, the description of the extensive range of colors used in the shade and the fine texture of its glass tells only half the story. The other half is supplied by the method of application and distribution, which in this case was done subtly and deftly, producing blending without monotony, contrast without ostentation. The end result is the accomplishment of an artist who was a great painter in glass. On a canvas of glass he created the picture of a lovely flower adorning the garden with its unforgettable beauty.

The bottom plate of the base is impressed with the number 22525, which is also found on the support sleeve of the shade.

Sunset Wisteria 293

Once again, an almost unprecedentedly bold background is employed to define and enliven the blue blossoms [293]. Basically a rosy orange, with red and orange striations and mottles, the background glass is gleamingly transparent, especially toward the bottom border. In the upper reaches of the shade, green and a denser red serve to dull the luster.

Many of the light green leaves are striated with red and could easily be mistaken for background glass.

The clusters, startlingly blue against the glowing background, consist of two types of glass. The topmost petals, in robin's-egg blue, are fabricated from a transparent glass, mottled with splotches of white and darker blue and shot through with innumerable small grayish specks. Lower in each cluster, the blue of the blooms becomes increasingly more intense.

However, though the density deepens, the actual blue color of the blossoms is almost uniform. If not for the sharp contrast furnished by the background, one cluster of this Wisteria would be indistinguishable from another. The attraction of the petals is intensified by their knobby texture; a magnetic purplish cast adds to the allure of the dark blue blossoms.

Throughout the shade, blossoms and background vie with equal vigor for the viewer's attention. In the crown and upper sides, the background attempts to dominate by looting leaves and blossoms, adding area to its own domain by interchange. Farther down, it fights the fascination of the flowers' purplish haze with more forceful contrast and brilliance. And so—happily for all beholders—the glorious battle of the colors rages on, never violent, never flagging, and never to be resolved.

293

INDEX

BIBLIOGRAPHY

MARIO AMAYA, *Tiffany Glass;* Walker & Company, New York, 1967
CHARLES DE KAY, *The Art Works of Louis C. Tiffany;* Doubleday, Page & Co., New York 1914
ROBERT KOCH, *Louis C. Tiffany, Rebel in Glass;* Crown Publishers Inc., New York, 1966